OUT OF
BOUNDS

OUT OF BOUNDS

INSIDE THE
NBA'S CULTURE OF
RAPE, VIOLENCE, AND CRIME

JEFF BENEDICT

HarperCollinsPublishers

HarperCollins books may be purchased for educational, business, or sales promotional use. For information, please write: Special Markets Department, Harper-Collins Publishers Inc., 10 East 53rd Street, New York, NY 10022.

FIRST EDITION

Designed by Joseph Rutt

Printed on acid-free paper

Library of Congress Cataloging-in-Publication Data
is available upon request.

ISBN 0-06-072602-4

04 05 06 07 08 ❖/RRD 10 9 8 7 6 5 4 3 2 1

AUTHOR'S NOTE

Jennifer Grogan graduated summa cum laude from the University of Connecticut in May 2003, where she double-majored in journalism and political science, and minored in criminal justice. She began as my research assistant in September 2003. I told her on day one that we had less than five months to research and write this book and that missing the deadline was not an option. Jennifer did not flinch. Within three weeks she familiarized herself with the names and vital information of more than 450 NBA players and underwent a crash course in public-records laws in most of the fifty states. Then she prepared and distributed document requests under Freedom of Information laws to over 150 law-enforcement agencies and courthouses throughout the United States. And this describes only her first month on the job. Before we finished, she assisted me in the research, reporting, writing, editing, and fact-checking for this book. Quiet and unassuming, Jennifer is a deceptively tough and relentless reporter, with a tireless knack for digging up one more fact, one more kernel of information that will cast further light on a subject of inquiry. She possesses the essential attributes of an investigative journalist: integrity, objectivity, tenaciousness, and a tireless attention to detail. I found her to be absolutely trustworthy, reliable, and unflappable under great pressure. I could not have asked for a finer, more competent partner. And we hit our deadline. Jennifer has been accepted into the Columbia University School of Journalism. She begins in the fall of 2004.

The other individual who played a critical role in the research for this book has requested anonymity. But it would be a crime not to note his contribution. A graduate of the FBI National Academy at Quantico and a magna cum laude graduate of Pace University's criminal justice program, he is currently a retired New York law-enforcement agent. I met him through a mutual friend in the investment-banking industry, who one day told me about an individual who was an endless reservoir of knowledge on how to find and obtain information about people via the Internet, as well as a stealth investigator. Armed with only a phone number, I called the man and persuaded him to come out of retirement to work this project with me. He started a few weeks before Jennifer and proved to be nothing less than a maestro when it came to tracking down addresses, phone numbers, and background information on people who seem to specialize in disappearing. I used him sparingly, almost as a troubleshooter. But some of the most important interviews I conducted never would have happened had he not navigated me through an electronic paper trail that led to the people on my "must find" list. Often the clues would come to me in a late night e-mail that would begin with words that said, more or less: "I think I found your man." Ultimately, I found a great investigator and a new friend, one who was an integral part of the team.

ACKNOWLEDGMENTS

One word best describes all who had a hand in this book: drive. Actually, *overdrive* is more accurate. This book was researched and written in less than six months, a breakneck pace unlike one I have ever encountered as an author. It required great sacrifice, a relentless work ethic and an absolutely dogged approach from the moment the first document was requested to the day the last pages were copyedited. Many people sacrificed along the way. No doubt, the highest price was paid by my dear wife, Lydia. Many days I arose at four A.M. or worked until midnight to hit the deadline. At one point, Lydia took our three children and went on an eight-day trip in order to enable me to work around the clock so that I could stay on the unforgiving schedule. She is the strongest woman I know, and I am blessed to call her my best friend, my confidante, and my greatest love.

The brain trust that I consulted with during every step of this project was my agent, Basil Kane, and my editor, Mauro DiPreta. No writer could have finer advisers. They are men who see the possibilities, men who know and understand the art of writing and the power of investigative reporting. I could not ask to be surrounded by better talent. Nor could I ask for better friends in the profession. I can say only thanks to them for their integrity, their character, and their vision. I am honored to call them my associates and most trusted colleagues.

My personal assistant, Donna Cochrane, epitomized speed and competence throughout this project. At times, my office was nothing short of insane, as I often maintained a "Let's get it done yesterday" approach to the book. Donna has the rare ability to work that fast—and to get it right. And her careful treatment of sensitive correspondence and confidential information is a treasure in itself.

I was also aided by Becky Greenhalgh in Seattle and Darla Collar in Portland, two very competent, smart, and thorough individuals who performed legal research for me in their respective cities.

Photo acquisition is an often overlooked yet critical part of a book of this nature. Joelle Yudin did a comprehensive job tracking down scores of player photographs and helped me select all of the noncrime photos contained in the insert. She was an absolute pleasure to work with.

Four individuals provided essential logistical and technical support: Johanna Freiheit was like a maestro booking all of my travel arrangements, most of which were arranged on a moment's notice. John Mikula set up my computer and e-mail security systems. Frank Chisholm monitored and maintained those systems. Ron Cochran designed and maintains my website and has been the ever-present consultant on using the Web to promote this book and previous ones.

Of course, none of this would have been possible without the support and enthusiasm of HarperCollins's publisher Cathy Hemming and president Susan Weinberg, both of whom took a personal interest in this project from day one and took time out of their busy schedules to meet face-to-face and discuss ideas. Attorney Kyran Cassidy was tasked with vetting this book. His legal eye and scrupulous attention to sourcing and evidence took the manuscript to another level. And publicist extraordinaire Justin Loeber was nothing short of a one-man firestorm of enthusiasm and passion, always looking and finding ways to better market and advance the manuscript.

Ultimately, a book like this is only as good as its sources. To that end, I'm an indebted to the countless law-enforcement agents, prosecutors, and court reporters and clerks who aided and trusted me in this project. The list is too long to mention. But a few sources merit mentioning: the Bellevue Police Department in Washington State; the Story County Prosecuting Attorney's Office in Iowa; the Monmouth County Prosecuting Attorney's Office in New Jersey; the Orange County Sheriff's Office in Orlando, Florida; the King County Prosecutor's Office in Seattle; Portland's Police Bureau; the Department of Public Safety at Arizona State University; and the Illinois State Attorney's Office, Cook County.

Finally, there are the women—victims at the hands of famous NBA players—who put their stories and their trust in my hands. Without them, this would be a different book altogether. Thank you for your faith.

To Jane Doe. She is nameless in court documents and press reports. She is faceless to those whose information about violence against women comes through television news and programming. She is frequently voiceless in the halls of Congress, state legislatures, and courtrooms, where laws governing violence against women are devised and enforced. But Jane Doe is many women across America, victims with real names who have been driven to silence, fear, and self-doubt at the hands of men carrying out the twin crimes of sexual assault and domestic violence. Jane Doe is a woman who has had something taken from her, something the justice system can't restore.

Jane Doe, this one's for you.

CONTENTS

PREFACE

Most people who are about to read this book probably view the NBA simply as a professional sports league featuring the world's most talented basketball players. On the face of it, this is true. But there is a dark, sinister side to the NBA, where criminal laws and social norms don't exist, a world where athletes are given license to be socially irresponsible. Nowhere are these conditions more apparent than in the relationships and interactions between NBA players and women.

In my career as a university researcher, a lawyer, and a journalist, I have personally reviewed more than five hundred criminal and civil complaints filed by women against college and professional athletes. I've written two books on violence against women committed by athletes. And six years ago I cowrote *Pros and Cons: The Criminals Who Play in the NFL.* That book, which examined the criminal histories of 509 NFL players, revealed that 21 percent of them had been formally charged with a serious crime. The lion's share of the victims in those cases were women.

Ever since publishing the NFL book, I've refrained from speculating on how NBA players would fare under a similar examination. I've also resisted numerous opportunities to write a book on the NBA and crime. Personally, I wanted to investigate and write about other topics, and I have. Moreover, I wasn't convinced that a book on the NBA was capable of going beyond the NFL book in terms of its reporting depth or its ability to shed additional light on the themes associated with celebrated athletes breaking laws. Kobe Bryant's arrest on rape charges last summer changed my mind.

Not since Mike Tyson's 1991 arrest for rape has a pro athlete of such prominence as Bryant been indicted for that offense. During the decade in between, little has changed attitudinally— on the part of athletes or the public. Criminal complaints concerning celebrated athletes abusing women are as common as ever, as is the fact that arrested players are rarely held accountable. And the public's skepticism toward women who file such complaints remains. Kobe's arrest has brought this point home. As soon as he appeared beside his gorgeous wife to deny the charges levied against him, I was repeatedly asked two questions by casual observers and the media:

Why would a man with such a beautiful wife rape another woman?

Why would a handsome young millionaire, a guy who could have lots of women, have to resort to rape?

These questions demonstrate that people have a hard time reconciling Kobe Bryant's public image with the vicious crime he's charged with. The press conference he held after being indicted, where his wife stood by his side as he shed tears, only made the charges against him seem more difficult to believe. Hence, the reaction: *Rape? Not Kobe. Anybody but Kobe.*

I watched Kobe's press conference too. It had a big influence on my decision to write this book. Denying rape, he said: "I made the mistake of adultery." Set aside the question of guilt or innocence for a minute and think about this. Bryant checked into a resort hotel shortly after ten P.M. on June 30, 2003, and a sexual incident was under way with a complete stranger by shortly after eleven P.M. How many people who travel can relate to going to a hotel in a strange city, seeing a complete stranger upon check-in, and having sexual intercourse with that stranger within an hour? This speaks volumes about the culture of the NBA and the mind-set of its players.

This book is not about Kobe Bryant, but rather about a lifestyle that is pervasive throughout the NBA, one that is typified in the Bryant case. Nor is the book limited to crimes involving women. It features dozens of NBA players—from All-Stars to journeymen—involved in many types of crimes, from armed robbery to domestic violence to gun possession to rape. The book's purpose is three-fold. First, to expose the environment and culture that encourages criminal behavior. Second, to explain the unique challenges the cases that grow out of this behavior pose for law-enforcement agencies and prosecutors. And, third, to take readers inside the hidden, yet critically vital role that lawyers, agents, and fame play in insulating criminally accused players from accountability.

I began my investigation by conducting a criminal background check on nearly two hundred NBA players who played during the 2001–02 season. This entailed supplying player names, birth dates, and other vital information to records clerks at ninety-four police departments and sheriff's offices and querying fifty-six municipal, state, and federal courts. In all, over 150 letters soliciting records under the Freedom of Information Act were sent. Those agencies and courts not queried by letter were either visited in person or contacted by telephone. The results revealed that 40 percent of the players in the NBA during the 2001–02 season have had a formal criminal complaint for a serious crime filed against them. That's right—40 percent! (The full results and the methodology for this investigation are detailed later, in the prologue following this section.)

It's a situation that is out of control and absolutely demands close scrutiny. This simply can't be ignored any longer. And the criminal-history research is just the starting point for the reporting done for this book. But a statistic doesn't tell a story. To drill down inside some of these cases, more than 5,000 pages of documents were obtained from police files and courthouses. Over 2,000 pages of trial transcripts, grand jury transcripts, and preliminary hearing transcripts were obtained. Twelve district attorney's offices provided access to an estimated 5,000 pages of documents pertaining to cases featured in this book. Law-firm billing records, college-grade transcripts, student records, and a variety of other confidential documents were obtained, all through legal and ethical channels commonly practiced by journalists. Nor was money paid, except for copying and shipping fees assessed by law-enforcement agencies and courts.

Additionally, over 400 interviews were conducted with police officers, prosecutors, criminal defense attorneys, player agents, players, victims, witnesses, and other individuals with knowledge about the cases covered in this book.

Secondary sources included over 1,000 press reports, primarily in the form of newspaper and magazine articles. A limited number of books were used for reference and background information.

As a result, what you are about to read is a painstakingly detailed look at cases that have largely been underreported or not reported at all. Crimes are recounted in graphic detail, and the narrative style I've chosen includes quotations and dialogue from the players involved in these offenses, their victims, and the law-enforcement officials who investigated and prosecuted these cases. The dialogue largely comes from tape-recorded transcripts of interviews conducted by police and prosecutors, transcripts of grand jury testimony, transcripts of pretrial and trial testimony, deposition transcripts, affidavits, police narratives, and arrest and incident reports. Over 12,000 police and court records were obtained or viewed for this book.

Quotes were also derived, in some limited instances, from court documents filed in civil lawsuits, including depositions and affidavits as well as press reports.

In addition to quotes and dialogue, my narrative style also involves the description of various crime scenes, in some cases with particular detail. I was able to do this through the assistance of crime-scene photographs, police drawings, and video surveillance tapes that I obtained or viewed. I was also aided by hundreds of documents in the form of arrest and search warrants, evidence logs, medical records, university records, police narratives, grand jury minutes, indictments, arrest reports, and incident reports. And in most cases, I conducted interviews with individuals who were directly or indirectly involved with the cases featured in the book. In cases where players' homes are described, that information was taken from photographs, diagrams, and detailed dimensions obtained through real estate and property records.

Every effort was made to report these stories without varnish—that is, names are named. In fact, 267 are factually identified in this book (players, lawyers, agents, coaches, law-enforcement officials, victims, and witnesses, among others). In rare instances—ten times to be exact—I used a pseudonym to protect an individual's identity, typically in situations involving sex crimes where the victim's identity was protected under rape-shield statutes, or if identifying a witnesses would put that person in harm's way. The following names are pseudonyms: Madison, in the prologue; sex-crime victim Jenny Stevens and her father, in chapters 1 through 3; sex-crime witness Susi Sanders, in chapter 1; Cathy Clark, an alleged rape victim, in chapter 3; Sammy Jones and Ray Scott, witnesses in a criminal investigation, in chapter 4; alleged rape victim Olivia Tamika, in chapter 11; and Tommy Harper and Dan Daniels, witnesses in a criminal investigation in chapter 14.

EVERY WOMAN'S FEAR

If I've learned anything in writing this book, it is that fear often triumphs over truth when women are abused by celebrated athletes.

In domestic violence and sexual assault cases, fear is the criminal athlete's best friend and turns the female victim into the reluctant, non-cooperative witness. What are women so afraid of? Becoming a celebrity by virtue of accusing a celebrity; seeing a private sex crime turned into a public media spectacle; being demonized by high-powered defense attorneys; and being victimized again by a justice system ill equipped to convict a defendant with endless financial resources. The biggest fear of all is that she will not be believed.

To illustrate these points, I offer two examples.

GOING UNDERGROUND

A few months into the research phase of this book, I received a tip that during the 2002 season, a young woman was sexually abused at a private party held exclusively for an NBA team that was in the midst of a road trip. During the party, one of the team's players pinned the victim against a wall and molested her.

I was provided the victim's name, Madison (a pseudonym), and the player's name, along with the date and location of the alleged incident. Although the source's credibility was exceptional, I was skeptical and had numerous questions. These kinds of incidents are not unusual at parties, particularly parties hosted or attended by celebrity athletes. Why was Madison at this party? Did she know the player previously? If she was truly assaulted, why hadn't this incident ever come to light? After all, the player involved is well known. And finally, did this incident really occur? Or was this just a rumor?

But a few facts intrigued me. A review of the NBA's game schedule for 2002 confirmed that the team in question was on the road and in the specific city identified by the tipster on the specific date in question. Next I confirmed that the facility of the alleged incident was legitimate. I then telephoned local law-enforcement agents in that city and inquired whether they had been dispatched to the address in question to investigate an alleged sexual assault on the date in question. They had not. Nor had Madison filed any complaint with law enforcement. Neither Madison nor the player's name was in the law-enforcement agency's computer database.

Toward the end of November 2003, I sent a package via UPS to Madison at her residential address with a letter of introduction, some previous materials I had published on athletes and violence against women, and my phone number. I waited for a response until December 9, when UPS returned the package, indicating that Madison's address was no longer current. A few hours later, I decided to catch a flight from Hartford, Connecticut, to the city in which Madison last resided in hopes of finding her. I brought the package with me. The only information I had to go on was her place of employment, a restaurant.

I drove straight from the airport to the restaurant where I ate dinner, looking closely at the nametags worn by the waitresses or hostesses. But none were marked with Madison's name. When I inquired, one waitress told me that Madison had unexpectedly quit three months earlier and had moved out of state. I asked to see the manager, who confirmed Madison had left months ago, but indicated that she had been in the restaurant earlier that day. She had come back to town to visit a friend, who lived nearby.

Provided with Madison's cell-phone number, I stepped outside and called her. I told her who I was and that I was at the restaurant with a UPS package for her. She was aware that UPS had tried to deliver to her old address and asked what the parcel contained. When I told her, she asked what I wanted to talk to her about. I only mentioned the NBA player's name provided to me by the tipster. I said nothing of the alleged assault.

She instantly became very angry and harangued me for tracking her down. Gradually she settled down, then admitted a one-time encounter with the player and insisted that he had taken inappropriate and offensive sexual liberties with her. Over the ensuing thirty minutes that Madison remained on the phone, she confirmed what I had been told in the tip and revealed additional details that were news to me, such as her motivation for not initially reporting the incident to authorities. She wanted no part of publicity and scrutiny that comes with accusing a high-profile athlete.

But it gnawed at her that she felt criminally violated. Eventually, Madison said that she could not contain herself after seeing the player on television following her run-in with him. Instead of calling the police, she picked up the phone and told her story to a prosecuting attorney. After reporting, however, she did not want to cooperate in any formal or public way with an investigation.

Madison said the prosecutors wanted a lot more out of her, however. She said that after her initial call to the DA's office, she received numerous follow-up phone calls and an investigator was dispatched to her job and home. Fearful that the incident and her identity would become public and her life turned upside down, Madison quit her job, moved out of state, and essentially went underground. "You have no idea what I have been through," she said.

At the end of the phone call, she agreed to take my package and read through my materials. Following her strict instructions, I left it in a safe, hidden location and drove off. One question I never got to ask Madison was why she was at this party in the first place? And now a new question arose: Why was she so scared when an investigator showed up at her place of employment seeking to speak with her?

There was only one place left to turn for these answers. Before contacting the prosecuting attorney's office, Madison confided in and sought advice from a retired judge who is now a lawyer in private practice. I called him. We engaged in a series of off-the-record preliminary conversations. He then checked out my background. He also informed Madison that I had called and discussed with her my request to speak with him. Ultimately we discussed Madison and her situation. He illuminated the story.

First, Madison had never met the player who accosted her. In fact, she didn't know any of the players on the team. She didn't follow basketball at all and wouldn't know a professional player if she saw one. Second, the party was not a party; it was a private dinner catered by the restaurant Madison used to work for-the same one I had visited. (I subsequently confirmed this with the restaurant.)

Did Madison report the incident to anyone in proximity to it happening? Yes. Even before leaving the facility that evening, Madison told a coworker and telephoned her mother. Then again, after leaving the facility, she elaborated on the details to her mother. Through family consultation and much thought, Madison and her family decided it was not in her best interest to file a criminal complaint. The idea of filing a civil suit was never discussed. Despite feeling violated and angry, Madison decided to do nothing.

So why did Madison seek out a retired judge and a lawyer? The lawyer is a family relative and she wanted guidance from someone who understood the law, someone she could absolutely trust.

The lawyer revealed that it was he who ultimately advised Madison to at least report her incident to the authorities. He assured her that this could be done in complete confidence and did not require her to follow through with a full-scale investigation. She acted on his advice.

The lawyer said he heard from the authorities shortly after Madison reported her incident to them. The authorities wanted Madison to do more than simply share her experience; they wanted her to cooperate more fully, a proposition that would certainly bring her into the public spotlight. "They called me and talked to me," the lawyer said. But when Madison decided she did not want to go further with the authorities, the lawyer made that clear to them. From that point forward his role has been to protect her privacy.

My interviews with Madison's relative and lawyer were conducted in January and February of this year, at the same time that Kobe Bryant's defense team was in court arguing for the right to introduce the victim's sexual history to jurors, and the victim's mother was begging the judge to schedule a speedy trial in order to put her daughter out of misery. Published reports indicated that Bryant's victim had been forced to move from state to state in an effort to protect her privacy. Madison's lawyer pointed to the Kobe situation as exhibit one for why Madison did not and should not come forward. Neither Madison nor her family wanted to be drawn into the media tsunami that her allegation would have unleashed. "The only thing Madison's trying to do is live a normal life," he said.

After completing my reporting on this incident, I placed my tape-recorded interviews, personal notes, and phone records in a safe deposit box, which is kept in a vault at a Connecticut bank. I then sent a letter to Madison and her lawyer, promising not to disclose her name in the book.

I include Madison's story here to illustrate a point: there are women out there, women who are simply going about their own business, who encounter celebrated athletes and become the recipients of unwanted sexual advances. Athletes will have you believe that they are constantly pursued by women seeking sex, and that any woman who files a rape complaint is either motivated by money, fame, revenge, or a combination of the three.

Surely there are groupies who pursue athletes for sex. But the notion that every woman who accuses an athlete of a sex crime is a groupie is a pernicious lie. But women who dare to press charges against an athlete are forced to live that lie; it's the price they pay for accusing a famous, wealthy man of a sex crime. And as Madison's experience shows, even women who choose not to press charges, file a lawsuit, or even talk to reporters can have their privacy threatened and their lives turned upside down.

Madison's experience says something else, too. The player who abused her is one who I have watched on television while writing this book. He runs up and down the court to the applause of thousands of cheering fans. Madison's story is a testament to the fact that we often know so little about the men we cheer loudest for. And when they are accused, we not only give them the benefit of the doubt; we doubt the accuser.

MR. ELUSIVE

According to records at Florida's Orange County Sheriff's Office, on October 5, 1998, Shaquille O'Neal and two male friends were outside BET Soundstage Club, a nightclub owned by Black Entertainment Television and located at Disney's Pleasure Island in Orlando, Florida. Twenty-three-year-old Kim Grant worked at the club. Around 11:15 P.M. she went on break and strolled outside. She was standing near the footbridge between Soundstage and Planet Hollywood when O'Neal and his friends approached. One of the men asked her name and what was going on at Pleasure Island. Grant talked up the Soundstage.

"There's nothing going on in Pleasure Island tonight," O'Neal said. Grant admitted that Mondays are a slow night, but suggested they return on the weekend. One of the guys said they would be back on Friday night. "I'll see you on Friday," Grant said.

"Hey, where are your friends?" O'Neal asked. Grant said she didn't have any friends.

"Yes you do," one of O'Neal's friends said. "You have friends you can call. Go call your friends." Grant said nothing.

"Come on," O'Neal said to his friends. "Let's go find us some white girls."

"Go ahead guys," said Grant, who is black. "Be my guest."

At that moment, Grant later reported in a written police statement, O'Neal grabbed her by the neck with his right hand, jerked her toward him, and said: "I was just playing. Can't you take a joke?" Grant said she panicked and screamed for him to let go. When he didn't she threatened to file a charge against him. Grant said this prompted him to tell her to go ahead. As soon as O'Neal released her, she ran back inside the club, where she encountered security guard Jon Vereen. She told him what had happened.

One week after she reported the incident to Disney security, the Orange County Sheriff's Office was notified. On October 13, Officer Roland Hernandez met with Grant, filled out an incident report, and had her write down what happened. The following day the case was assigned to Detective Bill Reynolds. When Reynolds started calling and leaving messages, Grant, who is West Indian, thought she needed a lawyer. People in her community referred her to the only West Indian attorney they knew, Shannon Baruch, a young lawyer who had only been practicing for one year. When Baruch listened to Grant's story, he knew enough to know that taking on Mr. O'Neal in court would be a tall order. "It wasn't just an ordinary person we were going up against," Baruch said. Worse still, the only witnesses to the incident were O'Neal's two friends, and Grant didn't know their names. "If it goes to court and it is she said-he said, that's not a very strong case," explained Baruch, "especially when the he is Mr. O'Neal."

Baruch advised Grant to cooperate fully with the sheriff's office.

Before Detective Reynolds got the opportunity to meet with Grant, however, he received a telephone call from prominent Florida criminal defense attorney Kirk Kirkconnell. A former Special Agent of the FBI, Kirkconnell was president of the Florida Association of Criminal Defense Lawyers and served on the Florida Bar Board of Governors. He is admitted to practice before the U.S. Supreme Court and the U.S. Court of Appeals. His specialty areas are white-collar crime, homicide, and forfeiture. Kirkconnell informed Reynolds that he represented O'Neal.

Reynolds told Kirkconnell that he wanted to speak with

O'Neal. Kirkconnell said that O'Neal had nothing to say and declined to produce him. Then Reynolds requested that O'Neal at least provide the names of the two men who were with him on the night of the incident. Again, Kirkconnell declined. The two men with O'Neal were the only other known witnesses to the incident between O'Neal and Grant. Without their identities, police had only two accounts to go on: Grant's and O'Neal's. And O'Neal wasn't talking. If an attorney tells investigators that O'Neal does not wish to say anything to them there is little they can do unless O'Neal comes forward himself.

Even if Reynolds arrested O'Neal on the basis of Grant's statement, O'Neal could not be compelled to talk or answer questions. He has the right to remain silent. Reynolds was frustrated. So was Grant, who initially remained adamant about pressing charges in her subsequent conversation with Reynolds. She also confirmed her willingness to testify against O'Neal. On November 13, 1998, O'Neal's agent at the time Leonard Armato told the press that the accusations are "completely false and without factual support." Nonetheless, on November 23, Reynolds charged O'Neal with battery and forwarded the case to the State Attorney's Office for prosecution.

The case was assigned to prosecutor Richard Parkinson on December 2, 1998. The next day, his office received a telephone call from Kirkconnell. Bill Vose, who is the chief assistant state attorney in Orange County and who supervises Parkinson, said that Kirkconnell asked them to hold off. "He said that he had some defense statements that could counteract whatever it is the victim is going to say," Vose said in an interview for this book. At Kirkconnell's request, the case was set aside pending the production of Kirkconnell's information. Then on August 10, 2000, nearly two years later, the case was dismissed. "This to me is a warning bell," said Vose. "When something takes this long it is because we are being Mr. Nice Guy and agreeing to wait for defense to provide information."

In this case, O'Neal's lawyer said they would provide information. But when asked, Vose said there was no record of any information being received. "If we got statements from Kirkconnell, they would have been put in the computer," Vose said. "And they are not. So we may or may not have received them." The documents from this case have been destroyed under the document retention policy of the prosecutor's office.

Vose could not explain the specifics for why this case was not prosecuted. He did say that his office handles around 80,000 juvenile, felony, and misdemeanor cases each year, about two thirds of which are filed for prosecution. The office had shown no reluctance to prosecute other high-profile athletes in the past. Vose himself had prosecuted Charles Barkley for resisting arrest in connection with an alleged battery. But the O'Neal case, besides lacking corroborating witnesses, did not involve much more than an alleged simple assault. "If this was a pushing and shoving case," Vose said, "we're not going to waste taxpayer dollars to prosecute it."

Long before the case was officially closed by prosecutors, Grant became frustrated when it was clear that prosecutors weren't going to indict O'Neal. She asked her lawyer what could be done. The only alternative was to sue. But without the district attorney's office at least prosecuting, Baruch was afraid to file a lawsuit against O'Neal. "It wasn't just an ordinary person we were going up against," said Baruch.

Baruch insisted he would not file an action unless she first produce an affidavit, a sworn, written statement detailing what happened to her. Baruch wanted protection against a countersuit in the event that O'Neal sued him. "I needed the affidavit so I could show the judge that I relied on the sworn statement of my client," said Baruch. "Without that I wasn't going to go forward."

Grant never produced the affidavit. In fact, Baruch said she virtually disappeared after that, not unlike the way the criminal case against O'Neal did-without a trace or an explanation.

When asked if Grant received a financial settlement from O'Neal, Baruch said he did not negotiate any settlement. So why did she drop her pursuit of the case? "That question remains with me today, and with her friends and family," said Baruch, who suspected that fear was behind it, not financial inducement. "She expressed fear of the power behind Mr. O'Neal." He added that when news of her complaint reached the press, television cameras and reporters camped outside her residence. Soon after that he lost contact with her.

Attempts to locate Grant to request an interview were unsuccessful.

When contacted for this book, Kirkconnell said he could not discuss the case, calling it "a client matter."

"Are you saying that you can't speak about this without your client's permission? Or are you saying you can't speak about this because there is some agreement that bars you from speaking about it?" I asked.

"I can't answer that," Kirkconnell said.

"Most defense attorneys don't answer that way," I said.

"I'm not most defense attorneys," he said, ending the call.

O'Neal's agent, Perry Rogers, also declined to talk. Multiple calls were placed to his office. E-mails were sent to him as well, along with a certified letter. All of these communiqués contained a request to speak with O'Neal. Rogers responded to none of them.

Baruch referred to O'Neal as "Mr. Elusive." Investigators in

Florida certainly found that to be the case. Yet O'Neal had the legal right to refuse to speak to police officers. But given O'Neal's publicly professed admiration and respect for law enforcement (in July 2002 the Port of Los Angeles Police Department designated him a second-class reserve officer and authorized him to carry a police-issued gun, ride as a second man in a police car, and work alongside senior officers to fight crime), as well as his status as an ambassador for the NBA and as a role model for so many children, investigators figured he would at least aid them in their attempts to complete a criminal investigation. Instead, investigators encountered layers of insulation around O'Neal.

Compared to the more serious and offensive crimes you are about to encounter, these are minor incidents. Still, they support a very clear point: law-enforcement officials tasked with investigating or prosecuting a celebrated athlete have little chance of seeing the player brought to justice, particularly if the victim is a woman.

UNDER ARREST

History will mark July 3, 2003, as a low point in NBA history, yet one that was utterly predictable, and equally unstoppable. That day, Portland Trail Blazers point guard Damon Stoudamire approached a security checkpoint at Tucson International Airport, carrying a boarding pass for a flight to New Orleans. It was three P.M. when a surveillance camera recorded him placing his carry-on bag in a gray plastic bin and sending it through the baggage X-ray machine. As Stoudamire stepped through the metal detector, an alarm immediately sounded. Wearing only a sleeveless black T-shirt, baggy white sweatpants, and untied sneakers, Stoudamire looked down toward his feet, then turned up his hands as he looked at Transportation Security Administration screener Robert McNew, who directed him toward the wanding area.

Stoudamire said he needed to return to the terminal. It was too late for that. McNew scanned his body with a metal-detection wand. Each time the wand passed Stoudamire's pants, it beeped. McNew asked Stoudamire if he had anything metal in his pants pocket. Stoudamire said he did not.

As McNew prepared to scan him one more time, Stoudamire wiggled his leg. An eight-inch-long piece of thickly wrapped aluminum foil fell out of Stoudamire's pant leg. McNew picked it up. He immediately suspected drugs but realized the foil wrap was also large enough to contain a weapon. He radioed for Airport Police assistance. A subsequent inspection of Stoudamire's backpack revealed a package of EZ Wider rolling papers.

Minutes later, police officers Michael Losada and Keith Kramer arrived. Kramer observed the aluminum foil package and the rolling papers inside a gray plastic bin beside Stoudamire.

"What's inside?" Kramer asked, examining the foil wrap.

"You know what it is," Stoudamire said.

Kramer, holding it up to his nose, detected the scent of fabric softener, then repeated the question.

"It's marijuana . . . mine," Stoudamire said. "It was in my pocket."

Kramer uncovered a clear Ziploc bag inside the foil that contained a green leafy substance. A scented fabric-softener sheet surrounded the bag, a common technique used by drug couriers to mask the odor from drug-sniffing dogs and security officers. Kramer handed the package to his partner, who donned latex gloves and opened a small briefcase containing portable equipment to field-test drugs. Kramer asked Stoudamire about the rolling papers. Stoudamire, noting the glance of travelers passing through the checkpoint area, revealed his identity to the officers and asked permission to move someplace out of public view. Kramer looked at Stoudamire's Oregon driver's license, then directed him and his female companion into a private room. Inside, Kramer informed them that they would not be catching their flight to New Orleans.

Within thirty minutes the leafy substance was confirmed to be marijuana. Stoudamire was arrested and charged with unlawful possession of marijuana and drug paraphernalia.

As officers were releasing Stoudamire to catch another flight,

Kobe Bryant was receiving word that he needed to catch a flight of his own, and quick. Only he wasn't headed for a holiday vacation. Colorado judge Russell Granger had just signed a warrant commanding Eagle County sheriffs to arrest Bryant and bring him without delay to Eagle to be booked in connection with a reported rape.

The next day, Bryant flew back to Colorado and surrendered to Lieutenant Mike McWilliam. After being photographed and fingerprinted, Bryant paid a surety bond of $25,000, promising to return to the state for further court proceedings. At 8:20 P.M. he was released and the NBA's summer of discontent officially began.

But it was actually well under way before Stoudamire and Bryant were arrested. The saturation coverage afforded to Bryant just overshadowed the fact that over twenty-five law-enforcement agencies in thirteen cities in the United States and Canada were simultaneously proceeding with arrest warrants, indictments, plea agreement proceedings, or trials involving more than a dozen other NBA players.

In Portland, Oregon, prosecutors were reviewing the contents of a lengthy police investigation into allegations that Scottie Pippen had harassed a Blazer fan following a playoff game on April 27, 2003. After being heckled, Pippen, according to police reports, said, "F— you," then threw a cup of water in the fan's face. "Meet me at my car," Pippen continued. "I'm going to kick your ass." A security guard then grabbed Pippen and ushered him toward the locker room. After reviewing a video surveillance tape of the incident that showed the fan laughing after being hit with the water, prosecutors declined to charge Pippen. Prosecutors also questioned whether the fan's police complaint was motivated by money, since he contacted Pippen's lawyer requesting compensation. (On July 15, prosecutors decided not to press charges.)

At the same time, Canadian authorities were weighing whether to upgrade a common assault charge against soon-to-be Los Angeles Lakers guard Gary Payton and his former Milwaukee Bucks teammates Jason Caffey and Sam Cassell. All three had been involved in an altercation outside a Toronto strip club on April 11, 2003, and had surrendered for booking a week later. On July 18, authorities upped the charges against Payton to two counts of common assault and one count of assault causing bodily harm. Cassell faces one count of common assault and one count of assault causing bodily harm. Caffey faces one count of assault causing bodily harm. Court officials will meet in June 2004 to decide whether the case will go to court.

Prosecutors in Houston, Texas, were reviewing a case filed against Rockets player Eddie Griffin after he was pulled over and arrested for possession of marijuana. Before authorities completed their review, however, Griffin would be arrested in a separate incident, this one for assaulting a woman and firing a gun at her. (In January 2004, after being released by the Rockets and signed by the New Jersey Nets in a $400,000 contract, Griffin was convicted on the marijuana-possession charge. Later, on February 2, 2004, he was arrested again and jailed in Houston for violating curfew requirements set by the terms of his probation. Then, on February 12, 2004, he was indicted on felony charges for assaulting his girlfriend and shooting at her. "None of this will interfere with Eddie re-entering the basketball world with the Nets," said Griffin's attorney Rusty Hardin. At the time this book went to press, Griffin was on leave from the Nets and undergoing treatment for alcohol abuse at the Betty Ford Center in southern California and awaiting trial on the assault and gun case. After completing substance abuse rehabilitation, Griffin has been ordered by a Texas judge to spend three months in a Houston halfway house.)

Prosecutors in Saginaw County, Michigan, were preparing to put Golden State Warriors star Jason Richardson on trial for domestic violence. On August 28, 2003, a jury convicted Richardson. On May 15, 2003, a jury in Cook County, Illinois, convicted Atlanta Hawks star forward Glenn Robinson of a similar crime.

Federal prosecutors in U.S. District Court in Michigan were making last-minute preparations for their trial of Sacramento Kings forward Chris Webber, who had been indicted for perjury, conspiracy to obstruct justice, and making false declarations before a grand jury. On July 14, the day before jury selection was to begin in his trial, Webber admitted to knowingly and intentionally lying to a federal grand jury and pleaded guilty to criminal contempt.

On July 7, Orlando Magic guard Darrell Armstrong was arrested for assaulting a female police officer in Orlando. One week later, Washington Wizards guard Jerry Stackhouse was arrested by police in Atlantic Beach, North Carolina, for allegedly assaulting a woman there. (In December 2003, the case against Armstrong was dismissed by a judge who ruled that it could not be proved beyond a reasonable doubt that Armstrong intentionally struck the officer. The case against Stackhouse was later dropped when he reached an out-of-court settlement with the victim.)

Authorities in Chapel Hill, North Carolina, were investigating NBA player Joseph Forte, who had an arrest warrant issued against him for assaulting a man. Forte eventually entered into a court-mandated dispute settlement with the victim.

In Oregon, the state's Division of Motor Vehicles lifted the driver's license of the Blazers' Qyntel Woods in July after he had been arrested a few months earlier for possession of marijuana, as well as for speeding and driving without a license or proof of insurance. (In January 2004, Woods pled no contest to the marijuana charge.)

And only four weeks before Kobe Bryant's arrest, prosecutors in Salt Lake City had decided, following a five-week investigation, not to indict Washington Wizards center Jahidi White for sexual assault. White had been accused of raping a twenty-four-year-old woman on February 14, 2003, at the Grand American Hotel in Salt Lake City, the same day the Wizards played the Utah Jazz. White's accuser, according to a published report, told police that she had met White the previous evening at a nightclub and had been drinking with him and his teammates before going with him to his hotel, where she eventually passed out. She said she was raped when she awoke. After a five-week investigation, Utah authorities determined there was insufficient evidence to indict White.

Seven of these cases involved violence against women, one of whom was a police officer. Two cases involved a gun. Three cases involved drugs. And these weren't just any old players. Nine of them—Payton, Robinson, Pippen, Bryant, Stoudamire, Cassell, Stackhouse, Webber, and Richardson—have been NBA All-Stars. Four of them will likely end up in the Hall of Fame.

Was this just a particularly bad month for the NBA? Hardly. Not these days, anyway. To be sure, during the Bob Cousy era, or in the days of Oscar Robertson, Bill Russell, and Bill Bradley, this would have been unthinkable. Even the more recent Magic Johnson–Larry Bird era did not see the rash of lawlessness that is currently gripping the NBA. A first-of-its-kind investigation into the criminal histories of current NBA players reveals that 40 percent of the athletes have had a formal criminal complaint filed against them for a serious crime.

To arrive at this percentage, I began by using the 2002–03 edition of the official NBA Register, which lists the names, birth dates, and places of residence for over 450 players who played during the 2001–02 season. Next I eliminated all foreign players (those who were born overseas and did not attend college in the United States). This left 417 players. Each of the 417 players' names and birth dates were sent to police departments and sheriff's offices in jurisdictions that the players have resided in, along with a written request seeking any arrest-history information on the players. So, for example, the complete player roster of the Portland Trail Blazers was sent to the Portland Police Department, along with a written request that each player be run through the department's computer system for arrest records. This procedure was followed in every city that hosts an NBA team. Similarly, the campus police departments at the universities and colleges attended by current NBA players were queried. For example, the names of current NBA players who attended the University of Michigan were sent to Michigan's campus police department for a records check. In all, arrest-history records were solicited from ninety-four police departments, including campus police departments.

Similar letters of solicitation were mailed or faxed to records clerks at forty state and federal courthouses, seeking information on whether NBA players had any criminal cases on file. Sixteen additional courts were queried by telephone.

Finally, twelve district attorneys' offices were queried in writing. Since prosecutors' records are not generally subject to Freedom of Information laws, this process required special permission from prosecutors to make on-site visits in order to view records, which included arrest-history information and conviction data for players.

Ultimately, over 150 letters seeking player arrest histories were sent under state and federal Freedom of Information laws. Due to state laws or agency policy, some agencies, such as the

Boston Police Department, declined to perform a records check on players. But many agencies and most courts complied with the records requests. In all, law-enforcement agencies and courts completed a records check on 177 of the 417 non-foreign-born players listed in the NBA Register. In other words, a records check was performed on 42 percent of the league's players. The results revealed that 71 (40 percent) of the 177 players researched had been arrested or otherwise recommended by police to prosecuting attorneys for indictment for a serious crime: namely, felonies or a misdemeanor involving violence, weapons, drugs, destruction or theft of property, or altercations with law-enforcement officials.

Forty percent is a stunning figure, particularly when compared to the results of a similar study I performed on NFL players six years earlier, which found that 21 percent of its players had been arrested for a serious crime. The NBA's arrest rate is roughly twice as high as the NFL's. The NBA's arrest rate is even more disturbing when one considers that it does not include players arrested for less serious offenses, such as routine traffic violations, urinating in public, violations of city noise ordinances, and other infractions. All of these cases were screened out.

Admittedly, since just under half of the league's players were subjected to a public-records check, it is conceivable that the 40-percent arrest rate for NBA players would drop if records could have been obtained on the remaining 240 players who did not undergo a records check. All unchecked players were run through LexisNexis, which tracks press reports. This process turned up an additional 29 players who had been arrested for a serious crime. These players are not included in the 40-percent figure, because police or court records were not obtained to corroborate the press reports. Nor is it accurate to suggest that merely running a player's name through LexisNexis satisfies performing a criminal-history check on a player. Many of the players whose arrest records surfaced through police and court record checks did not surface in the LexisNexis search.

Without question, this first-of-its-kind canvassing of law-enforcement agencies and courthouses is not as thorough as the sort of official criminal background check that would be performed by law-enforcement agencies and therefore has its limitations. Nonetheless, it represents an attempt to complete a records check on every non-foreign-born player in the league. And the 40-percent arrest figure avoids minor offenses and excludes all players whose arrest history could only be confirmed by a previously published press report.

In an attempt to respond to these findings, the NBA will likely trot out the usual suspects: *faulty statistics,* *"arrests don't equal convictions,"* and *racism.*

Faulty Statistics. The statistics are not faulty. They are the product of a sample predicated upon record availability, which is determined by state law and individual record-disclosure polices, as adhered to by police departments and other law-enforcement agencies. To put this in perspective, most public-opinion surveys performed in the United States sample less than 1 percent of the U. S. population. *Here almost half of the NBA population was sampled for their arrest histories.*

"Arrests don't equal convictions." This is the NBA's see-no-evil approach to the problem. In the NBA's eyes, arrests are not a problem unless they result in a conviction. Never mind those crime-scene photographs depicting blood on the floor and bruises on a battered woman, or the seized handgun with a player's initials engraved on it. Of course arrests don't equal convictions. But "not guilty" pleas don't equal innocence. And neither the NBA nor this book can judge whether a player's alleged criminal actions satisfy the elements of a particular criminal

statute. That is the role of the courts. Without a doubt, due process should be afforded to every player, and judgment reserved until the court process has run its course. But while justice may be blind, that doesn't mean the rest of us outside the justice system need to close our eyes to the reality playing out before us.

Who can deny that a league whose players are getting younger and richer is seeing those same players getting arrested with increased frequency for such serious offenses as rape, assault, domestic violence, illegal use or possession of guns, and use or possession of a controlled substance? Of the fifteen NBA players in contact with the criminal justice system in July 2003, only two of them saw their cases dismissed by prosecutors due to lack of evidence. The other thirteen were formally charged with crimes. One entered a court-ordered settlement and one reached an out-of-court settlement with the victim. One went on probation. Two more pleaded guilty. And two of them were convicted by a jury and sentenced. The remaining six players' cases are pending. To simply say that an arrest is not a conviction is not an adequate response.

Racism. When all else fails, cry racism. It is, of course, ironic when the wealthy white businessmen who, for the most part, run the NBA and its teams complain of racism. Nevertheless, it's an allegation that must be addressed. In fact, 81 percent of the NBA players sampled in this book are black; 91 percent of the players with an arrest history are black. That's not evidence of racism. That's the result of an honest, hard look at a league that is predominantly African American. A similar examination of the National Hockey League, which is composed almost exclusively of white players, would surely demonstrate that most, if not all, of its players, with a criminal history are white. There is no news bulletin in any of this.

Nor is it surprising that the NBA and many of the players featured in this book declined to be interviewed. After contacting

Damon Stoudamire's agent, Aaron Goodwin, and requesting to speak with Stoudamire about his drug arrest at the Tucson International Airport, I received a call back from Goodwin's assistant, who said: "I spoke with Aaron and he had a question. Is this an NBA-sanctioned book?" "No," I replied. "Then at this time they will decline an interview."

The message was clear: unless the NBA is controlling the message, the players won't speak. The NBA may be able to influence what its players say. But the volume of run-ins between players and law-enforcement officials indicates that the league is either unable or unwilling to control what its players are doing. And players' actions speak far louder than words. Stoudamire is a perfect example. His arrest on marijuana charges was not his first, nor even his second.

On February 23, 2002, Stoudamire's Portland neighbor called the police and reported that a home-security alarm was going off at Stoudamire's house. When police arrived, they found the front door open. Stoudamire was miles away, playing in a game at Portland's Rose Garden Arena. Following standard police procedure, officers entered the home, deactivated the burglar alarm, and searched the unoccupied home for intruders. While searching, they spotted a bag containing more than 150 grams of marijuana. The police seized it and later charged Stoudamire with a felony.

But before the trial took place, Stoudamire's lawyer challenged the constitutional grounds on which the police conducted their search, insisting that officers should have had a search warrant. The police responded that an inability to search potentially burglarized homes without first getting a warrant from a judge would compromise public safety. Stoudamire's lawyer prevailed when an Oregon Appeals Court ruled that the search was improper and therefore the marijuana was inadmissible as evidence.

The NBA's approach to this kind of case is: No conviction, no problem. But Stoudamire had a big problem. Nine months after police found a bundle of pot in his home, Stoudamire got arrested again, this time for possessing marijuana in his vehicle. On November 22, 2002, he and teammate Rasheed Wallace were on their way back to Portland following a game in Seattle. They were riding in Stoudamire's yellow Humvee, which was stocked with Smirnoff Ice, marijuana, and cigarette rolling papers, and driven by Stoudamire's friend Edward Smith.

Eighty-five miles south of Seattle, State Patrolman Rob Huss sat in his cruiser on Interstate 5, operating a radar gun just outside Chehalis, Washington. At two minutes to midnight, he observed the Humvee speed past at 84 miles per hour. Huss pulled the Humvee over and approached the passenger's side. When Stoudamire put down his window, marijuana odor poured out. Huss asked about the smell and all three men acted as if they didn't know what Huss was talking about and denied having any marijuana. Russ asked Stoudamire to step out of the vehicle.

"Man, I can't believe you're going to play it this way," Smith said.

"You have the right to remain silent," Huss said as Stoudamire got out. His eyes were bloodshot and glazed. He smelled of marijuana and alcohol. Huss asked him where the marijuana was located in the vehicle. Stoudamire hesitated, and then admitted pot had been smoked inside the Humvee. But he insisted it had all been burned up or smoked. He turned his pockets inside out, revealing only money.

A second trooper, Officer Brian Dorsey, arrived and asked Wallace and Smith to exit the Humvee. In the process, he asked Wallace about the marijuana smell.

"We had smoked a jay as we were driving down the freeway," Wallace said.

The odor was far too overwhelming to result from one or two joints. Dorsey wanted to know where in the vehicle the rest of the marijuana was hidden.

"We smoked it all," Wallace insisted.

The smell in the vehicle was so strong that the officers could not use the K9 dog that had been brought to the scene; his senses would simply have been overwhelmed by the odor. Meanwhile, Stoudamire kept denying the presence of marijuana in the vehicle. Still, without the aid of the K9, officers found marijuana on the floorboard beneath the front seat and in front of the passenger's-side seat, where Stoudamire had been sitting. They also found it in the glove box in front of Stoudamire's seat, on the floor near the center console, and in the seat pouch in front of where Wallace had been seated. Stoudamire and Wallace were arrested and in March 2003, Lewis County prosecutor Jeremy Randolph agreed to place them both on probation and ultimately drop the charges if both men committed no criminal violations in any state for a one-year period.

But Stoudamire's subsequent arrest at the Tucson International Airport threatened his probation in Washington. Stoudamire's lawyers filed a motion to get the marijuana suppressed, arguing that the airport police conducted an unlawful search when they opened the foil without a warrant. This time it didn't work. Arizona judge Paul Simon ruled that by entering an airport security checkpoint, Stoudamire consented to an administrative search of his person and his carry-on items. "Since the search was lawfully initiated," said Judge Simon, "an officer need not close his eyes to evidence of other crimes which he may uncover."

As this book went to press, prosecutors in Washington were preparing to take action against Stoudamire for violating his probation. And authorities in Arizona were preparing to prosecute him in connection with the airport arrest, for which the Blazers fined Stoudamire $250,000. But the team later decided that he didn't have to pay the fine; instead, he donated $100,000 to a Portland-area child-education program.

But if the NBA finds the Stoudamire situation embarrassing, it is easy to see why the Kobe Bryant case is far more threatening. Besides being a much more serious crime, rape complaints open the door to the dark, sordid sex life of athletes, one that is rarely seen by the fans. When prosecutors in Colorado indicted Kobe Bryant, they didn't just indict the league's brightest star. They indicted the NBA culture.

PART I

SEXUAL LIBERTIES

ONE

GROSS FELONY

Besides money, life in the NBA offers vast amounts of two other things: free time and sex. A pro game takes two hours to play. Throw in a couple hours for preparation and travel, and that leaves a tremendous amount of discretionary time. Much of that time is spent on the road, where NBA players play a minimum of forty-one games a year and spend as many as a hundred nights in hotels. This lifestyle leads many players to spend great amounts of time at strip clubs, topless bars, and other such nightspots. And players' celebrity status attracts a steady stream of opportunities for consensual sex. It is an environment hot-wired to produce allegations of sexual assault. This environment also makes it nearly impossible for a rape victim to file a criminal complaint against an NBA player without being labeled a groupie or a gold digger.

To overcome these labels, a rape victim's reputation must be clean enough to survive a relentless, well-financed effort to discredit her. Simply put, it takes a victim nothing short of Snow White to obtain a conviction in a sexual assault case against a celebrated athlete and emerge with a reputation still intact.

•   •   •

Twenty-three-year-old Jenny Stevens said yes when the owner of A Nanny For You—a Seattle-area nanny agency—called on January 4, 2000, and asked if she would accept an interim position with a family in nearby Bellevue. A permanent nanny had already been placed with the family but couldn't begin work for about two weeks. Jenny had previously done short nanny stints with two other wealthy families. She needed the money. She had finished two years of study at a community college, completing a medical-assistant training program, and was trying to save enough to return to school.

The agency told Jenny that the husband in the family she would be working for was an NBA player on the Seattle Sonics named Ruben Patterson. The name meant nothing to Jenny. She didn't follow sports and had little interest in basketball. Despite growing up in Washington, she couldn't name one Sonics player.

The next day, Jenny went to the Patterson home for an interview and to meet with Ruben's fiancée Shannon and their three children: a thirteen-year-old boy, a seven-year-old boy, and a five-month-old baby girl. The oldest boy was, in fact, Ruben's brother (Ruben is his legal guardian). The seven-year-old was Shannon's child from a previous relationship. Ruben was the biological father of the baby.

Although they were close in age, Jenny and Shannon's situations were quite different. Jenny is white; Shannon is black. Jenny lived in a cramped apartment and hustled for part-time jobs. Shannon lived in a spacious home in a gated community in Seattle's wealthiest suburb and did not work. Jenny and her fiancé, who worked with at-risk youth, had just postponed their marriage plans. Shannon was about to marry a twenty-four-year-old celebrity making $1 million a year playing basketball.

Yet none of this seemed to matter. Jenny and Shannon hit it off instantly, as if they had known each other for years. And

Shannon observed that the children were immediately comfortable around Jenny, an experienced daycare worker who handled the Patterson baby with ease. After talking for two hours, Shannon decided against hiring the other nanny and offered the permanent position to Jenny. Her duties would include being home during the day with the baby; picking the boys up after school; doing homework with them; cooking dinner; delivering the boys to doctor's appointments and sports practices; and doing the grocery shopping and housecleaning. There would be some overnights, as well as opportunities to travel with the family. Her hours would range between forty and sixty per week. The pay was $12 per hour. Jenny accepted on the spot, without even meeting Ruben, who was away.

When Jenny told her parents she had landed a full-time job, they were pleased. Her mother, a registered nurse, was glad her daughter was in a home with a baby. Mr. Stevens, a career social worker who investigated child-abuse cases for the state of Washington, was intrigued that his daughter would be employed by an NBA player. Mr. Stevens followed the Sonics and knew of Patterson's on-court reputation. An All-American out of the University of Cincinnati, Patterson had been drafted by the Lakers in 1998 before signing with the Sonics in1999. In his first season in Seattle he had established himself as one of the league's premier defenders, considered one of the few players in the league capable of guarding Kobe Bryant one-on-one. He was nicknamed "Kobestopper." The scouting report on Patterson was that a "nasty attitude drives his game" and "he doesn't back down," both traits highly sought after by NBA coaches and fans.

Jenny's father knew nothing of Patterson's off-the-court reputation or his background. Neither did Jenny.

Before he became a wealthy NBA star, Patterson grew up in the Cleveland area, where he had experienced violence from all perspectives: as a victim, a witness, and a perpetrator. According to records on file at the Cleveland Police Department, Patterson was held up at gunpoint and robbed while walking on a Cleveland street during his senior year of high school. An incident report indicates that two men pulled up alongside him in a car, aimed a long-barrel handgun at him, and demanded that he remove his shoes and hand over the gold chain around his neck and the cash in his pockets. "Don't run or I'll shoot you in the back," one of the thieves threatened Patterson, who complied with their demands. The men then sped off.

In 1997 Patterson witnessed a vicious domestic-violence incident in which his mother was attacked by an individual armed with scissors and shouting: "I'll get all you f—ers." Patterson stepped in and was able to disarm the suspect and the police were called. Patterson's mother declined to press charges.

Also in 1997, police were called after Patterson's sister reported being assaulted by him. The report said that Patterson "punched victim in face with closed fist and when victim tried to defend herself, named suspect then grabbed victim by her throat and lifted victim up in the air and then dropped victim on top of her vehicle and she rolled off and fell to the ground." No arrest was made in this case, which was forwarded to prosecutors for review and dropped.

Jenny officially began working in the Patterson home in January 2000. With her roots in a rural Washington town and her upbringing in a practicing Christian home where dating was not allowed until her sixteenth birthday, Jenny found the lifestyle of an NBA family new and at times exciting. She occasionally sat in reserved seats near the Sonics bench with Shannon. She got to drive the kids all over Seattle in the couple's new Ford Explorer.

She traveled with the family. And she attended some social events where Sonics players were present.

But her love for the job centered on her relationship with Shannon and the children. She and Shannon had become close friends, and the children regarded Jenny as a surrogate mother. When Jenny did overnights on a regular basis during the season, the baby sometimes slept with Jenny in her bed.

Her interaction with Ruben was more limited. He was often on the road or occupied with basketball and his friends. After the season, however, she saw a lot more of him. That's when the Pattersons returned to Cleveland for a month to get married and visit family and friends. They rented an apartment in the Cleveland area and Jenny stayed with them for the month.

After returning to the Seattle area in September 2000, Shannon elected to have cosmetic surgery on her stomach—a "tummy tuck." The procedure required an overnight stay at the surgery center and a few days of home bed rest afterward. Shannon asked Jenny to sleep at the house for the week to take care of the children.

It was close to ten P.M. on September 25 when Jenny stepped out of the shower, dried off, and put on her pajamas, adding an oversize sweatshirt for added warmth. It had been a long, tiring day; but a good one. Shannon's surgery went well and she would be returning home the following morning. The boys were tucked in bed. And the baby, sick with a cold, had been given her medicine. Before retiring to bed herself, Jenny had just one task left; retrieve the baby from Ruben, who had agreed to watch her while Jenny showered.

Jenny stepped from her guest room and headed down the hall to the master bedroom. As she reached the door, it was partway open. She raised her hand to knock. It was too late. Just inside the door she saw Ruben, completely naked, facing the television and masturbating. He turned and saw her.

Embarrassed, she turned her head, covered her face, and backed out of the doorway. She headed back down the hall. But before she had taken a few steps she could hear him coming up behind her. A chill overcame her. Then he did. He grabbed her from behind, firmly gripping her upper arms with his hands.

"Come on, Jenny," he said in a seductive voice. "Let's do it."

Jenny stiffened.

"I've been looking at you for so long," he said, reaching around her, trying to touch her breasts and her pubic area.

"No, Ruben. You don't know what you are doing."

"You know you want it," he said, assuring her he had a condom.

"No," she told him. "Shannon's one of my best friends."

The more he tried to touch her intimate parts the more she squirmed and tried to get away. But she had no chance. Ruben is six-five and weighs 225 pounds. She is five-eight and weighs 130 pounds.

He grabbed her by the upper arms again, squeezed her tight, and lifted her off the ground.

Jenny's feet flailed in the air. Afraid the boys were going to wake up and witness what was happening, she kept her mouth shut until he carried her into the nearby entertainment room.

"Come on," he said, his seductive tone shifting to a threatening one.

He fell back onto the couch as Jenny dropped to the floor between the couch and a glass coffee table. She was scared. He was frustrated.

For the first time in the encounter Jenny was facing Ruben. He had an erection. He did not have a condom on. He put his hand underneath her pajamas and touched her breasts. Then he reached inside her underwear and touched her vaginal area. She tried to squirm away and stand up, but banged against the glass table.

Ruben used his legs to box her in. He grabbed her head with his hands so that she could not turn her head side to side, let alone move the rest of her body. When she tried, he squeezed her head harder. She was trapped.

"Come on," he said forcefully.

He guided her head down toward his penis. She felt it against her face. She tried to turn her head. His grip was too tight.

Jenny cried as he put his penis in her mouth. He ejaculated into her mouth within seconds.

Then he let go of her head and she fell backward.

"Don't tell anyone," he said as he stood up and nonchalantly walked out of the room and went to bed.

In a heap on the floor, Jenny wept, alone.

After she gathered herself, she wondered, Should I run? Should I tell someone? Should I call the police? Should I stay? What about the children? Questions and fears raced through Jenny's mind. She wanted to flee. But Shannon had convinced her early on to never leave the baby alone with Ruben. One time early in her employment Jenny had, and Shannon reprimanded her, explaining that Ruben did not know what to do if the baby cried or how to properly feed her.

She had to stay. She cared too much about the children to just up and leave. Jenny reasoned that she would not encounter Ruben again that night. And Shannon would be home in the morning.

She went to the bathroom and washed off her face and rinsed out her mouth. Then she went to sleep in the guest room, hoping to wake up and find out she had had a nightmare.

•   •   •

That's the account that Jenny told officers and detectives from the Bellevue Police Department. It is documented in over fifty pages of transcribed, tape-recorded interviews conducted with her by sex crime investigators. It is corroborated by over 200 additional pages of reported evidence and transcribed interviews with witnesses directly involved in this case. These witnesses were those who first saw and spoke to Jenny following the incident. Days went by before Jenny first told the police. Initially, she wasn't going to report the assault. But a chain of events ultimately convinced her that she had to.

The morning after the assault, Jenny saw Ruben before he left to pick up Shannon from the surgery facility. He said nothing about the night before and acted as if it were any other morning. When Shannon returned to the house, Jenny stayed with her and nursed her during recovery.

Ruben packed and flew home to Cleveland, where a grand jury had returned an indictment against him for felony assault. Patterson was scheduled to appear in a Cleveland courtroom to answer the charges, which stemmed from an incident that took place on June 11, 2000. On that night, according to police and court records and interviews with the prosecutor, Patterson and his friends exited Top of the Flats, a Cleveland hip-hop nightclub, sometime after midnight. When they reached Ruben's brand-new, two-door, black Mercedes-Benz, they discovered that someone had used a key to scratch the paint.

Patterson was furious. Kevin Lewis, a thirty-six-year-old black male, came up and told Patterson that he saw the man who keyed his car. Lewis worked for a clothing store and had been in the parking lot, placing clothing advertisement flyers on car windshields. He provided a description of the alleged vandal.

Patterson wanted a name, but Lewis said he did not know the man's name. Patterson and his entourage suddenly accused Lewis, then punched him, knocked him to the ground, and beat and kicked him repeatedly after he was down. An incident report indicates that Lewis suffered bruises on his body, a broken thumb, and had his jaw broken in two places. He was taken to a nearby hospital, where he underwent oral surgery and had his jaw wired shut for two months.

With Ruben away, Jenny tried to figure out what to do next. First she told her best friend, Susi Sanders. Then she told her ex-fiancé, Isaac Vicknair. At first she felt too embarrassed and too guilty to speak about the details. Ultimately she did speak and Vicknair gave her the number for the crisis hotline for women and encouraged her to call.

They both urged Jenny to quit her job at once. But that would require an explanation to Shannon. She and Jenny were too close for Jenny to simply walk away. Nor did she want to. The thought of losing an intimate friend and never seeing the children again tore at her.

For the next few days she helped pack up the Patterson's home in preparation for a weekend move to a new home three blocks away. Shannon was due to sign the lease on Saturday, September 30. That was also the day Ruben would return from Ohio. Jenny knew she had to be gone by then.

Shannon and the children chose to stay in an Embassy Suites hotel the night before moving into their new home. When Shannon asked Jenny to stay overnight with them, Jenny agreed and decided to use the opportunity to break the news. Jenny asked her girlfriend Susi to come with her for moral support, while Isaac agreed to take the Patterson boys from the hotel and entertain them for the morning. Before telling Shannon, Jenny called Rebecca Vidmore, the owner of the nanny agency, to explain why she would no longer be working for the Pattersons. She told Vidmore that Ruben had tried to rape her and this would be her last day as their nanny.

It was roughly nine-thirty when Jenny faced Shannon. With her friend Susi looking on, Jenny told Shannon she had something to tell her. Shannon already knew that. She could read Jenny's face. Something was wrong.

"I'm going to be mad, aren't I?"

"Yeah, you're going to be mad."

"Did you wreck the truck?"

"No."

Jenny dropped her head and began to cry. Then she recounted the details of what transpired the night Shannon was in the surgery center. Shannon said nothing until Jenny got to the part about being forced to perform oral sex. Then something happened. In a rage, Shannon grabbed Jenny by the hair and jerked her head from side to side as she shouted obscenities at her. She punched Jenny in the head and the face with a closed fist.

Stunned, Susi froze in silence.

Jenny sobbed, not bothering to defend herself or retaliate.

Finally Shannon let go. She picked up a garbage can and kicked it in the air. "Shit," she said, before picking up the telephone and punching in the number for Ruben's agent, Dan Fegan, in California. She told Fegan to tell Ruben not to bother coming back. She was filing for divorce.

Fegan had no idea what was going on. The Pattersons had been married less than two months, so the phone call seemed to come from out of the blue. Shannon explained that Ruben had tried to rape their nanny.

Still upset, she hung up the phone and picked up her baby,

clutching her as she paced around the room. Then she tried Ruben on his cell phone. But she kept getting his voice mail, and finally just left him a message: "How did you think Jenny wouldn't tell me? How did you think you could get away with it?"

She hung up and approached Jenny. "I'm sorry," Shannon said. "I'm sorry." Both women wrapped their arms around each other and cried. Susi slipped out of the room, sensing they needed some time alone. When she returned a while later with coffee, Susi observed that Shannon still had tears in her eyes. "She knew that it was true," Susi later told police. "And she didn't want it to be."

Shannon had to go to the new house and sign the lease papers. She asked Jenny and Susi to ride over with her. Before they got there, Shannon told Jenny that the two of them would sit down with Ruben when he returned and sort things out. After they got to the new house, Shannon handed Jenny the keys to the Explorer and asked her to take the baby with her and go do some light grocery shopping. The cupboards were bare and everything was in boxes.

Jenny was shocked by Shannon's approach. She was acting as if everything would return to normal, as if the sexual assault were just a little speed bump in their lives. "She just doesn't get it," Jenny told Susi as they drove away. "I can't work there anymore. I can't."

Susi agreed. But neither of them knew what to do. They were driving the Pattersons' SUV with the Pattersons' baby in the backseat. Ruben was on a flight back from Ohio. By the time they finished grocery shopping and returned to the house, Ruben might be there.

Desperate, Jenny used her cell phone to call home. Her father spent his career counseling and helping children and teenagers who had been abused. He worked with the police and courts. She knew he would know what to do, but embarrassment and guilt had kept her from calling him sooner.

The phone rang at Jenny's home. It was just after noon. Her mother answered.

"I need to talk to Dad. I need to talk to Dad right now."

"Why, what's wrong?"

Jenny hesitated. "Ruben tried to rape me."

"What? What did you just say?"

Jenny started crying.

Jenny's father took the phone from his wife and asked Jenny what was going on.

She told him.

As a professional, Jenny's father had encountered many horrible stories about abused children. But no training, no experience, prepared him for this. He felt like shouting and crying at the same time. But both emotions would have to wait. His daughter needed sound advice, now.

"You need to go to a police department, the nearest one," her father said. "Take the child. Don't return to the residence at this point." He explained that the police could escort her to the Patterson residence. Once there, the police could return the baby and the car keys while Jenny waited in the police car.

She agreed to do it.

He had one more piece of advice: be sure to make a formal statement, a complaint to police. Tell them what happened.

This she was less sure about. "It will be in the paper," she said. "No one's going to believe me. Who's going to believe the nanny?"

"Please," he said, "make a statement."

•   •   •

Jenny drove to the police station in Issaquah, a town bordering Bellevue. While she waited there for a Bellevue officer to arrive, she fretted. What Ruben had done to her was bad enough. But reporting it to the police, she feared, would make her life a living hell and trigger a media firestorm that would turn her private nightmare into a public spectacle. At two-thirty that afternoon she told her story in graphic detail. The officer listened and took notes. "At times during the interview," he wrote, "Jenny was fearful, crying, sobbing, and having trouble completing sentences. This was especially apparent when she was talking specifically about the assault."

When Jenny finished making her statement, the officer had one question: Will you cooperate in a criminal prosecution if Ruben is charged?

Jenny paused. She knew he had done wrong. She wanted him held accountable. But she doubted she could face him in court. Besides, she said, he is a highly visible professional basketball player and a criminal case would attract tremendous media attention. That was the last thing in the world Jenny wanted.

The officer asked a follow-up question: Will you speak to a detective?

Jenny asked to speak with her father first. The officer obliged. "What should I do, Daddy?" she said over the phone.

Her father told her to go forward, meet with the detective.

Jenny hung up and told the officer she would do it.

Less than an hour later, Bellevue detective Jerry Johnson joined Jenny and the officer and accompanied them to the Pattersons' new home. At the door, Detective Johnson handed the baby to Shannon and spoke to her briefly.

Later Jenny told Detective Johnson something she had remembered. On the night of the assault the Pattersons' baby was badly congested and coughing. After giving her Robitussin, Jenny took the baby into the upstairs children's bathroom, shut the door, and turned on the hot water in the shower to humidify the room. While she sat holding the baby in the steam, the bathroom door opened unexpectedly. She looked up and saw Ruben.

"Oh, I thought you were in the shower," he said.

But she wasn't. Both Jenny and the baby were sitting in the bathroom, fully clothed.

"I didn't think of it until after the attack," Jenny told the detective. "Why was he—why would he be coming in if I was in the shower?"

When the baby saw her father, she went to him. While the baby was briefly with Ruben, Jenny quickly got ready for bed. It was when she returned to get the baby that Jenny encountered Ruben in the nude.

In retrospect, she found it hard not to blame herself for not seeing what was coming.

There's something that happens inside a father when his daughter is sexually violated. Fury and anguish collide, making even the most peaceful man want to turn violent. Stevens felt all that. But by the time he got to Jenny the next day, he wanted simply to comfort and protect her. When she told him she still had Shannon's ATM card, he immediately said he would return it. Both Jenny's parents knew Shannon. She and the children had accepted an invitation to spend the upcoming Thanksgiving with Jenny's parents while Ruben was out of town on a road trip.

En route, Stevens wondered what he would say, what he would do if he encountered Ruben. He approached the house and knocked on the door. Moments later Ruben opened it. Stevens stood face-to-face with the NBA player he had watched run up and down the court on television. Now all he saw was a man who sexually abused his daughter. He wanted to unleash a verbal tirade. He wanted to take him apart. Staring up into Ruben's eyes, he introduced himself as Jenny's dad.

A look of fear swept over Ruben's face. Stevens said he had come to return Shannon's ATM card. His hand trembling from anger, he extended it, holding out the card.

"Shannon, get over here," Ruben shouted into the house.

Jenny's father turned and walked away, leaving Ruben in the doorway holding the ATM card. Nausea wrenched his stomach as he reached the car. He got in, drove off, and wept.

TWO

THE PROBLEM SOLVERS

"She's full of shit," Patterson said into his phone. On the other end, Rebecca Vidmore, the owner of Jenny's nanny agency, had just told him about her phone conversation with Jenny earlier that morning, explaining why she had abruptly decided to quit working for the Pattersons. Ruben's flight back from Ohio to Seattle on September 30 had barely touched down when he called Vidmore, wanting to know what Jenny was saying.

By the time Ruben hung up with Vidmore, Jenny had already been to the police. He knew he had a major problem on his hands; in fact, he had two problems. He was also under indictment in Ohio for assaulting the man in the parking lot.

But this wasn't the first time Patterson had faced dual charges. While leading the University of Cincinnati Bearcats to a number one ranking in college basketball, he was arrested and charged with aggravated burglary following an incident with a former girlfriend. Also while at Cincinnati, the National Collegiate Athletic Association (NCAA) launched a comprehensive investigation into the Cincinnati program for all sorts of alleged violations. Patterson was at the center of the probe, accused of improper associations with agents and receiving prohibited payments.

At that time, Patterson had little need to worry. He played for a college team that freely gave scholarships to players with troubled backgrounds and routinely turned a blind eye when players had run-ins with the law. Among them were Nick Van Exel, Art Long, Danny Fortson, and Dontonio Wingfield.

Van Exel was offered a scholarship to Cincinnati even after it had been reported that during a fight he kicked an unconscious teammate and allegedly assaulted his girlfriend, a charge for which he was not arrested. Long, despite a prior conviction for selling marijuana to an undercover police officer, was given a scholarship to play for Cincinnati, too. After he arrived, he was charged with assaulting his girlfriend, for which he pleaded no contest. Then Long and teammate Danny Fortson were arrested for getting into an altercation with police officers. According to police reports, Long, who is six-foot-nine, 250 pounds, "walked up and whacked" a police horse four times. Fortson was charged with being disorderly while intoxicated. Both Long and Fortson were acquitted. And Dontonio Wingfield, just before enrolling at Cincinnati, pleaded guilty to two counts of misdemeanor obstruction and one count of criminal trespass after an altercation with police in Georgia.

Not one of these players graduated with a degree from Cincinnati. But every one of them made it into the NBA. In a 1996 cover story about the Cincinnati program, *Sports Illustrated* revealed that only one player who had exhausted four years of eligibility under Cincinnati coach Bob Huggins had graduated. "As long as a young man is talented enough on the basketball court, the Cincinnati administration will . . . enroll him despite untoward incidents in his past," *Sports Illustrated* concluded.

Patterson was no different. His burglary case was dropped after a grand jury declined to indict him. But the NCAA determined that Patterson had indeed received improper financial gifts and had engaged in prohibited contacts with two sports agents. The NCAA also concluded that Patterson had "repeatedly changed his story to investigators" in the course of the probe. As a result, the NCAA issued a fourteen-game suspension and ordered Patterson to pay $1,434 in restitution for the improper benefits he had received. The university appealed this decision on Patterson's behalf, arguing that the penalty was too harsh. At the time, Patterson happened to be the team's leading scorer. The NCAA rejected the university's appeal and Patterson sat out the first fourteen games of his senior year. But he returned to the lineup halfway through the season, reemerged as the team leader, and went on to be drafted by the Los Angeles Lakers.

According to a close friend, when Patterson left Cincinnati he could barely read and was unable to do even high school–level math. But college did teach him one thing: *athletic superiority is a way to escape accountability*. There is no better course to teach this lesson than big-time college athletics, except for the NBA, which only builds on this approach, overlooking off-the-court incidents in the backgrounds of college players.

But now Patterson faced implications far more serious than those that come with NCAA rules infractions. Felony charges in two states could land him behind bars and sever his ability to earn millions in the NBA. A rape charge in particular would bring an onslaught of bad press, too. Fortunately for him, his salary enabled him to attract some of the top problem solvers in the areas of public relations and criminal law.

Approximately 400 agents are certified by the NBA Players Association to represent players. This amounts to almost one agent for every roster spot in the NBA. Why so many agents? Money. NBA players are cash cows for agents. NBA players average $2.3 million in salary per year. Top-tier players have contracts in the

$80-million range and endorsement deals that exceed $25 million. The standard agent fee is 4 percent.

Yet player agents today are responsible for so much more than negotiating multimillion-dollar contracts, securing endorsement deals, and managing players' finances and business affairs. Today, the most vital function of an NBA agent is crisis management, which usually means navigating players through their legal problems. This is the function that enhances agents' earning power as much as it protects players. It is also the function that earns agents the nickname "handlers." When players get in trouble with the law, agents handle it.

For some agents, handling a player's legal problems means identifying and retaining the best criminal defense lawyers money can buy. But sometimes it also involves consulting on the legal defense strategy and crafting the public-relations approach that goes with it. Since many agents are lawyers themselves, this is a natural extension of their other agenting activities.

Patterson's agent was among the best at handling legal problems. Dan Fegan was graduated from Yale Law School in 1989 and went on to practice at the prestigious Los Angeles law firm O'Melveny & Meyers. From there he went on to establish himself as one of the top-ranked sports and entertainment lawyers in the country. Boasting a stable of NBA players as clients, Fegan signed both Patterson and Patterson's college teammate Kenyon Martin, who was the number one pick in the 2000 NBA draft. To handle Patterson's problem, Fegan needed a game plan to attack two criminal investigations simultaneously.

Priority number one was getting the Ohio case resolved quickly. Primary responsibility for this fell on two Cleveland defense attorneys: Robert Rotatom and Susan Gragel. They negotiated with Cuyahoga County prosecutor Brendan Sheehan. The lawyers reached the following agreement: Patterson's felony charge would be reduced to a misdemeanor, to which Patterson would plead guilty. In exchange, a recommendation was made to the court that Patterson receive a six-month suspended jail sentence. In other words, he would do no time as long as he did not violate probation for one year. He would also perform community service and testify against his friend Melvin Scott, who had been arrested alongside him in the incident.

On January 29, 2001, an Ohio judge accepted these terms and ordered Patterson to pay a $1,000 fine. The judge also permitted Ruben to perform his community service obligations at a youth basketball program in Cleveland, and have his probation transferred to Washington.

When Ruben testified at Melvin Scott's felony assault trial, he did not, according to prosecutors, make a good impression on jurors. "He came in dressed with his Armani suit and his gold chains," prosecutor Brendan Sheehan recalled. "The jury was told that Scott threw the jaw-breaking punch. The jury didn't believe Ruben, who testified to this fact. So the jury acquitted Melvin Scott."

Sheehan also said that his office had no idea at the time they negotiated Patterson's plea bargain that he was under a felony investigation for attempted rape in Washington. He indicated that had his office been made aware of this fact, the plea negotiations and the terms of probation would likely have been approached quite differently by the prosecution. But as it stood, under the deal Patterson received in Ohio, even if he were later convicted of sexual assault in Washington it would not qualify as a violation of his probation, since the date of the alleged attempted rape in Washington preceded the date of Patterson's conviction in Ohio.

"After this case I don't even watch the NBA, I was so disgusted by what I saw," Sheehan said.

For their part, the NBA suspended Patterson for three games

on account of his assault conviction, which cost him $34,000 in salary. The Sonics took no additional action. And like that, the Ohio problem was solved.

The sexual-assault case posed a much bigger challenge and threatened to derail Patterson's career. Even without a conviction, the mere mention of a celebrated athlete in conjunction with a sex crime allegation can trigger an avalanche of scrutiny and negative publicity. For this reason, when high-profile athletes are accused of a sex offense, the strategy for countering the allegation can be summed up in one word: containment. Fortunately for Patterson, neither of the two things that normally alert the press to such incidents—a 911 call or an arrest—had taken place. Patterson and Fegan hoped to keep it that way.

As the police were tracking down witnesses and building their case, Patterson and Fegan started calling witnesses too, reaching some of them even before the police did. Patterson's first calls were to Rebecca Vidmore, Jenny's boss. He told her that the incident didn't happen the way Jenny had claimed. And he informed Vidmore that when Shannon wasn't around Jenny had a habit of telling him how sexy he looked.

Vidmore tried to remain neutral—she had a business to run. But she was torn. She had become close friends with Shannon, and to a lesser extent with Ruben. She had gone out socializing with them and shown them around Seattle. She was one of the only friends the couple had made since moving to the Pacific Northwest. The Pattersons were also her clients. Now Ruben stood accused by one of Vidmore's employees and the Patterson marriage was on the rocks. "Your wife needs your attention right now," she told him, hoping to end the conversation. "I don't need to talk to you about this anymore."

Shortly after hanging up with Patterson, Vidmore got another call, this one from Fegan. She later told police in a recorded statement: "Dan Fegan called me over the weekend because he knew Jenny had called me. And he asked me questions."

Fegan did more than ask questions. He gave instructions. Fegan knew that Vidmore had a direct line to Jenny. He told her to find out what Jenny wanted out of this.

"Dan had offered for me to get information," Vidmore told police, "such as, 'What does Jenny want? What is she looking for?'"

The next time Vidmore talked with Jenny on the telephone, she took notes when Jenny indicated that all she wanted monetarily was to collect the remaining $8,000 that would have been owed her had she been able to complete her one-year employment contract. "I did relay that information to Dan," Vidmore later told police.

But according to Vidmore, there was something else Fegan asked her to do. "He wanted me to offer her ten thousand dollars to just go away," Vidmore said in an interview for this book.

Vidmore said she did not comply with Fegan's request because she thought it was illegal and because Shannon Patterson was opposed to it.

Fegan did not respond to repeated attempts to be interviewed for this book.

The police soon discovered that Vidmore wasn't the only witness who had been approached. A Seattle businessman with ties to numerous Sonics players and team officials received a call from Patterson too. The businessman had previously been introduced to Jenny by the Pattersons at a social event.

"He [Patterson] called and told me that something had happened and wanted to get together with me," the businessman said when questioned by police.

It quickly became apparent to investigators why Patterson wanted to talk to the businessman. Patterson knew that on the evening in which the businessman had met Jenny at the social event, she had accused him of something too, albeit something far less serious. Nonetheless, it was sexual in nature, and if the businessman's version of events were believed, it might discredit Jenny as someone who had falsified a sexual complaint previously. The incident happened during a break in the social event, when the businessman approached Jenny while she was separated from others and asked if she was interested in getting together sometime to have a drink. But Jenny soon reported to Shannon, who was at the social event, that the businessman did more than invite her out for drinks. Jenny said that he took her hand and placed it on the outside of his pants, against his penis.

As soon as she heard this, Shannon confronted the man. "Shannon asked me if I had groped her or if I had tried to make her perform some act of sexual indecency on me," the businessman later told the police. "I told Shannon that wasn't true."

When police called the businessman to question him in connection with the sexual-assault complaint filed against Patterson, the businessman insisted that Jenny wrongly accused him of placing her hand on his crouch.

The police asked the businessman if he ever told his wife that he had been falsely accused by Jenny. He said that he had never mentioned it to his wife. "Did you have to explain why the cops were calling?" a detective asked him. "No," the businessman said. "Because, um, we had never . . . we had not had any conversations about that incident. Uh, I kind of just, you know, there was nothing to talk about, there was nothing going on."

The police didn't believe the businessman's story. He told police that Jenny had approached him in hopes of getting access to other Sonics. But he could not provide an instance in which

Jenny had engaged in the slightest bit of sexual activity with an NBA player. Meanwhile, the police had found a corps of witnesses who supported Jenny's account of events, including her parents, her ex-fiancé, and her best friend. Although none of them was an eyewitness, each of them was an "outcry witness," meaning they had received a fresh account of the incident from Jenny in close proximity to the event. Police tape-recorded and analyzed each outcry witness's statement, comparing what Jenny told each of them to what Jenny told police. The police concluded that Jenny's story had been very consistent no matter whom she told. "The story rung true," one investigator said.

Ruben and Jenny, however, were the only two people who knew what happened between them on the night in question. Ultimately, it would come down to her word against his. Credibility and personal reputation would go a long way to decide who was more believable. Patterson had a criminal record and was already on probation for a violent crime in Ohio. Jenny was a young nanny who had grown up in a home where dating before age sixteen had been discouraged. She had nothing in her history to suggest she was a sports groupie or even had an interest in athletes. Prior to working for the Pattersons she had never even met a professional basketball player, let alone had a sexual relation with one. Portraying her as a promiscuous groupie would be a tall order, as would the suggestion that she was a gold digger. After all, she had not filed a civil lawsuit seeking money from the Pattersons.

Patterson had still another problem. From the standpoint of an accused sex offender, there is probably no worse place in the United States to be charged than King County, Washington. King County prosecutor Norm Maleng's office has a reputation for being one of the most aggressive prosecuting agencies on sex offenses in the nation. It was the first prosecuting attorney's office in the United States to create a special division to prosecute sex crimes. Many of the sex crime units now common throughout the nation are patterned after King County's.

To counter this, Fegan needed to find Patterson more than a top-flight criminal lawyer; he needed someone adept at helping high-profile people defuse high-profile problems. Fegan found his man: John Wolfe, a private attorney whose fee is over $400 an hour. He was the go-to guy for powerful and wealthy men accused of sex offenses. When talk of impeachment swirled around Washington State governor Mike Lowry after his deputy press secretary resigned in 1995 and accused Lowry of fondling her and making improper and salacious suggestions, Lowry called Wolfe. The end result was a quick out-of-court settlement in which Lowry paid his former aid $97,500. No lawsuits. No criminal charges. No impeachment. Problem solved.

Wolfe became the lawyer of choice for criminally accused athletes in the Seattle area after he successfully defended Seattle Seahawks quarterback Gale Gilbert in 1987. Gilbert had been charged twice with sexual assault within a six-month period and faced separate trials for raping one woman and sexually molesting another. After winning an unlikely acquittal in the rape trial, on June 1, 1988, Wolfe disposed of the second case for Gilbert two days later by convincing prosecutors to let the quarterback plead guilty to second-degree attempted assault. Then Wolfe succeeded in persuading the judge to spare Gilbert any jail time, and instead sentence him to 240 hours of community service.

From then on, sports agents around the country called him for help. Most of Wolfe's clients have been NBA players, and most of Wolfe's cases have never seen the light of day. That's why players and their agents hire him.

One such case involved Chris Mullin, the former 1992 U.S. Olympic "Dream Team" member and NBA All-Star who played for the Golden State Warriors and Indiana Pacers. On April 2, 1994, Mullin and the Warriors were in Seattle to play the Sonics. The team stayed at the Stouffer Madison Hotel. On the day of the game, two women—ages twenty-six and thirty-six—met Mullin in the team's hotel lobby. The twenty-six-year-old accompanied Mullin to his room at around one P.M. Sometime after two P.M. she emerged from Mullin's room and called 911 to report that she had been assaulted.

Seattle police officer Dan Whelan and his female partner responded to the hotel. The female officer interviewed Mullin's accuser. She said that she had been attending a craft fair held at the hotel when she and her girlfriend met Mullin in the lobby. He offered them complimentary tickets to that evening's game. The women went to his room to pick up the tickets. At that point, the accuser went inside with Mullin, while the other woman left. Once inside his room, the accuser said that Mullin tried to seduce her with a kiss. She said that when she resisted, Mullin pulled her toward him and onto the bed, causing a minor injury. She revealed a scratch on her left breast. After he made further advances that were rejected, she said that she left the room.

Meanwhile, Officer Whelan contacted Mullin at the hotel. Mullin immediately indicated he wanted to speak to his attorney. He called his agent in Washington, D.C., Bill Pollak, who got on the phone with Officer Whelan. Pollak introduced himself as Mullin's agent, a lawyer and a former member of President Jimmy Carter's administration. Then Pollak told Whelan he wanted to have an off-the-record conversation. Whelan informed him that he does not do off-the-record conversations during formal police investigations. Pollak explained that Mullin had a game to get to and promised that Mullin would be available to answer questions after the game.

The minute Pollak hung up with Mullin he started calling sources in Seattle seeking referrals on Seattle's top criminal defense attorneys. He was told to hire Wolfe. But Wolfe was on vacation, skiing with his family in Canada at the time. Pollak called Wolfe's office and left his name, phone number, and an urgent message: *This is an emergency. I've got a problem in Seattle and you're going to solve it.*

Wolfe returned the call from Canada. Pollak explained the situation and said he needed Wolfe in Seattle right away.

Wolfe was five hours away and could not get there that fast. Pollak offered to dispatch a helicopter to Wolfe at once. Finally, Wolfe convinced Pollak he could handle the situation over the phone until he returned to the city.

When Mullin stepped off the court at the conclusion of the Sonics game, Officer Whelan and his partner, both in plain clothes so as to appear inconspicuous, were waiting for him. They escorted him directly into a private room and read him his rights. Then they asked him to give his version of events. "He said they kissed and that was about it," said Whelan. "And she became uncomfortable and left."

Whelan asked Mullin if he would put his statement in writing. Mullin said no. After less than an hour the interview concluded. Mullin pulled sweatpants over his uniform and the police escorted him to the team bus, which was waiting for him beside the arena. Whelan and his partner concluded their preliminary investigation and turned things over to the sexual-assault unit for further investigation.

Then Wolfe took over. Other than one small press report that said an unidentified woman had made an accusation against Mullin, word of the investigation did not get out. Mullin was married, enjoyed one of the best reputations of anyone in the league, and had no criminal record. Pollak wanted to keep it that way. Wolfe did not disappoint. He launched a thorough investigation into Mullin's accuser.

Meanwhile the police forwarded their investigation to the prosecutor's office for review. A police supervisor who was familiar with the accuser had recommended against arresting Mullin, unwilling to charge him solely on the basis of her statement. Before prosecutors made a final decision, Wolfe finished his investigation, which turned up information in the accuser's past that would challenge her credibility. On July 30, 1994, four months after the complaint was filed, prosecutors quietly dropped the case. An eight-page internal screening memorandum at the Seattle City Attorney's Office made available for this book did not explain why, other than to suggest that the required elements for criminal assault—an intentional touching of another person that is harmful and offensive, and which would offend an ordinary person who is not unduly sensitive—could not be proved in this case.

When contacted, Wolfe declined to comment on the Mullin case or the Patterson case, citing the nature of the attorney-client relationship that prohibits him from discussing client matters without the client's permission. Mullin, who now works as an assistant in the Golden State Warrior organization, did not respond to interview requests, or to requests for permission to talk to Wolfe.

Nonetheless, Wolfe's representation of Mullin produced a double victory: no charges and no publicity. Even the decision to drop the case did not receive any press. The whole case just disappeared.

Fegan hoped for the same result for Patterson. Wolfe went right to work. First he hired Seattle area private investigator Roger Dunn, who oversees a top-flight team of investigators, former Seattle area police officers with expertise in surveillance and criminal investigations, including one retired sex crimes detective.

In such cases the role of the investigator is to turn up anything and everything that could discredit Jenny or her account of
what transpired between her and Patterson. And find out
whether she had a motive to lie.

Their approach: leave no stone unturned.

Interviews were conducted with people close to Jenny, including her past employer. Records were checked to find out if she
had ever previously accused anyone of sexual assault, whether she
had a criminal record, and whether she owed anyone money—
from creditors to someone who may have won a judgment
against her in a lawsuit. Jenny was even put under surveillance
and followed, although Wolfe categorically denied that he or his
private investigator had any role in the surveillance.

The results convinced Wolfe that Patterson's case wasn't
going away without charges being filed. He had seen enough
athlete-acquaintance rape cases to know that the decision
whether to file charges hinges more on the accuser's actions and
her credibility than on the athlete's. A woman who willfully goes
to a player's bedroom, hotel room, or any other intimate place
and then claims rape puts prosecutors in the position of having
to explain to a jury why she went to an famous athlete's bed, if
not for sex. In a he said, she said situation, this gives defense attorneys the upper hand.

But there were two glaring problems in the Patterson case.
Patterson insisted that the sex act that took place was by consent,
that Jenny went to his bedroom with the intent to participate in
sex. However, if this was true, it raised the commonsense question: Then why didn't the act take place in the bedroom? Why did
Jenny run to the opposite end of the house and end up with her
back against a glass table on the floor of the recreation room?

The other problem was that unlike women who meet an athlete once and accompany him to a hotel room, Jenny worked for

Ruben and slept at his home often by way of her job responsibility. And there was no evidence that she had ever had sexual contact with him, or any other athlete, previously.

Wolfe decided that the best Patterson could hope for was to get the charges reduced (down from a felony), keep him out of prison, and dispose of the case without any publicity. Normally defense attorneys don't start talking with prosecutors until after a client has been charged with a crime. Not Wolfe. Not when the client is an NBA player under investigation for a felony sex crime that threatens to trigger a media firestorm if discovered by the press. Wolfe wanted to talk to prosecutors right away.

King County deputy prosecutor Lisa Johnson had been reviewing the Bellevue Police Department's investigation, which classified Patterson's actions as a felony. But Johnson had to determine whether Jenny's claim and the supporting facts turned up by the police investigation could convince a jury beyond a reasonable doubt that a felony had taken place. She hadn't yet made up her mind when she and Wolfe began talking. He wanted three things: the case treated as a misdemeanor, no jail time, and minimal public exposure of the allegations supporting the charge. He had a number of facts and arguments on his side. There were no witnesses other than the accuser and the accused. Patterson's position would be that consensual oral sex took place. And there was no compelling physical evidence to refute this position.

Johnson decided that if she couldn't arrive at a mutually agreed upon resolution with Wolfe and the case went to trial, she would charge the case as a felony. But her main objective was to get a conviction and jail time. Before any charges were filed, Wolfe and Johnson went into private negotiations. Ultimately, Wolfe and Johnson agreed to the following: Patterson would be charged with a misdemeanor, not a felony, and he would enter a plea under the "Alford doctrine," which would allow him to deny guilt while admitting sufficient facts for a jury to convict him. Wolfe liked to refer to the Alford plea as "a problem-solving mechanism." Both sides got something here. Patterson could stand up and insist that he committed no crime. But since Washington treats an Alford plea as a guilty plea, Patterson would have a conviction on his record and he would be required to register as a sex offender, both of which the state wanted.

The timing of the plea would coincide with the filing of the indictment, snuffing out the chance for extended media coverage from a drawn-out legal saga.

For punishment, both sides understood that Johnson would recommend a one-year jail sentence, with all but fifteen days suspended, two years' probation, restitution to the victim, and Patterson's registering as a sex offender. Wolfe would recommend that the one-year sentence be suspended in entirety. He would also seek community service in place of probation.

Wolfe and Johnson were willing to live with the judge deciding on whether to impose a fifteen-day jail sentence, as well as the issue of community service versus probation. The objective was to avoid a trial. For Patterson, the risks of a trial were too great: he would be tried for a felony carrying an eight-year prison term, and he could lose.

There were other factors to consider. The Sonics were aware of the nature of the allegations against Patterson and the looming charges. And they had made it clear to him that they had no interest in re-signing him after the season. Fegan's prospects of landing a contract for Patterson with another team would be slim if he were headed into a full-blown criminal trial for a sex crime. The dollars associated with any contract signed under those conditions would be even slimmer. And the prospect for future endorsement deals would be dead. There was simply too much money at stake—for Patterson *and* for Fegan—to risk a trial.

For Jenny, a trial guaranteed massive media exposure, which she feared. More than anything, she wanted to keep this incident out of the newspaper. It was the one goal she shared with Patterson. Besides, she was tired of being followed, and tired of the uncertainty of it all.

When Wolfe notified Patterson of the deal, he was pleased. When Johnson notified the police, they were not. Investigators felt that Patterson should be charged with a felony, and they resented the fact that he was receiving what appeared to them as preferential treatment. For example, before Patterson could be arraigned and plead guilty he had to be booked, photographed, and fingerprinted by the agency that investigated him. But Wolfe had worked out an arrangement with prosecutors whereby Patterson would go around standard police procedure and be booked by another agency far removed from the Bellevue police station. For the officers who spent six months on the Patterson investigation, it represented the first time in their collective careers that a suspect had been permitted to be booked by an outside agency.

Nonetheless, the police recognized that the deal was done. Patterson would be arraigned in court and plead guilty without any fanfare. The press would not know about it until it was over. The court date was set for Friday, May 11, 2001.

THREE

HUSH MONEY

"The guy's got a zillion dollars." Jenny's ex-fiancé, Isaac Vicknair, made this point to her more than once.

"To tell you the truth, I brought it up," Vicknair told the police. "I tried my very best to convince her to go for that because I feel like she got done really wrong, and that would be good compensation."

Vicknair just couldn't convince her. But he did help her find someone who could—a lawyer. The idea that she needed a lawyer of her own had not occurred to Jenny or her family; they figured that working with the district attorney was sufficient. Jenny had no personal experience with the criminal justice system from a victim's standpoint. She didn't know what to expect. Nor did she or her parents know any lawyers from the Seattle area, or what kind of lawyer to contact, or how to go about finding the answer.

Isaac Vicknair's father, Richard Vicknair, is the former executive director of the Family Values Alliance and the founder and pastor of the Westside Church, one of Seattle's largest congregations. Mr. Vicknair is a longtime friend of Seattle private attorney Roger McKinstry, a highly respected trial lawyer who had also been rated as one of the best business litigation lawyers in the

United States. One of his specialties was mediating settlements in civil lawsuits. Jenny agreed to meet with McKinstry.

For Jenny, two things were clear. Patterson had committed a serious offense against her, for which he needed to be held accountable. When contacted for this book, Jenny did not discuss her incident with Patterson. She did say, however, that after months of a difficult criminal investigation, she wanted no part of a civil lawsuit against him. "I told him [McKinstry] I never wanted to go that route," Jenny said. "I didn't want money at all. It upset me that people would think that's what it was about."

Jenny said that McKinstry's response was: "You're not going to get the kind of justice that you should. This is the way we get justice today." Justice meant a great deal to Jenny, too. In her view, Ruben had always escaped consequences. "I've seen other things that were wrong happen and how it never affected him," she said. "The consequences never hit him. It was just a mild inconvenience at most."

Jenny retained McKinstry, who first approached Wolfe a couple of months before Wolfe had negotiated the plea agreement with the prosecutor. A source familiar with the initial discussions between McKinstry and Wolfe said that McKinstry wanted close to $2 million to avert a potential lawsuit by Jenny against Ruben. It was clear that if Ruben pled guilty to a sex crime, winning a civil suit against him would be a virtual slam dunk. The plea would be a clear admission of wrongdoing. The question would be a matter of how much a jury would award for damages. McKinstry felt it would be well over $2 million. Wolfe disagreed and rejected the deal.

As a result, negotiations broke off. Meanwhile, McKinstry introduced Jenny and her family to his partner, attorney Jan Olson, whose role would be to resume negotiations with Wolfe after Ruben's plea bargain was finalized.

•   •   •

It was early in the day on Monday, May 7, 2001, when the phone rang at the Bellevue Police Department. A Seattle reporter wanted a copy of the police report in the Ruben Patterson attempted-rape investigation. Up to that point, not a word had been printed about the investigation, which had gone on for nearly eight months. That was about to change.

Washington State has a fairly liberal approach toward public access to police and court records, although reports from active investigations are generally withheld and sex offense reports are sanitized. From the police perspective, the Patterson investigation was closed. And since a representative from the media had requested a report, the police released one. Holding back the hundreds of pages of reports filed in the Patterson investigation, the police instead put out a three-page summary. It mentioned Patterson by name. It did not name the victim.

By late afternoon, the Seattle print, television, and radio journalists were chasing the story. Wolfe, Fegan, and Patterson were outraged. Forced to respond, Wolfe issued a statement on Patterson's behalf:

> Ruben Patterson denies that he engaged in any criminal conduct. Nonetheless he wishes to apologize for his act of marital infidelity. He wishes to apologize to his wife, to his team and to the complaining witness to the difficulties that he has created.
>
> In order to bring closure to this incident, and avoid the significant emotional and financial burden that it would create for he [*sic*], his family and the complaining witness were he to go to trial, he will be entering an Alford plea.

The approach was simple: admit sex, confess to adultery, and deny attempted rape. The Sonics issued a statement too. CEO and general manager Wally Walker sidestepped the sensational allegations and said simply: "As an organization, any legal situation regarding an employee, including Sonics . . . is treated very seriously."

The following day, under the headline SONICS' PATTERSON FACES RAPE CHARGE, the *Seattle Times* reported that the Pattersons' twenty-four-year-old nanny "found Patterson . . . naked and masturbating" and that "Patterson overpowered her and forced her to perform oral sex."

The story dominated Seattle talk radio and was made fodder for the newspapers until Patterson's appearance before Judge Brian Gain in Superior Court on May 15 to plead guilty and undergo sentencing. It was the first and only time that Patterson spoke publicly about the incident. "Your honor, I did not commit any criminal act last summer with the complainant witness," he began. "But I did participate in consensual sexual acts and cheated on my wife. I would like to apologize to everyone that I have hurt by my stupid decision, including my wife, my family, and my team and my fans. I made a terrible mistake cheating on my wife. I have learned a painful lesson."

Despite her initial fury toward Ruben when she first learned of the incident, Shannon Patterson stayed with Ruben and defended him before the judge. "I am here today because I do not believe that Ruben raped or attempted to rape our former nanny," she said. "If I honestly believed that he committed those crimes, I would have taken our children and left a long time ago. Ruben and I have talked about him cheating on me and we have worked that out between us."

Immediately after the incident she was demanding a divorce. Now she was Ruben's staunchest and most credible defender.

This would not have surprised Wolfe. Speaking generally about his experience as an attorney, Wolfe said that in almost every case he handled involving an athlete accused of rape, the initial reaction by the wife was consistent with Shannon's. But after a brief cooling-off period, usually a few days, the wife would rechannel her anger toward the victim. Why? It is easier to believe that a woman preyed on your husband than to come to grips with the opposite.

Fegan told the judge that the NBA would surely punish Patterson with a multigame suspension and a six-figure fine. Then he spent most of his time railing against the Bellevue Police Department for releasing portions of the police report that included information about Patterson masturbating. Fegan said he had received more than six phone calls from around the NBA regarding the allegations that were reported in the press. With Patterson a free agent at the time, Fegan was trying to land him a contract. "At this point," he told the judge, "it would be difficult to calculate the harm, the potential harm Mr. Patterson has suffered regarding this information in terms of his value around the league."

When Wolfe made his case for a lenient sentence, he wasted no time going after the police. "Two good lawyers sat down and recognized we had a problem," he said. "We solved it. This was a routine case until the Bellevue Police Department determined that they didn't like the deal." Wolfe resented the police department's decision to release its report before the case could be resolved in court. "It resulted in our not receiving the benefit of the bargain we thought we were going to get," complained Wolfe.

Before closing, Wolfe asked that Patterson receive no jail time and be required to perform community service. He added that Patterson would pay a price with his wallet and implied it would come via lawsuit. "There will be a civil trial in this case, it appears," Wolfe told the judge, as Jenny's lawyer, Jan Olson, sat silently in the courtroom.

Through all of this the judge heard little from Team Patterson about the reason they were all in court: because a sex crime had been committed. Jenny and her family did not attend the hearing and Olson did not address the court. Only prosecutor Lisa Johnson spoke in Jenny's behalf.

"The defendant is not the victim here," she told the judge. "Mr. Patterson is no more or less culpable because of his celebrity. He is, however, like anyone else, responsible for his actions." She asked the judge to impose a fifteen-day jail term.

After listening to both sides, Judge Gain made clear that in his mind the case was not about the Bellevue Police Department, its conduct, the NBA, or Patterson's celebrity status. "Mr. Wolfe, you have talked about the benefit of the bargain," Judge Gain said. "Celebrity carries with it positives and negatives. And unfortunately Mr. Patterson, I'm sure, benefits from a lot of those positives but he also has to live with the negatives."

Contrary to Wolfe's characterization of the case as "routine," the judge said there was nothing routine about it. "The question is whether or not Mr. Patterson should be treated differently because of his celebrity and it is my feeling that he should not be."

But Patterson's celebrity status had already afforded different treatment. From the outset of the police investigation he had an agent coaching him and telephoning at least one key witness. Second, he had one of the top criminal defense lawyers in Seattle working aggressively on his behalf. That was a direct result of his status and income. Rarely do accused sex offenders have such talented counsel. Finally, Patterson had press releases issued and spokesmen talking for him. Rarely do accused sex offenders get such opportunities.

The judge sentenced Patterson to one year in prison, suspending all of it but fifteen days. He ordered Patterson to begin serving the fifteen days' jail time no later than July 17. He required him to register as a sex offender. He imposed a two-year period of supervised probation and ordered him to commit no criminal acts during that time or he would be required to serve the 350-day portion of his jail term that had been suspended. And he imposed a $5,000 fine on Patterson.

On July 17, Ruben Patterson began serving his jail term. But he didn't do it inside a Washington jail, or any other jail. Instead, the court allowed him to serve his sentence in the privacy of his off-season home in Ohio, with some time knocked off for good behavior.

Paul Allen, the cofounder of Microsoft with Bill Gates, is the third-richest man in America, worth $22 billion. And he still has a $5-billion stake in Microsoft, prompting *Forbes* magazine to write that he "has plenty of room for risk." Only the NBA could bring a pair like Allen and Patterson together. Allen owns the Portland Trail Blazers. And while Patterson was serving time for a sex crime, Allen's management team began negotiating with Dan Fegan to sign Patterson to a contract. But there were some issues to resolve.

First, Blazers general manager Bob Whitsitt telephoned Wolfe to get a handle on the terms and conditions of Patterson's probation. There were two legal issues. Arrangements would have to be made for Patterson to complete his probation in Oregon. Also, as a registered sex offender in Washington, Patterson would have to join the sex offender registry in Oregon. But neither of these were deal breakers for Allen and the Blazers; lawyers could work out those details.

There was, however, a third issue that got the Blazers' attention: the unsettled matter of Jenny and the need for Ruben to enter into a confidential settlement agreement that would pay her money in exchange for her silence. But Allen quickly learned that NBA team owners take risks that are a little different from those taken by entrepreneurs in the high-tech industry, such as whether to invest millions on a gifted young player with a rap sheet. If Allen wanted Patterson, he would have to be willing to live with the risk. He was.

Before Patterson finished his "jail term," Allen and the Blazers had agreed to pay him $33.8 million over six years; he had been making a mere $1 million per year prior to his sex crime conviction. As soon as Patterson completed his in-home jail term, the Blazers called a press conference in order to introduce the media to Patterson. "I'm not a bad guy," Patterson told the Portland press. "I'm not a rapist. I'm a great guy."

The NBA is one place where a registered sex offender can get a $33-million increase in salary the day he gets out of jail, and then be introduced to the public as a "great guy" without any questions being asked. But Allen could only hope that his risk didn't backfire. The organization had previously taken a beating in the press following a string of arrests and disciplinary problems by players, all of which caused local media to dub the team the "Jailblazers."

The irony was that Patterson had just served time for an offense far more serious than any of the incidents that had caused the Blazer organization so much bad press. But few people in Portland realized the full extent of what had taken place in Seattle. Allen could only hope things would stay that way now that Patterson was wearing his team's uniform.

Whether that information remained forever hidden hinged on conversations taking place in Seattle between Patterson's lawyer, John Wolfe, and Jenny's lawyer, Jan Olson. The Blazers had a big stake in the outcome. Both lawyers had a problem.

Wolfe had a client who was extremely vulnerable in a civil suit, both financially and from a publicrelations standpoint. And Olson had a client who did not want to go through with a lawsuit. Wolfe and Olson agreed to meet with a mediator in hopes of pounding out a confidential settlement.

One summer day before the start of the 2001–02 season, Jenny filed into a conference room in a Seattle high-rise. She was accompanied by her parents, who were asked to wait outside. A group of lawyers were present, including Wolfe, Olson, and a professional mediator. Inside, the session was testy and bitter. Lawyers yelled. Jenny cried. And the negotiations quickly turned into a one-on-one battle between Wolfe and Olson, two lawyers with large egos. Finally, after ten contentious hours, a settlement was reached, the terms of which required Ruben to pay slightly over $400,000 in exchange for promises that Jenny would bring no future claims against him and both sides would never discuss the incident or the amount and terms of the settlement.

The money was transferred to an account at McKinstry and Olson's law firm. After their legal fees and expenses were deducted, the roughly $250,000 remaining went to Jenny. Patterson's rich contract with the Blazers enabled him to pay Jenny, a substantial portion of which went to lawyers.

Shannon Patterson was furious when she learned how much Ruben had paid. But given the circumstances, Patterson may have gotten a bargain. He had forced Jenny to perform oral sex on him and pleaded guilty. A review of jury verdicts in similar cases, in addition to interviews with plaintiffs' lawyers, indicates that a jury would have awarded no less than a million dollars had the case gone to trial. "If she was sexually assaulted in a real way and she's clean, those cases are worth a lot more than a half a million dollars," explained Los Angeles attorney Larry Feldman, who had represented the boy who accused Michael Jackson of molestation in 1993. Feldman negotiated with Johnnie Cochran the financial settlement between the boy and Jackson that resulted in the boy receiving millions of dollars. The boy also stopped cooperating with prosecutors, and the criminal complaint against Jackson was dropped.

When briefed on the Patterson settlement in an interview for this book, Feldman said that the Patterson case, on account of his guilty plea, would have been a lock for Jenny to prevail at trial. "It is an admission, and you win," Feldman said, referring to Patterson's guilty plea. "It is just a question of how much you've been damaged. The jury would give an awful lot of money and punish him with damages."

It is not unusual for NBA players to enter into confidential, out-of-court settlements to extinguish sexual-assault complaints. Feldman represented former Los Angeles Laker center Elden Campbell, who was sued after Pebbles Salcido attended a party at Campbell's Redondo Beach home on September 1, 1996. While there she allegedly had sexual contact with Campbell. On April 22, 1997, Salcido filed a police complaint against Campbell, but no charges were filed. One year after the incident, she sued him, claiming he had raped her. Campbell denied the charge. Feldman negotiated a settlement with Salcido's lawyer, in which Campbell paid her $20,000 to dispose of the claim.

Similarly, Los Angeles Clippers star center Michael Olowokandi entered into a confidential settlement agreement after a sexual-assault suit was filed against him on June 1, 1999. Like Campbell, Olowokandi was never charged with a crime. According to documents filed at the San Joaquin County Superior Court, Olowokandi was accused of raping Cathy Clark, a student at the University of the Pacific in Stockton, California, on June 5,

1998. Olowokandi was the most successful basketball player in the school's history and a senior at the time of the alleged incident; Clark was a junior. They had an ongoing relationship that preceded the incident in question.

According to the complaint, Olowokandi, who is seven feet tall and weights 270 pounds, "physically overpowered" Clark and "forced his body, including his sexual organs, onto plaintiff and completed an act of sexual intercourse." In her lawsuit, Clark claims that she begged and pleaded for him to stop, and that the assault resulted in an unwanted pregnancy.

Three weeks after this incident, on June 24, 1998, the Los Angeles Clippers selected Olowokandi as the number one overall pick in the NBA draft. He signed a four-year, $15-million contract. The lawsuit was quickly settled. "It was worth paying her a little bit of money rather than going through the trial," Olowokandi's lawyer, Daniel Sullivan, said. "He would have spent more money going through the trial to establish his non-wrongdoing. It was a matter of business."

Athletes who settle sexual-assault allegations with money routinely claim that the decision was a business one. But rape claims are unlike any business dispute over property, money, equipment, or stock. A rape allegation carries with it a stigma and a potentially permanent stain on a man's character. There are issues that far exceed money and efficiency to consider when settling these cases. "These things are never settled for business reasons," said Clark's attorney, Stewart Tabak. "There is reputation, ego, and honor at stake. Nobody pays money out as a business decision when these things are involved."

Both Sullivan and Tabak are bound by the confidentiality agreement they negotiated in a judicially supervised settlement conference in a judge's chambers. No transcripts or formal records were maintained of the conference. But both sides agree that the decision to settle came after Olowokandi hired a private investigator that dug up information on Clark. Among other things, the investigator tracked down women from Clark's sorority house and conducted tape-recorded interviews with them. Some of them said that Clark viewed Olowokandi as her ticket to money, which Sullivan was prepared to use to discredit her if the case proceeded. "They were on their knees and we had a whip in our hands," Sullivan said.

"I heard the tape," said Tabak, who conceded that Olowokandi's superior financial resources and the work of his investigator contributed to his client's decision to settle. "When the Kobe case broke, I had recurring thoughts that we did the right thing by not pursuing the case. Her reputation would have been absolutely decimated." According to Olowokandi's lawyer, he "made a nuisance value settlement" that was "not even remotely close" to what Ruben Patterson paid.

Tabak insisted that his client had settled to avoid public humiliation. He said Olowokandi's motives were different. "The reason this was done was: 'We better pay money so the jurors never see the light of day.'"

This proved not to be the last time Olowokandi claimed he was the victim of a false allegation. Just over a year after settling the rape case, on December 1, 2001, Olowokandi was arrested by Manhattan Beach police for allegedly assaulting another woman. This time he was charged with three felonies: domestic violence, false imprisonment, and robbery. Olowokandi was held on $50,000 bail. Within two days, however, the woman who had accused him declined to cooperate further with the authorities. Olowokandi's agent, Bill Duffy, immediately issued a press release through the Clippers that said that the woman had "expressed sincere regret in making these false accusations." Manhattan Beach police took issue with the statement. "I'm not a judge, but the victim did not beat herself up, nor did she rob herself of property," said Detective Karl Nilsson.

But the district attorney's office released a statement saying: "We reviewed the case and determined there is insufficient evidence to prove the allegation beyond a reasonable doubt, so we are not prosecuting."

To be sure, the Campbell and Olowokandi settlements are dramatically lower than what Patterson paid. But there is also a dramatic difference between their situations and that of Patterson. Neither Campbell nor Olowokandi was charged with a crime, much less convicted. Patterson was a registered sex offender, and therefore far more vulnerable. Regardless, immediately after negotiating Patterson's settlement agreement, Jan Olson wanted to celebrate. But Jenny and her parents did not. For an entire year they had dealt with lawyers, investigators, and agents. At times they felt like they had taken on the entire NBA by pressing charges against one of its players. Now they were exhausted. Feeling like roadkill, they got in their car and drove away from Seattle as fast as they could.

But Ruben Patterson's story wasn't over. As soon as the Pattersons moved to Portland, they telephoned an old friend back in Ohio, retired Cincinnati Bengals standout wide receiver Tim McGee. Criminal cases, civil settlements, team changes, and contract negotiations had both Ruben and Shannon feeling as though their financial and personal lives were out of control. They also became convinced that their best interests weren't being looked out for by all the handlers around them. McGee agreed to take over the management of Ruben's money and oversee his personal and business affairs. "Ruben needed someone to treat him with respect as a human being," said McGee. "He did not need another yes-man or someone trying to use him as a vehicle for financial gain. I came in and started telling him no before yes. Although these guys are twenty-seven years old, they are not the most mature people in the world. He just needed proper guidance."

With McGee on board, Patterson had no legal problems for the first year he was in Portland. McGee also helped him get his finances in order and eliminated all outstanding debts. Then, on November 25, 2002, McGee was on the telephone with Shannon when an argument erupted between her and Ruben. McGee tried to de-escalate the situation by talking to both of them. But while he was on the line with Ruben, Shannon called 911. According to police reports, when officers arrived at the Patterson home, Shannon answered the door, crying and holding a cell phone. Blood was dripping from her finger, which she had wrapped in a cloth. Shattered glass was visible on the floor behind her. She reported that she had been on the telephone when Ruben approached and put his hands around her neck and that she had been unable to breathe for about five seconds, before being shoved into a pantry area and held against her will.

But then, when Ruben went upstairs, Shannon followed him and started yelling at him for choking her. Shannon said he attacked her again. "He grabbed her by the throat and threw her onto the bed, and again began choking and smothering her with a pillow so that she was unable to breathe [*sic*]," the report said.

Shannon told police that during this altercation Ruben yelled at her, calling her "nigger," and "bitch." The children were crying in the bedroom doorway. Ruben didn't stop, Shannon reported, until she threatened to call the police. "Ms. Patterson added that Mr. Patterson has been physically abusing her for the last 6 years and that she was 'sick of being abused,'" one of the officers wrote in the police report. "Ms. Patterson said that she was so upset this time because on the last occasion she was abused by Mr. Patterson, Mr. Patterson promised to never abuse her again."

When questioned by police, Ruben admitted there had been an altercation but laid the blame on his wife. It began, he reported, when he heard her saying disparaging things about him on the telephone to McGee. "Mr. Patterson said he got angry with Ms. Patterson and went downstairs to confront her about her comment," according to the police report. He admitted restraining her in both the kitchen and the bedroom, but insisted he did this only because she was destroying property inside the home.

Ruben was arrested and charged with felony assault under Oregon's Domestic Violence Abuse Prevention Act. McGee continued to talk to Ruben via cell phone right up until the moment when the police put him in the back of a police car and took him to jail for booking. Patterson was released when teammate Derek Anderson posted bail for him. If convicted he faced up to five years in prison and a $100,000 fine.

As soon as he heard what happened, Patterson's agent, Dan Fegan, telephoned John Wolfe in Seattle and asked him to determine how this would impact Ruben's probation status in the sexual-assault case. Even Ruben placed a personal call to Wolfe in Seattle, seeking help. "I was called and asked to drop whatever I was doing at the time to focus on this problem," Wolfe said in an interview for this book. "And relying upon Mr. Patterson and Mr. Fegan, I did so, under engagement." Meanwhile, Tim McGee talked to Shannon right after Ruben's arrest and convinced her to go and speak with the county prosecutor to try to get the charges dropped. In an interview for this book, McGee said, "I was on the phone [with the Pattersons] . . . and Ruben did absolutely nothing to provoke [the incident]. I will never defend a client who is abusive, and I won't lie for them. But that was a domestic argument, the same as any other husband and wife have an argument. Ruben never engaged in any physical contact toward her."

On December 2, Shannon Patterson issued a formal statement to the media. It said: "I made a statement that was accurate, but in the heat of the moment was incomplete. Ruben and I had a disagreement this evening. I want the public to know that Ruben did not assault me."

The same day Shannon released her statement she met with District Attorney Bob Hermann's office and asked that formal charges not be brought against her husband. Without her cooperation, Hermann dropped the case. "There are some situations where the State of Oregon can proceed with other admissible evidence in the absence of a completely cooperative and willing victim," Hermann said. "This is not one of those situations."

Ruben escaped prosecution. But neither he nor the Blazers could escape the bad press generated by the arrest. The Blazers went ahead and fined Patterson $100,000 anyway, citing "conduct detrimental to the team." And Paul Allen issued a statement of his own: "Let there be no mistake that unacceptable conduct will not be condoned. Everyone at the Blazers will tackle these issues head-on—and we are prepared to suspend players, levy heavy fines and trade or release a player if that becomes necessary."

Considering all the other players Allen had on the team with criminal records, his words following the Patterson case rang hollow. "The team fined him, which was horrible," said McGee, who acknowledged that Ruben had committed criminal acts prior to moving to Portland. "But when you're guilty in one case, that doesn't make you guilty in everything," McGee said.

Once the domestic-violence case was dismissed, Wolfe billed Patterson for the work and legal research he had performed at the direction of Fegan and Ruben. When McGee saw Wolfe's bill for

$2,806, he told Ruben not to pay it. Then McGee called Wolfe, told him not to expect a dime from Patterson, and dismissed him as his lawyer. Wolfe wasn't the only one that McGee terminated. He got rid of Patterson's criminal lawyers in Ohio and his business manager. "If you're not in trouble, you don't need an attorney," said McGee. "I cleaned out the whole team except Dan Fegan. Ruben has no more bills. And now Ruben sees his checks before they go in the bank. He doesn't have a business advisor."

Postscript: In the summer of 2003, Ruben and Shannon Patterson sold their home in Portland, and Shannon and the children moved back to Ohio. The Blazers tried to deal Patterson to another team that summer, but his status as a sex offender, particularly in the wake of the Kobe Bryant arrest, left the team unable to deal him. Tim McGee continues to manage all of Ruben's personal affairs, except contractual matters, which are still handled by Dan Fegan. Since McGee has begun managing Patterson's affairs, he has had no run-ins with the law besides the domestic-violence arrest.

Jenny Stevens is now married and training to become a registered nurse. She and her husband have a one-year-old daughter and live in the Northwest.

FOUR

SOMETHING BAD HAPPENED

Ruben Patterson's conviction for sexual assault is an anomaly. Usually, when a police complaint is filed against an NBA player for rape, the player never ends up being charged, much less convicted. For this book, twenty-two formal police complaints alleging felony rape against an NBA player were examined. (This does not include other sexual assaults or sex crimes treated as misdemeanors, or any alleged felony rapes that went unreported to law enforcement.) Of the twenty-two felony police complaints, three cases were closed following the police investigation. The remaining nineteen cases were forwarded to prosecutors to be screened for indictment. Of those nineteen, prosecutors declined to prosecute fourteen. Of the five players who were indicted for rape, four pleaded guilty and one player—Kobe Bryant—is awaiting trial. Based on the records reviewed for this book, if Bryant is acquitted, he would become the only NBA player in the last decade to be found not guilty after undergoing an indictment for rape.

These numbers suggest a couple of things. Most rape complaints against athletes that are filed with the police are deemed credible enough to survive a thorough police investigation. In other words, law-enforcement officers find probable cause to forward the case to prosecutors, who must then determine whether a charge can be proved beyond reasonable doubt. When prosecutors take the step of indicting a player for rape, the conviction rate is 100 percent. But roughly 75 percent of the time, prosecutors decline to indict.

Yet interviews with the prosecutors in these cases, along with a review of the court documents, reveal that in only one instance did the authorities determine that a complaint was false. That one instance also represented the only case in which the accused player's contention was that he did not have sexual contact with his accuser, which was supported by the evidence. In every other instance, the accused player admitted having sex with his accuser, and the legal question was consent. Three out of four times in this situation, prosecutors opted not to indict.

Accused players and defense attorneys are often quick to categorize any complaint that doesn't lead to a conviction as false. But a closer look at these cases reveals that the false complaints are easily detected during the police-investigation stage. And if the complaint advances to prosecutors for review, there are facts sufficient to persuade investigators that a crime probably occurred. But "probably" is not good enough to bring an indictment.

Equating dropped charges with a false claim is no more appropriate than saying that every accused athlete who isn't convicted got away with rape. Clearly, when sex assault cases against athletes are closed without an indictment or a formal finding of innocence, there are often more questions than answers. But a few things are certain. A woman who goes to an athlete's bedroom, whether for sex or otherwise, takes a big risk that if she is sexually abused she will not see her abuser arrested, much less convicted. Similarly, an athlete who takes a woman to his room in anticipation of having sex risks being criminally accused and seeing his name splashed across news headlines in association with rape charges.

These are risks that women and players take night in and night out in the NBA.

Detective David McGann was off duty when his supervisor at the Waltham Police Department called him at home at nine A.M. on November 11, 1997. A nurse at the Boston Medical Center had telephoned the Waltham PD and reported that a rape victim had come in the previous night, suffering from shock. A rape-kit examination revealed injuries to her throat, cervix, and rectum, along with bruising on her back consistent with someone being dragged across a rug. Sperm had been retrieved from her vagina. The victim had been referred to a nurse-psychologist and was scheduled to be discharged to her home later in the morning.

For McGann, an experienced sex crimes investigator, brutal details were nothing out of the ordinary. What he heard next, however, was. The victim in this case reported that her assault took place inside a Waltham luxury condominium belonging to Boston Celtics superstar Antoine Walker. And she had accused Walker's teammates Ron Mercer and Chauncey Billups, along with Walker's roommate, of raping her.

This wasn't the first time McGann had been assigned to investigate a Celtics player in connection with rape charges. Waltham, a Boston suburb, is home to numerous Celtics. On March 18, 1993, McGann went to the Boston Celtics practice facility at Brandeis University and escorted Celtics reserve forward Marcus Webb from the building and arrested him for first-degree felony rape. Webb had been accused of returning to his Waltham condominium following a game against the San Antonio Spurs on March 3 of that year. His victim, a Boston-area college student who had a relationship with Webb, reported that he had forced her onto her stomach and raped her anally. A medical exam at

Boston's Beth Israel Hospital revealed severe tearing and abrasions around her anal opening. The district attorney's office assigned their top homicide prosecutor, David Meier, to try Webb. The Celtics released Webb and he eventually pleaded guilty to indecent assault and battery, and was sentenced to three to five years, but ordered to serve just thirty days in jail.

McGann quickly realized this case would be much more complicated. After reading the report filed at the hospital, McGann and his partner drove directly to the victim's home in Boston, in one of the city's blighted neighborhoods. Her apartment looked more like a shanty. Her story wasn't pretty, either.

She said she had known Walker and dated him on and off for about six months and had visited his home numerous times. As a result, she was also acquainted with his two roommates, Sammy Jones and Ray Scott, both of whom grew up with Walker in Chicago and had moved in with him after he made it to the NBA.

On the evening of November 9, the victim and other women had met up with Walker, Billups, Mercer, Jones, and Scott at a comedy club in Boston. There she was introduced to Billups and Mercer for the first time. Before leaving the club, Scott approached her and told her that Walker wanted her to visit his home. She said that Walker and Scott left in one car, while she went with Mercer and Jones in a vehicle driven by Billups. Once at Walker's home, she reported that Jones led her to his bedroom, where he and Mercer and Billups performed a series of unwanted sex acts on her. Jones, in particular, gripped her head tightly with both hands and forced his penis into her mouth, causing her to gag and choke. "Yo, who wants some? Who wants some?" she reported him saying, before someone else shouted, "Yo, who's next?"

She blacked out at one point. When she woke up early the next morning, she found herself in bed, completely naked. Jones was asleep next to her, also naked. Used condoms and condom wrappers littered the floor. She immediately got up and called a girlfriend, telling her: "Something bad happened."

But figuring out exactly what happened in these cases is difficult, even for experienced sex crimes investigators like McGann, whose job was to determine whether there was probable cause to believe that what happened was criminal. He called Middlesex County assistant district attorney Judy Carroll for assistance. If a crime had been committed, Carroll would have to determine whether it could be proved beyond a reasonable doubt. Before going for arrest warrants, McGann and Carroll wanted to talk to the players.

Billups and Mercer immediately retained criminal defense attorney Dennis Kelly, a highly respected former prosecutor in the U.S. Attorney's Office in Boston under former governor Bill Weld. Kelly accompanied Billups and Mercer to the Waltham Police Department. In a private room, with a tape recorder running, the two players talked to the police. While we have no confirmation on what they said, their answers to a subsequent civil complaint tell a story that began the same way as their accuser's did. But the ending was quite different. Mercer denied going to Walker's home after leaving the comedy club. He said that he went to Billups's home. There, he said, his accuser initiated and performed oral sex on him. Billups also denied going to Walker's home after leaving the club. And he denied having sexual contact in his home with his accuser. But he admitted putting his penis inside her mouth after she initiated and consented to the oral sex act while in his automobile.

Neither player could explain how the victim ended up naked in Walker's condominium hours after they were with her.

Investigators hoped an interview with Antoine Walker might clear up the discrepancies. Walker hired another former federal prosecutor, Nick Theodorou. Walker had not been accused of sexual assault; his roommate and teammates were. Theodorou advised him to talk to the investigators. While there is no confirmation of what Walker told the police, he subsequently answered a civil complaint by admitting that he knew the accuser and had seen her on the night in question. But Walker claimed he did not see an assault take place in his condominium. His interview with the police did little to clear up the questions.

Despite no arrests being made, word of the investigation reached the press. The news could not have been worse for Rick Pitino, who had a personal connection to all three players. He coached Walker and Mercer in college at Kentucky, where they helped him win a national championship before he left to take the Celtics job. And only months earlier, Pitino enjoyed the rare luxury of having both the third and sixth picks in the first round of the NBA draft. He chose Billups, a sophomore out of Colorado (third), and Mercer (sixth). Now the three twenty-one-year-old players whom Pitino planned to build a new Celtics foundation on were embroiled in a rape investigation.

"All I know is he [Walker] has absolutely nothing to do with it," Pitino told reporters on December 3, 1997, after word of the investigation leaked. "We found out the facts of the situation, that Antoine had nothing to do with it. When we first heard about this, we checked it out, and to the best of our knowledge, it doesn't involve anyone on the Celtics."

It is unclear where Pitino got his facts. According to the Waltham Police Department, neither Pitino nor anybody else from the Celtics ever contacted them about the case. And both Mercer and Billups had admitted sexual contact with their accuser. The legal question was whether the acts were the result of force.

Even if a criminal act could not be proven, it would be difficult to deny that a public-relations nightmare was looming. Pitino had two players whose own admissions indicated they were taking turns pulling down their pants and inserting their penises into the mouth of a woman they had barely met for the first time. But none of those details had been made public. Before the district attorney's office could decide whether or not to indict the players, Pitino traded Billups to the Toronto Raptors, on February 18, 1998. His lawyer insisted that the ongoing criminal investigation had nothing to do with the trade.

By April, the district attorney's office still had not decided whether to prosecute. But the fact that it still had not presented the case to a grand jury suggested they had serious doubts about their ability to prove the allegations. Meanwhile, the alleged victim retained Boston attorney Margaret Burnham and on April 15, 1998, filed a civil lawsuit accusing Mercer, Billups, and Jones of assault and rape. She also sued Walker for negligence, claiming he had a duty to come to her aid when he knew she was being assaulted in his home.

Before the lawsuit was resolved, Mercer and Billups paid an undisclosed amount of money to settle the case with the accuser. Walker subsequently reached an out-of-court settlement with the woman, too.

Billup's and Mercer's lawyer, Dennis Kelly, wouldn't discuss the settlement. But he did express his view for the motivation behind the suit. Money. Kelly is not alone in this view. A chorus of defense lawyers interviewed for this book said that NBA players are easy targets for women who prey on them for money. Of course, if players were not so quick to engage in sexual relations with random women, their potential risk of being targeted for lawsuits would be significantly reduced, if not eliminated altogether. Nonetheless, the conduct of some of the women who have sued players, not to mention that of the lawyers who represent them, gives credence to the notion that athletes are sometimes targets.

The lawsuit filed against Elden Campbell, for example, contained highly sensational allegations. Accuser Pebbles Salcido claimed in court papers filed at the Los Angeles Superior Court that she lost consciousness after drinking alcohol that had been secretly laced with a drug. She claimed she awoke nude from the waist down and bleeding from the vagina. She accused Campbell of raping her while up to twenty men watched. She also alleged that five other men took turns having forced intercourse with her.

But no criminal charges were filed, and a year later, Salcido hired Pasadena attorney Joe Hopkins and sued Campbell, on August 29, 1997. Campbell, who refused to discuss the case for this book, hired Larry Feldman to represent him. The case settled quickly. "With a little cross examination they folded like a cheap suit," Feldman said. "She was very vulnerable legally and factually."

When interviewed for this book, Salcido's lawyer was blunt about having no interest in taking this case to trial. "I wanted to get in and out of a lawsuit as quickly and quietly as I could," Hopkins said. On January 21, 1998, Feldman and Hopkins agreed to a settlement agreement whereby Campbell paid Salcido $20,000 to drop the lawsuit. "I'd take ten of those cases any day," Hopkins said.

Was this case financially worth his while? "If I didn't make any money," Hopkins said, "I wouldn't take ten of them, would I?"

The authorities never charged Campbell. After waiting seven months to file a police report, Salcido filed a lawsuit against Campbell one year after the alleged rape. According to Campbell's lawyers, she then resisted being deposed about the incident.

And the minute a settlement was proposed, Salcido's lawyer took the first deal and ran.

This doesn't mean that Salcido could not have been victimized. But this approach only lends credibility to the idea that athletes are targets. It also contaminates the credibility of rape victims who go to the police, undergo a rape-kit exam, and submit to interviews with investigators. The fact that athletes are sometimes the subject of specious claims enables defense attorneys in criminal cases to more easily depict women who accuse athletes as gold diggers chasing after money. Prosecutors are often sensitive to the prospect that complaints filed against wealthy celebrities and athletes may be motivated by greed.

"There is an added concern when the subject of the investigation is someone famous," said Florida chief assistant state attorney Bill Vose, whose office handled numerous criminal complaints filed against pro athletes "One of the warning signs for us is when the defendant is high profile and the victim hires a civil lawyer." When NBA star Charles Barkley was arrested for assaulting a man at an Orlando club in 1997, Vose reviewed the charges for prosecution. "The victim was a Mexican migrant who was an illegal alien," Vose said. "He got a hotshot attorney, settled for quick money, and left the country." Vose said he declined to prosecute Barkley for the alleged assault, but Barkley pled no contest to resisting arrest.

When women file criminal complaints against athletes for rape, it is less common for them to also hire a civil attorney. Usually prosecutors will discourage this, as it taints the credibility of the victim. It also compromises the integrity of the criminal prosecution by attaching a monetary interest to the outcome of the case.

It would be naive to deny that NBA players are sometimes falsely accused of rape. But when judging the veracity and credibility of rape complaints against celebrated athletes, it is important to distinguish civil suits from criminal complaints. Women who go to the police are far less likely to fabricate a complaint. And when they do, the criminal investigation will usually uncover it. In 1994, New Jersey Nets forward Derrick Coleman was accused of raping a woman in a Detroit hotel on July 14 of that year. Coleman denied having any sexual contact with his accuser. He provided a blood sample. A DNA test performed on semen found on the accuser and on her clothes showed that it did not come from Coleman. The Detroit Police Department held a press conference to announce that there would be no charges against Coleman.

And in June 1998, Washington Wizards forward Juwan Howard sued Melissa Reed, a Connecticut woman, for defamation, intentional infliction of emotional distress, and malicious prosecution after Reed called 911 and reported being sexually assaulted at Howard's home in Potomac, Maryland, on April 6, 1998. The police did not arrest Howard, and after completing a thorough investigation, authorities found no basis to charge him with a crime. Howard filed the lawsuit to publicly demonstrate his innocence. On November 12, 1998, a Maryland judge entered a default judgment against Reed, ordering her to pay Howard $100,000 in damages.

The Coleman and the Howard cases demonstrate that players can be subjected to questionable rape claims. But the more important point here is that law enforcement did not advance these claims. After proper investigations, the authorities did not arrest either player. Nor was either player recommended for prosecution.

In the majority of rape accusations where the alleged attacker claims to have had consent, the case turns into a he said, she said contest. But only in cases involving athletes does that dispute so often hinge on the scene of the alleged crime. Most often, these incidents take place in an athlete's hotel room, dorm room, or place of residence. And most of the time the accuser admits going to the scene willfully. Legally, of course, merely walking into a man's bedroom doesn't convey consent to sexual intercourse. Practically, however, a woman who goes to the bedroom of a star athlete—an athlete who is, typically, a complete stranger—has to answer the question: If not for sex, why were you there?

That question kills many complaints against athletes. There are some exceptions. In the Ruben Patterson case, the victim worked in his home and slept there as a condition of employment on a regular basis. In 1995, a Milwaukee County jury convicted Kansas City Chiefs star wide receiver Tim Barnett of sexually assaulting a fourteen-year-old girl in his hotel room. The victim was a housekeeper at the hotel who had gone to the room to clean and supply fresh towels. In both of these incidents the accuser had a legitimate reason, a professional responsibility for being in a celebrated athlete's bedroom.

The other exception is the presence of freshly reported physical injuries that are inconsistent with consensual sex. Mike Tyson and former Boston Celtics forward Marcus Webb were convicted of sexually assaulting women who went to their bedrooms by choice. In Webb's case, his victim had even had consensual sex with him on prior occasions. But the incident in question produced compelling injuries. Both Webb's and Mike Tyson's victim underwent rape-kit exams that documented their injuries.

Absent one of these two scenarios—a legitimate reason for being in an athlete's bedroom, such as employment, or a well-documented, timely report of physical injuries—a woman who enters an athlete's bedroom and is raped has little chance of seeing her perpetrator formally charged, much less convicted of a crime.

FIVE

NO STRINGS ATTACHED

While it is often difficult for prosecutors to prove beyond a reasonable doubt that an accused NBA player actually committed rape, it is no mystery as to why players are repeatedly accused of abusing women. Many players develop an extremely warped perception of women, viewing them as nothing more than sexual prey. This distorted view is shaped by the impressive number of consensual sexual encounters that players have with women, particularly when their team is on the road.

Once source of these sexual encounters is strip clubs. NBA players spend half of their season on the road. For many players, strip clubs and nude-dancing establishments become a home away from home. Why? There are three essential reasons, which I refer to as the three S's: sex, secrecy, and security. First, strip clubs make sexual gratification for athletes as easy as a layup. All players need to do is show up. Second, these clubs promise image-conscious athletes a private environment, where the deeds they participate in are shielded from the view of wives, the press, and fans. Third, players are secure from lawsuits, paternity claims, and police reports of sexual assaults inside strip clubs. The women employed by these clubs are there to stimulate and satisfy the players, and they come with no strings attached.

As a result of all this, visiting such venues is as much a part of some players' travel itinerary as visiting the other teams' arenas. While there is nothing illegal about visiting such establishments, these places tend to foster in players the false perception that the role of women is to cheerfully satisfy their demands and urges. This sometimes can lead to unforeseen problems, including crime and abusive treatment of women.

It was eight minutes to midnight on April 6, 1998, when Patrick Ewing, the New York Knicks' seven-foot center, entered Atlanta's Gold Club, an adult entertainment nightclub. An escort immediately whisked him away from the crowd on the main dance floor, leading him up to Gold Room number 7, the largest, private VIP room in the place. Inside, a sectional couch wrapped around two of the room's four walls. Ewing took a seat in the dark and waited while a security guard stood watch outside the door. Moments later a couple of voluptuous nude women filed in.

Before they started to perform there was a knock on the door. The guard announced that the owner of the club and a top club executive had arrived and wanted to meet Ewing. Steven Kaplan and Thomas "Ziggy" Sicignano entered, introducing themselves to Ewing as Steve and Ziggy. The two told him that they were from New York and were longtime Knick fans. Kaplan, a New York businessman, had taken over the Gold Club in 1994 and turned it into one of the most prominent, financially lucrative nude-dancing establishments in the United States, with reported profits of roughly $20 million a year. Kaplan made his club famous by catering to celebrity clients, most notably athletes. Word quickly spread through the NBA and the NFL that the Gold Club had the prettiest dancers in town and provided preferential treatment to athletes: complimentary food, drinks, and dances, all in private VIP rooms. Everything was free, including, as it turned out, sex. The combination drew in lots of pro athletes.

Kaplan and Ziggy took seats on the couch near Ewing. Then two more dancers, Frederique and Diva, arrived in Ewing's room. Out of the club's one hundred dancers, Frederique was the one most frequently requested by NBA players. She had never performed for Ewing, however. The room was so dark it was hard to see anything more than the shape of his tall figure. With shoulder-length blond hair, penetrating dark eyes, and long fingers, Frederique approached him and was introduced. Frederique, Diva, and the other girls started dancing.

First they pressed their flesh together. Then some of the dancers took turns performing oral sex on one another. As they did, Kaplan used a flashlight to illuminate each dancer's private areas. This went on for ten minutes and had the effect of getting Ewing completely aroused.

"Take care of Mr. Ewing," one of the men said.

Two of the dancers then approached Ewing and took turns performing oral sex on him, as Kaplan and Sicignano looked on. The whole affair lasted about forty-five minutes. Ewing's tab was $991.24. But he paid nothing. Ewing figured he would at least tip the dancers—he typically gave $20 to $30 to a nude dancer. But on this night even that was covered. Before Ewing left, Kaplan and Sicignano assured him that if he ever wanted the girls to go to his hotel room they would take care of that, too.

Certainly Ewing, who is married, didn't expect his private affairs inside the Gold Club to become public. But in March of 1999, the FBI raided the club and the federal government subsequently filed a 100-page racketeering indictment against Kaplan and sixteen club employees, alleging that the club had become a den for prostitution, illegal drug use, money laundering, extortion, credit-card fraud, and tax evasion. Federal authorities also accused Kaplan and club executives of having ties to the Gam-bino crime family. Dozens of athletes—including Denver Broncos running back Terrell Davis, Atlanta Braves slugger Andruw Jones, and a slew of NBA stars—were implicated in the case as recipients of illegal sexual favors. No athletes were indicted. But a handful of players received subpoenas ordering them to testify, Ewing among them. Prosecutors wanted to know exactly what he and the other athletes experienced in the club.

Few people knew the answer to that question better than Jana Pelnis, the dancer known to Ewing and scores of other NBA play-ers only as Frederique. Pelnis knew the names of more pro ath-letes than some ESPN sports anchors. And she had seen enough of them in a state that was unfit for television. But Pelnis could not have cared less about their fame or their athletic prowess. She viewed the players the same way they viewed her: as an object. The players' aim was sexual gratification. Her aim was earning money. For her the club was nothing more than a temporary layover until she landed a career in modeling.

Ever since graduating from high school in Wisconsin, Pelnis dreamed of being a fashion model. From a physical standpoint, she had all the credentials. But in the highly competitive model-ing industry, she lacked the connections. Right after graduating, she landed a part-time modeling job in Wisconsin. But she earned more money working nights as a topless dancer at a club called Heartbreakers in Milwaukee. She never intended to dance for very long. But in 1997 two things happened that pushed her toward full-time nude dancing: she filed a domestic-abuse tem-porary restraining order against a man in Milwaukee, and she traveled to Atlanta with other Heartbreakers dancers to audition at the Gold Club. Pelnis got offered a job and moved to Atlanta in 1998. She adopted a stage name and quickly began earning far more than she could ever earn in Milwaukee. That spring, Pelnis had her encounter with Ewing. Before long she became the most sought-after dancer among NBA players and traveled as far as Las Vegas to entertain sports personalities. She participated in lesbian shows, performed oral sex on athletes, and even participated in three-way sexual encounters.

Yet her dream to become a fashion model stayed with her, and she was always looking to leave the nude-dancing industry. Before she did, however, the FBI raided the Gold Club and Pelnis got swept up in the indictment and charged in connection with the prostitution scheme alleged by federal authorities. She was stunned when the government alleged that a part of her employment duties was illegal and that by doing that she had helped advance a larger criminal enterprise. But in Georgia, oral sex can qualify as "intercourse." When performed for money, oral sex can come under the state's criminal prohibition against prostitution. If convicted, Pelnis faced time in a federal penitentiary. Pelnis needed a criminal defense attorney.

Barbara Moon is a forty-eight-year-old lawyer in private practice. A single parent who put herself through law school at night while raising two children, she developed a successful practice, splitting her time between divorce and criminal cases. Moon had seen her fair share of domestic violence, sex abuse, divorce, and child custody disputes. Little in the world shocked her. But she knew nothing about the world of the NBA or the business of nude dancing. After the Gold Club got raided and Steven Kaplan was indicted, Moon received a call from Kaplan's attorney, Steven Sadow, a close friend of Moon's. Sadow told her that one of Kaplan's dancers needed a lawyer and asked Moon if she would represent her. Moon agreed to meet with Pelnis.

The minute Moon laid eyes on Pelnis she was struck by her

beauty. She had never seen a woman so striking. Equally compelling was Pelnis's determination to fight the charges against her. Nearly twice Pelnis's age, Moon quickly took a more protective role toward her than lawyers typically take with clients. She assured Pelnis she would vigorously defend her in court. But she made one thing clear up front. "I'm not going down for any client," Moon told Pelnis the first time they met. "We deal with the truth and the truth only." Pelnis agreed.

Moon quickly got up to speed on how business inside the Gold Club was done. Customers who pay the standard entrance fee are given access to the main dance floor, where they can buy dances from dancers. Customers who pay an enhanced fee can go upstairs to a more private setting. Then there's a super-enhanced fee for patrons who want to go into a "Gold Room," an isolated room with private nude dancers. The NBA players and other professional athletes were always brought to the private Gold Rooms. But unlike other customers, they never had to pay the steep fees. They were good for business; their presence brought the club prestige.

The athletes got special treatment inside the rooms, too. The dancers were asked to do erotic dances and perform sex acts one another to arouse the players. Then the dancers would take turns performing oral sex on the athletes. The more the dancers did for the athletes and other VIPs, the more the dancers got paid. Sometimes things got out of hand behind closed doors. Alcohol flowed. Men got carried away. The dancers fed into it; the more excited the man got, the more money the dancer made. It was not unusual for the dancers in the VIP rooms to make between $2,000 and $3,000 per night. And no one said a word when it was over.

To Moon, all of this was a little hard to believe, much less visualize. In order to best represent her client's interests, Moon decided she had to see it for herself. Since the Gold Club prohibits female patrons, she had to get special permission to enter. The moment Moon stepped inside, she noticed that every woman in sight was young, wonderfully built, and completely naked. Yet they walked around the club as carefree as a baby in a bathtub. Moon felt like a fish out of water.

Everything about the work atmosphere conflicted with Moon's experience. Female employees at the Gold Club were not only allowed to drink on the job, they were encouraged to. Dancers had no limit on how much alcohol they drank.

The girls would typically stay up all night. After work they'd go to breakfast, then go home to sleep for the day. They returned to work around four or five in the afternoon. Everybody they interacted with was there to see them nude.

The longer she observed the more Moon realized that the women at the club thought they were on top of the world—men wearing expensive suits and driving expensive cars were paying big money to be with them. But Moon could see it was all a cruel illusion. The girls inside the Gold Club had only one thing going for them: their bodies. She came away convinced that the whole arrangement was a concerted attack on women. "This is a means of survival with these girls," Moon said. "Some of them didn't know where to draw the line. These women are very vulnerable." Pelnis was as vulnerable as any of them. Despite making thousands to entertain top jocks and celebrities, she didn't have enough money to afford her own apartment. Instead, she lived with a group of other dancers at Kaplan's Atlanta home.

Soon the case began absorbing Moon and she could not wait to defend her client in court. As Moon geared up, Pelnis got the news she had been hoping for since high school: a modeling agency in Paris called and expressed interest in hiring her. The end of nude dancing was suddenly in sight, and at the same time the criminal case took on added importance. But in August 2000, as pretrial hearings in the Gold Club case started, Pelnis got another piece of unexpected news: she was pregnant. She could have gotten an abortion to protect her modeling opportunity, but Pelnis never entertained the thought, even when she experienced morning sickness so severe that she was unable to stay in the courtroom during hearings.

After Pelnis left the court numerous times due to illness, prosecutors approached Moon and offered her client a deal. If she would agree to plead guilty to a reduced charge and cooperate by testifying against the club executives, Pelnis would be spared jail time and be free to get on with her life. The government would make repeated overtures of this sort to Moon for months. Pelnis rejected them every time. Moon was sure Pelnis would reject this one, too. Now, however, Pelnis said she would take the deal and plead guilty.

Moon was shocked, but nonetheless supported her decision. The pregnancy had changed Pelnis's priorities. Modeling didn't matter anymore. Being free to raise her child did. On August 18, 2000, Pelnis pleaded guilty to one count of interstate transportation in aid of racketeering and agreed to cooperate fully with the government. In addition to helping prosecutors convict Kaplan, Pelnis's testimony would become a public-relations nightmare for the NBA.

NBA players and other professional athletes are quick to point out that women and sex are readily available to them on account of their celebrity status. The story is that when players travel for road games, women come to their hotels and offer themselves up for the players' sexual gratification. And there is some truth to this. But there's more to the story, too. Some of the women who seek out athletes for sex do so not by choice but rather by the nature of their employment. The Gold Club case offered a sordid view of the pervasive, exploitative practice of NBA players getting sexual favors from exotic dancers. It also exploded the myth that strip clubs are a perfectly legal, harmless form of recreation. While strip clubs are lawful, they are poorly monitored places where criminal behavior, from prostitution to drug use, can go undetected. They also cultivate an image of women that reduces them to disposable pleasure toys.

The combined testimony of Ewing and Pelnis laid these facts bare. The two of them came to court on the same day, July 23, 2001. Ewing, in a conservative pinstripe suit, blue shirt, and gray tie, took the stand first. Only five days earlier he had signed a free-agent contract with the Orlando Magic. But prosecutors wanted to talk to him about his time with the Knicks. They began by asking him what happened inside Gold Club Room number 7 on April 6, 1998, the first night he met Kaplan and Thomas "Ziggy" Sicignano.

"Where were Kaplan and Ziggy in the room with respect to you?" Assistant U.S. Attorney Glenn Baker asked.

"They were sitting beside me," Ewing said.

"And what happened after the conversation you had with them?"

"The girls danced, started fondling me; I got aroused. They performed oral sex. I hung around for a little bit longer, talked to them, then I left."

"Did you tip the dancers any money that night?"

"No. I was told that it was taken care of."

The moment they display athletic superiority as a child, athletes begin receiving preferential treatment. In college it translates into scholarships, easy courses, and perks—from free sneakers to excused absences from classes on account of road trips. By the time they reach the pro ranks, agents come calling and millions of dollars are lavished on players, enabling them, if they choose, to be free of any ordinary responsibilities, from grocery shopping to bill paying. And despite their inflated incomes, players are inundated by offers from businessmen of complimentary suits, meals, jewelry, and even automobiles. In this environment, sex can be just another freebie, arranged for and taken care of like any other aspect of a player's life. Ewing didn't have to go out and find a girl. He didn't have to pay money. All he had to do was show up and sit there with his pants down. In his testimony, Ewing admitted going to Gold Club ten times within the span of a few years in the mid-1990s. To put this in perspective in terms of frequency, that's just one club in one city. The Knicks travel to twenty-seven other cities, repeatedly, during the playing season.

U.S. Attorney Baker wanted to demonstrate that the scenario Ewing described from 1996 was not an aberration at the club. He asked Ewing about another visit he paid to the Gold Club, in 1997, this time with a group of other Knicks players. Prior to Ewing testifying, Ziggy Sicignano, who ended up cooperating with prosecutors in their case against Kaplan, testified that one night in 1997 Knicks players were taken to a semiprivate room with six to ten dancers. Someone yelled, "There are no rules tonight," Sicignano testified. "Girls were having a good time, jumping on the players. . . . Girls were getting groped. Girls were groping."

Ewing confirmed that he and a group of Knicks went back to the club and that Kaplan and Sicignano were present in the room again, as Sicignano testified. Baker asked Ewing what happened. "The girls danced," Ewing said. "They fondled me again. I'm not sure which one told them to go ahead and take care of [me]. They gave me oral sex again."

"Were there other Knicks present in the club?" Baker asked.

"There was a lot of us," Ewing said. "I know Larry Johnson, I think John Starks . . . Charles Oakley. I don't remember the rest." Ewing said that Johnson was in a room adjacent to his. But when Ewing tried to enter, a security guard stopped him.

There was one more thing Baker wanted to ask Ewing about. Sicignano had testified that he and Kaplan had a squad of dancers who put on sex shows and performed sexual acts for members of the Knicks, the Charlotte Hornets, and the Indiana Pacers. He described an instance when Kaplan took dancers to an Atlanta hotel where the Pacers were staying. Baker wanted to know if dancers were ever brought to the Knicks' hotel.

"Did there come a time where you actually saw an employee that you recognize as an employee at the club at your hotel?"

"Yes, there was," said Ewing. "There was a knock on my door and it was one of the dancers. She was looking for one of my teammates."

While Ewing testified, Pelnis was sequestered in a private room in the courthouse, clutching a picture of her new baby girl, who had been born five months earlier. When a court officer told her it was time to take the stand, Pelnis tucked the picture in her pocket and walked into the courtroom. Under oath, she confirmed that she and a group of other dancers had performed lesbian shows and sexual acts on Ewing. Prosecutor Art Leach then asked her about other NBA players who had received similar treatment. "I want to direct your attention to a man by the name of Dikembe Mutombo," Leach said. "Did there come a time when you saw Mr. Mutombo at the Gold Club?"

"I was sent up into his room," Pelnis said, and confirmed it was room number 7, the same room where she had met Ewing. When Pelnis entered, there were multiple dancers performing for Mutombo. She said that her boss told her: "Just put on a show and take care of the customer, Mr. Mutombo."

"Were there any flashlights present?"

"Mr. Kaplan had a flashlight."

"And what was he doing with that flashlight?"

"Shining it on . . . whoever it was giving oral sex. He would shine it on the . . . on your private area where it was being done."

The prosecutor asked Pelnis if she recalled Kaplan saying anything while she performed oral sex on Mutombo. "After I was finished giving oral sex to Mutombo he was making comments about how it was such a great thing what I did."

"How did that make you feel at that time?"

"Good."

"Now, did you receive any payment on that occasion?"

"Yes, I did." She said that after leaving Mutombo's room, she received a handful of cash from Kaplan.

Before prosecutors were finished with Pelnis, she testified about several other athletes, most of whom were NBA players who had been to the club and who had received similar VIP treatment. In his cross-examination, defense attorney Bruce Harvey humiliated Pelnis further.

"When you get into those four walls of the Gold Club, that's a whole 'nother world, isn't it?"

"Yes."

"Because you know that the folks that come into that world are looking for people like yourself. They are looking at you, right? They're looking to you to entertain 'em, right?"

"Correct."

"And they're looking for you to fulfill, at least in some degree, their fantasy. Not yours, but theirs, right?"

"I would imagine."

"Well, you've done it for long enough to know that that's precisely what they're looking for, correct?"

The more defense attorneys pressed Pelnis, the more difficult the experience became. Finally she broke down in tears. Now the differences between Pelnis and Ewing emerged. He was not indicted for his role in the encounter. She was. Nobody insulted or demeaned him for exploiting dancers for oral sex, despite the fact that he was married at the time the incidents took place. Pelnis had been labeled a prostitute. When Ewing left the stand, he stepped smoothly from the courtroom to the basketball court, where he continued to make millions as a highly respected basketball player. Pelnis would leave court with a criminal record, no money, and no job.

Pelnis left the witness stand humiliated and embarrassed. She couldn't wait to return home to her baby and get as far away from Atlanta, NBA players, and the trial as fast as possible. "All I wanna do is get on that plane," Pelnis told Moon after leaving the courtroom. But her flight back to the Midwest was still hours away. Moon searched for some encouraging words. None came. "C'mon," she said. "I'll buy you lunch."

After seeing Pelnis off at the airport, Moon called lead prosecutor Art Leach and asked him to drop the single charge that Pelnis had pleaded guilty to prior to the start of the trial. Moon argued that Pelnis had done everything the government had asked and deserved a clean slate. Shortly thereafter the government took the necessary steps to clear her name, ensuring that Pelnis walked away with no criminal record.

The Gold Club trial ended when Steven Kaplan pleaded guilty to racketeering involving credit-card fraud and prostitution and was sentenced to sixteen months in federal prison and ordered to pay a $5-million fine, plus $300,000 in restitution. As part of the settlement, Kaplan had to sell the club, and four other defendants pleaded guilty to charges associated with prostitution stemming from sex that occurred at the club. By this point, however, trial witnesses had linked many prominent NBA players to the Gold Club, putting all of them in the awkward position of having to defend themselves publicly rather than allow the stain of the club's reputation to remain with their name.

Knicks guard John Starks confirmed, through his lawyer, that he had sex with club strippers, but that he had since "rededicated his life to Christ."

Toronto Raptors forward Antonio Davis held a press conference with his wife by his side to explain that although he had gone to the club, he had not actually received sexual favors. Thomas "Ziggy" Sicignano had testified that Davis had requested and received strippers at his hotel room. Davis called this a lie and sued Sicignano in a $50-million defamation suit. "Let Antonio Davis go on TV and say what he wants," Sicignano said after Davis's press conference. "But others will corroborate that at his request we took women to his room." (The case was dismissed on July 26, 2001, without cost or other award to either party.)

Former Knicks forward Charles Oakley is another one of the players whose name surfaced in the Gold Club case. When the press asked him, he didn't deny it. Instead, Oakley expressed surprise that the club and what went on inside it would cause the public to be concerned. "What's the big deal?" Oakley said at the time. "It's a public place; it's like going to a mall. You go to the mall to shop. You go there [the club] to relax and cool out."

The fact that Oakley—and probably plenty of other players, if they were to speak candidly—could equate receiving sexual favors inside a strip club with shopping at, say, Wal-Mart says a great deal about how warped his perception had become. It also is an indication of how normal such behavior becomes for some players.

Oakley, as it turns out, is also among the many players who have been arrested for abusing a woman. His arrest took place in Atlanta, not far from the Gold Club. According to police and court records and interviews with one of the officers who arrested him on June 29, 1998, Oakley struck Sharonda Smith in the face after she refused to participate in a three-way sexual encounter with Oakley and another woman. Oakley was charged with battery and simple assault. After a pretrial hearing, Oakley entered into an agreement with prosecutors on November 20, 1998. Eighteen months later, and at the prosecutor's request, the court dismissed the case on May 30, 2000.

Postscript: Today Jana Pelnis is the mother of two daughters, ages three and one. She is raising them in the Midwest, where she earns a modest wage working for a company associated with the food industry and is preparing to begin taking courses in the fall of 2004 to become certified as a radiology technician. Since becoming a mother, Pelnis has not gone to a club or gone out socially without her children at her side. Nor has she had any contact with any NBA players or anyone connected to the Gold Club since the trial. "That was a horrible chapter in my life," she said. "I never want to go back to it."

Patrick Ewing's wife, Rita Williams-Ewing, who is a lawyer, retained nationally renowned divorce lawyer Raoul Felder and filed for divorce around the same time that published reports surfaced that Ewing had been seeing a twenty-six-year-old Knicks City Dancer, who told the press she "didn't have anything to do with [the marriage breakup]." The Ewing divorce was finalized amicably. Rita went on to write a novel about the infidelities of NBA players entitled Homecourt Advantage. *Patrick retired from the NBA after the 2001–02 season. He is now an assistant coach with the Houston Rockets. He is expected to be inducted into the Hall of Fame.*

In February 2004, the Gold Club building was taken over by a Christian congregation and is now dubbed "The God Club."

PART II

ABOVE THE LAW

In 2002 and 2003, Portland Trail Blazers point guard Damon Stoudamire was arrested three times on drug-related charges.

Ruben Patterson is considered one of the toughest defensive players in the NBA and is nicknamed "Kobe stopper." As a member of the Seattle Sonics, he pled guilty to assault in Ohio and served fifteen days of a suspended one-year sentence for attempted rape in Washington.

SUPERIOR COURT OF WASHINGTON FOR KING COUNTY

THE STATE OF WASHINGTON,   )
)
                    Plaintiff,   )   No.   01-1-04295-1 SEA
)
    v.   )
)   INFORMATION
RUBEN N. PATTERSON   )
)
)
)
                    Defendant.   )
)

I, Norm Maleng, Prosecuting Attorney for King County in the name and by the authority of the State of Washington, do accuse RUBEN N. PATTERSON of the crime of **Attempted Rape in the Third Degree**, committed as follows:

That the defendant RUBEN N. PATTERSON in King County, Washington, on or about September 25, 2000, did attempt to engage in sexual intercourse with another person, named NZ who was not married to the defendant under circumstances where NZ did not consent to sexual intercourse with the defendant and such lack of consent was clearly expressed by NZ's words or conduct; attempt as used in the above charge means that the defendant committed an act which was a substantial step toward the commission of the above described crime with the intent to commit that crime;

Contrary to RCW 9A.28.020 and 9A.44.060(1)(a), and against the peace and dignity of the State of Washington.

NORM MALENG
Prosecuting Attorney

By:_____
Lisa D. Johnson, WSBA #16336
Senior Deputy Prosecuting Attorney

Norm Maleng
Prosecuting Attorney
W 554 King County Courthouse
Seattle, Washington 98104-2312
(206) 296-9000

INFORMATION- 1

A copy of the attempted-rape complaint filed by the King County, Washington, Prosecuting Attorney's Office.

STATE OF WASHINGTON)
)
          Plaintiff,)   No. 01-1-04295-1 SEA
)
          v.)   APPENDIX J
)   JUDGMENT AND SENTENCE –
Ruben N. Patterson)   SEX OFFENDER NOTICE OF
)   REGISTRATION REQUIREMENTS
         Defendant.)
)

SEX AND KIDNAPPING OFFENDER REGISTRATION. RCW 9A.44.130, 10.01.200. Because this crime involves a sex offense or kidnapping offense (e.g., kidnapping in the first degree, kidnapping in the second degree, or unlawful imprisonment as defined in chapter 9A.40 RCW where the victim is a minor and you are not the minor's parent), you are required to register with the sheriff of the county of the state of Washington where you reside. If you are not a resident of Washington, you must register with the sheriff of the county of your school, place of employment, or vocation. You must register immediately upon being sentenced unless you are in custody, in which case you must register within 24 hours of your release.

     If you leave the state following your sentencing or release from custody but later move back to Washington, you must register within 30 days after moving to this state or within 24 hours after doing so if you are under the jurisdiction of this state's Department of Corrections. If you leave this state following your sentencing or release from custody but later while not a resident of Washington you become employed in Washington, carry out a vocation in Washington, or attend school in Washington, you must register within 30 days after starting school in this state or becoming employed or carrying out a vocation in this state, or within 24 hours after doing so if you are under the jurisdiction of this state's Department of Corrections.

     If you change your residence within a county, you must send written notice of your change of residence to the sheriff within 72 hours of moving. If you change your residence to a new county within this state, you must send written notice of your change of residence to the sheriff of your new county of residence at least 14 days before moving, register with the sheriff within 24 hours of moving and you must give written notice of your change of address to the sheriff of the county where last registered within 10 days of moving. If you move, work, carry on a vocation, or attend school out of Washington State, you must send written notice within 10 days of establishing residence, or after beginning to work, carry on a vocation, or attend school in th new state, to the county sheriff with whom you last registered in Washington State.

     If you are a resident of Washington and you are admitted to a public or private institution of higher education, you are required to notify the sheriff of the county of your residence of your intent to attend the institution within 10 days of enrolling or by the first business day after arriving at the institution, whichever is earlier.

     Even if you lack a fixed residence, you are required to register. Registration must occur within 24 hours of release in the county where you are being supervised if you do not have a residence at the time of your release from custody or within 14 days after ceasing to have a fixed residence. If you enter a different county and stay there for more than 24 hours, you will be required to register in the new county. You must also report in person to the sheriff of the county where you are registered on a weekly basis if you have been classified as a risk level II or III, or on a monthly basis if you have been classified as a risk level I. The lack of a fixed residence is a factor that may be considered in determining a sex or kidnapping offender's risk level.

I have read and understand these registration requirements.

X _____
Defendant   Date   Judge

_____
Deputy Prosecuting Attorney   Defense Attorney

APPENDIX J (rev 4/00)

A copy of Ruben Patterson's sex offender notice of registration requirements.

After joining the Portland Trail Blazers, Ruben Patterson was arrested on felony domestic violence charges on November 25, 2002, by the Tualatin Police Department. The charges were later dropped when his wife declined to press charges.

Two of the wealthiest men in the world, Microsoft co-founders Bill Gates and Paul Allen, talking during an NBA game. Allen owns the Portland Trail Blazers, which the press dubbed the "Jailblazers" following a rash of player arrests and disciplinary problems.

Former New York Knicks center Patrick Ewing with his agent
David Falk. Ewing testified that nude dancers performed oral sex on him
at the Gold Club, a strip club in Atlanta that was popular among many
NBA players. It was later shut down by the FBI on racketeering charges.

COURTESY OF THE DELAWARE COUNTY SHERIFF'S DEPARTMENT, MUNCIE, INDIANA

As a college star at Indiana's Ball State University, Bonzi Wells was arrested for assaulting his girlfriend. The charges were later dropped. After joining the NBA, Wells refused a Portland police officer's demand to leave private property, saying, "F— you, man. You don't just walk over here and tell me what to do. You even know who you are talking to?"

AP PHOTO/AARON HARRIS

While playing for the Blazers, Wells was involved in a number of on-court incidents, including spitting in the face of an opponent, cursing out his coach, and physically striking a referee. The Blazers traded Wells to the Memphis Grizzlies on December 3, 2003.

Anthony Mason, now a Milwaukee Bucks forward, pleaded guilty to endangering the welfare of a child after being charged with statutory rape in New York. Authorities in New Jersey and North Carolina also investigated him when women in both states filed separate criminal rape complaints. Neither case resulted in formal charges being filed.

While a member of the Iowa State University basketball team, Sam Mack and a member of the school's football team were arrested for kidnapping, armed robbery, and terrorism. Mack was acquitted of all charges by a jury.

A copy of the criminal complaint filed by the state of Iowa against Sam Mack appears on the following two pages.

IN THE IOWA DISTRICT COURT IN AND FOR _____Story_____ COUNTY

THE STATE OF IOWA

THE CITY/COUNTY OF ___Story___

vs.

Samuel Charles Mack

Before Magistrate_____

Criminal Number ___14599-0389___

Ct.2 & Ct.3

COMPLAINT AND AFFIDAVIT

The defendant is accused of the crime of _Ct II - Kidnapping in the second degree;_
Ct III - Terrorism _____ in violation of Section
Ct II - 710.1(4) + 710.3
Ct III - 708.6 of the Iowa Criminal Code/ _____ in that the defendant
on or about the _30th_ day of _March_ ,19_89_ (at approximately _11_ o'clock
_P_.M.), at _209 Lincoln Way, Ames_
(location as definitely as known)
in _STORY_ County, did _confine three persons without their knowledge_
or consent, + with the intent that such confinement be secret; Ct IV - shoot a
dangerous weapon in a building, thereby placing people under apprehension of serious injury
THEREFORE, Complainant requests that said Defendant, subject to bail or conditions of release where applicable.
(1) be arrested or that other lawful steps be taken to obtain Defendants appearance in court; or
(2) be detained, if already in custody, pending further proceedings;
and that said Defendant otherwise be dealt with according to law.

Complainant _Mary E. Richards_
Signature of Complainant

STATE OF IOWA, County of _STORY_ ss., **AFFIDAVIT**

I, the undersigned, being duly sworn, state that the following facts known by me or told to me by other reliable persons
form the basis for my belief that the Defendant committed this crime.

Count II
This defendant and an accomplice, during the commission
of a robbery at Burger King, each put some of the other
persons present on the premises into the walk-in cooler where
they could not be seen or heard by anyone else.

Count III
This defendant aided and abetted his accomplice who
shot a rifle inside the premises ~~and directing~~ of Burger King,
causing other persons to believe they were in imminent danger
of serious injury.

Mary E. Richards
Signature of Affiant

Subscribed and sworn to before me by the person(s) signing this Complaint (and affidavit(s)) on this the _3rd_
day of _April_ , 19 _89_

Kathy J. Tiffany
Signature of Notary

Complaint and affidavit(s) filed and probable cause found that the defendant committed the offense charged.

Steve Van Marel
Magistrate

Clerk to issue Warrant.
Bond $100,000.00 cash
~~only~~ or surety.
Steve Van Marel 4/3/89

SUMMONS/WARRANT ISSUED
DATE 4/3/89
BY

Koch Brothers, Des Moines Form KB 601

White Court, White Prosecutor, Yellow Defendant.

IN THE IOWA DISTRICT COURT IN AND FOR ___STORY___ COUNTY

THE STATE OF IOWA
vs.

SAMUEL CHARLES MACK

Criminal No. _____14599_____

INFORMATION

Comes now ___Mary E. Richards___ , (Assistant) County Attorney of

___Story___ County, State of Iowa, and in the name and by the authority of the

State of Iowa accuses___Samuel Charles Mack___of the crime of
Count I: Robbery in the First Degree, A Class "B" Felony; Count II:
Kidnapping in the 2nd Degree; Count III: Terrorism ___committed as follows:

The said___Samuel Mack, on or about the 30th day of March, 1989, at approx.
(Time and date as definitely as known)

___11:00 p.m., at the Burger King Resturant, 209 Lincolnway, Ames,
(Location as definitely as known)

___in the County of___Story___and State

of Iowa, in violation of Section Ct.I: 711.1, 711.2; Ct.II:710.2(4),710.3; Ct.III:708.6 of the Iowa Criminal Code, did

Count I:
purposely put other persons in fear of immediate serious injury to further
the commission of an intended theft, and while so doing, was armed with a
dangerous weapon, towit: a knife; and aided and abetted another who was armed
with a rifle.
Count II:
confine persons without their consent and with the intent that such
confinement be secret, with the purpose of furthering the commission of a
robbery and enabling escape without detection, while armed with a dangerous weapon,
Count III:
aided and abetted another who shot a dangerous weapon in a building, thereby
placing people under apprehension of serious A TRUE INFORMATION
injury.

Mary E. Richards
(Assistant) County Attorney

This Information and the minutes of testimony accompanying it have been examined by me and found to contain sufficient

evidence, if unexplained, to warrant a conviction by a trial jury; the filing of this information is approved on this the __14th__

day of ___April___, 19_89_

Bail is fixed in the amount of __$128,750__

~~and the Clerk of Court ordered to issue a warrant.~~

Dale E. Kuigh
Judge or Magistrate

Dale E. Kuigh
District Judge
District Associate Judge
Magistrate having jurisdiction of the offense

List of witnesses
NAME   ADDRESS   OCCUPATION

SEE ATTACHED MINUTES OF TESTIMONY

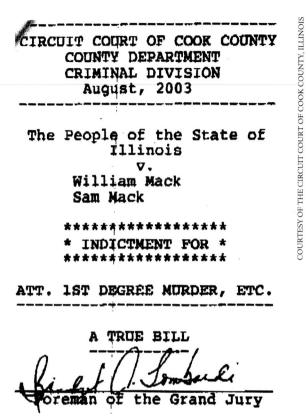

CIRCUIT COURT OF COOK COUNTY
COUNTY DEPARTMENT
CRIMINAL DIVISION
August, 2003

The People of the State of
Illinois
∇.
William Mack
Sam Mack

★★★★★★★★★★★★★★★★★
★ INDICTMENT FOR ★
★★★★★★★★★★★★★★★★★

ATT. 1ST DEGREE MURDER, ETC.

A TRUE BILL

Foreman of the Grand Jury

WITNESSES
OFF. W. ROLNIAK

A copy of the criminal complaint filed against Sam Mack
by the state of Illinois. After retiring from the NBA,
Mack was charged with attempted first-degree murder.
The charges are pending.

All-Star Glenn Robinson was arrested after a run-in with police outside a Miami Beach nightclub. The charges were later dropped.

On May 15, 2003, a Cook County, Illinois, jury found Glenn Robinson guilty of domestic battery and assault, after police charged him with attacking his former girlfriend and threatening to shoot her.

Pennsylvania authorities touched off a firestorm of controversy when they filed a fourteen-count indictment against league MVP Allen Iverson in July 2002. A judge later dismissed most of the charges and prosecutors later withdrew the remainder of the charges.

In 1993 Iverson spent four months in a Virginia prison following his conviction for his part in a brawl. But Virginia governor Douglas Wilder granted him clemency, enabling him to enter Georgetown University on a basketball scholarship. His conviction was later overturned on appeal.

Boston Celtics star Paul Pierce was jumped and repeatedly stabbed by gang members at a Boston nightclub on September 25, 2000. As a result, three men were charged with attempted murder.

Left to right: William "Roscoe" Ragland and Trevor Watson were found guilty of assault and sentenced to prison; Tony Hurston was acquitted.

SIX

DO YOU KNOW WHO I AM?

Why have so many of today's NBA players been handcuffed, photographed, and fingerprinted by law-enforcement personnel? A partial explanation may be found in the new profile of the NBA players. More and more of today's NBA players are boys, literally. The average age of the fifty-eight players selected in the 2003 NBA draft was twenty-one. Six players were just eighteen years old. Seven players came directly from high school and would still be considered too young to drink and classified as minors in some jurisdictions.

Yet they entered a place where the minimum starting salary is $348,000 and the average annual salary is $2.3 million. With this sudden wealth comes an added sense of power and entitlement. And everything about the experience of an NBA player cultivates the idea that players are kings. But when confronted by a police officer, players suddenly face a new experience: accountability and consequences. For many players, encounters with law-enforcement officials represent the rare instance of someone telling them no. Judging by the way players react when confronted by a police officer, it is no wonder why women who tell them no end up being abused.

• • •

"I've never broke the law in my life and I don't want to start today." That's what Portland Trail Blazer team captain Bonzi Wells told an Indiana sportswriter who was profiling him in July 2003. At the time, Wells was conducting a summer basketball camp for youth in his home state, Indiana. His declaration of innocence came in response to a reporter's query about the litany of charges filed against Wells's Trail Blazer teammates for crimes and on-the-court outbursts. "It hurts all of us," Wells said in reference to the negative image fostered by players' legal problems.

"Wells, it should be noted," the article reported, "says he's never had an off-court problem."

Fortunately for Wells, he wasn't under oath when he made this statement and the reporter he spoke to apparently didn't dig any deeper into his history.

On September 6, 2001, Portland police officer Mark Friedman was on routine patrol in downtown Portland when he observed a group of private security officers dealing with a disturbance outside the nightclub Polyesters. The club had just closed and about fifty people had spilled into an adjacent parking lot, where a verbal confrontation had started between patrons. The parking lot where the incident was taking place was well known to Friedman. The lot was private and its owner had entered into a policing agreement with the Portland PD. Friedman had been there many times to break up fights and remove loiterers after the area clubs and bars closed.

After consulting with private security guards, Friedman got into his patrol car and pulled into the lot. Several car stereos were blaring and people were shouting at one another. "Leave the area!" Friedman said into his loudspeaker. He repeated the command two more times, prompting most people to head toward their cars.

But six men standing around a silver Mercedes ignored Friedman. He shined his spotlight on the group, moved closer, and repeated his request for them to leave the lot. At that, one of them turned and started shouting obscenities at Friedman. It was Wells, who was accompanied by his Blazers teammate Erick Barkley.

Friedman didn't recognize Wells or Barkley. He could see, however, that they were both over six feet tall and acting hostilely toward him. He radioed for backup before exiting his car to talk to the group.

"Look, it is time to go," Friedman said as he approached.

"You gotta ask me please," Wells said.

Friedman again said they had to leave. Wells called him rude, then shouted that he wasn't going anywhere, which he emphasized with a string of obscenities.

Friedman explained that the lot was private property. Wells and anyone else refusing to leave would face criminal trespassing charges.

"F— you, man," Wells said. "You don't just walk over here and tell me what to do. You even know who you're talking to?"

Friedman still had no idea that Wells played for the Blazers.

"You're rude," Wells continued. "You want me to leave, say please. You ain't talking to no regular nigger. I'm the richest f—ing nigger in this place."

The louder Wells got, the more people who had been leaving began congregating around him and Friedman. People started laughing and mocking Friedman, who told Wells that he would not ask him please and reiterated that he would face citation if he didn't leave.

"Then cite me. Write me every citation you can. You couldn't bury me in tickets."

Friedman demanded to see each man's identification. Then Barkley got in the act of berating Friedman, shouting some obscenities and calling him a "pig" before surrendering his New York driver's license. Wells handed over his Indiana license.

Despite enduring some of the worst verbal abuse of his career, Friedman opted not to handcuff the men and haul them down to the station to be fingerprinted and photographed. It was the middle of the night and officers were spread thin, with multiple police calls coming over the radio. Instead, Friedman issued Wells, Barkley, and the two others citations, charging them with criminal trespass and ordering them to appear in court. When Wells realized he had, in effect, been arrested and charged with a crime, he apologized. "I'm sorry I disrespected you," he told Friedman. "That was wrong of me." He and Barkley then climbed into the silver Mercedes and drove off.

This is not the first time Wells had been arrested. Before becoming a first-round pick in the 1998 draft and joining the Blazers, Wells attended Ball State University in Indiana, where he was the school's all-time leading scorer and the Mid-American Conference Player of the Year. Near the end of Wells's sophomore season, Ball State police arrested him and charged him with battery after Erika Thompson, a sophomore at the university, reported that Wells had abused her for refusing to have sex with him. According to the police report, marks were visible on Thompson's neck and her jewelry had been broken as a result of the incident. Wells was jailed and later released after posting $2,000 bond. Ball State chose not to suspend Wells and prosecutors ultimately dropped the case, citing insufficient evidence.

Wells declined to discuss his arrest history or what prompted him to challenge the Portland police officer in the trespassing case. But Barkley, who has changed agents since the incident and now plays in the NBA's developmental league, did explain what happened. "He tried to talk down to us," Barkley said in an interview for this book. "Police officers talk to you like they are bigger than you sometimes. I've been stopped in Portland plenty of times because I was in an expensive car. They tried to talk down to me until they knew who I was."

Barkley suggested that the youthful age and luxurious cars driven by athletes make them prime targets for police harassment. But he also did something most unusual among NBA players today: he took responsibility for his actions and admitted he was wrong for saying some of the things he said to the officer. "Looking back," Barkley said, "with the words that were exchanged, if I was the cop I'd be mad too."

When he was arrested, Barkley worried there would be repercussions from the Blazers. He and Wells were called in to see the team management, and both players were informed they would likely be fined and miss a game. "I didn't even do nothing," Barkley told the team. "Why do I have to get suspended?"

In the end, neither Wells nor Barkley was suspended or fined, according to Barkley. Instead, the team went to work to shield both players from any accountability. "We had to get lawyers for the whole situation," Barkley said. "The team helped us with that. It was a team lawyer. They did their job, because it went away."

The case went away because the Portland police were stymied by a refusal on the part of the parking-lot owner (which also held a lucrative contract to manage the parking facilities at the Rose Garden, where the Blazers play) to press charges against Wells and Barkley. As the lot is private property, the police have the authority to order people to leave the premises, and they can arrest those who fail to do so. But their authority stops there. Under the business trespass agreement between the police and downtown property owners, it is up to the private property owner to swear out a formal complaint against a trespasser, otherwise the case is dropped.

"It wasn't that big of a deal," Barkley said, looking back on the incident. If he were comparing this incident to the other crimes detailed in this book, Barkley would be absolutely right. Trespassing hardly stacks up to rape, domestic violence, or the unlawful use of a firearm. But this incident demonstrates how young, rich players react when someone tries to hold them accountable. Most people in society would never dare mock or verbally berate a police officer, much less find it amusing as Wells did. But the culture of the NBA fosters the perception in these players that they are above the law and the officers who are sworn to enforce it. The NBA experience helps convert that perception into reality. The Blazers quickly snuffed out any worries Wells or Barkley may have had with respect to consequences by using the team's resources to make the altercation with the Portland police disappear.

Wells and Barkley weren't the first Blazers to challenge the authority of Portland police officers. On April 29, 1990, Blazer Cliff Robinson, in the midst of his rookie season, was arrested for aggravated assault and disorderly conduct after striking a female police officer. That night Portland police were responding to a fight inside Goldie's Restaurant and Lounge. Robinson, who was at the restaurant with his brother, some friends from New York, and his teammate Mark Bryant, had gone after another patron, Carlos Barfield, who stands five-nine and weighs 150 pounds. Robinson is six-ten and weighs 225 pounds. When security guards tried to restrain Robinson, he swung at them, too. The guards tackled Robinson and a brawl ensued between the security officers and Robinson and his entourage. Security ultimately managed to push Robinson and his friends outside.

But more fights quickly erupted in the street between the Robinson group and other patrons. By the time the police arrived, over thirty people were involved in the melee and Robinson had, according to police reports, assaulted at least seven people outside the restaurant. One security guard tried to deter Robinson by reminding him that as a Blazer he shouldn't be involved in a public display of violence. Robinson was not fazed.

Severely outnumbered, the police used a PA system to order people to stop fighting and clear the scene. Most did. Robinson and his group did not. Instead, Robinson continued to pursue Mr. Barfield, who ran to Officer Elaine Sloan and pleaded for help. No matter; Robinson charged Sloan. And while her head was turned toward Barfield he struck her in the side of the head with such force that Sloan dropped to the ground and was later treated at a nearby hospital for injuries. Robinson then assaulted Barfield, who was left bleeding from the facial area.

As more officers streamed onto the scene, one of Robinson's friends from New York had gone to the car and returned with a baseball bat. He dropped it only after police threatened to shoot him. Mark Bryant tried to whisk Robinson from the scene, but police apprehended Robinson and arrested him. After being assisted by her fellow officers, Officer Sloan read Robinson his Miranda rights. He mimicked her the entire time. He was then transported to the station for booking, where he was issued four citations for assault and disorderly conduct. "If I had known you were giving me all these tickets," Robinson told her, "I would have made the hit worthwhile." He also made derogatory ethnic comments to Sloan's female partner. Robinson ultimately pled guilty to assault and was placed on probation and ordered to undergo anger-management counseling and perform fifty hours of community service.

This was not Robinson's last contact with Portland police. On July 30, 1997, the police received a report of males in a Hummer waving guns. Police quickly spotted the vehicle and stopped it. Robinson was the driver. He, along with three other occupants, were removed from the Hummer and handcuffed. While searching the vehicle for guns, which turned out to be four paintball guns, the officers found marijuana. Robinson was charged with possession. The charge against him was later dropped when his brother claimed responsibility for the marijuana and pleaded guilty to possession.

A review of all the police records examined for this book reveals that while women are most frequently the victims of crimes committed by NBA players, police officers are their second-most common group of victims. And female officers are no exception. Neither badge nor gender means much to out-of-control players. Orlando police officer Teresa Joyce was assisting with crowd patrol outside Club Firestone in Orlando on July 7, 2003, when she observed Orlando Magic guard Darrell Armstrong standing in the middle of the street, preventing a taxicab from passing through. Joyce asked Armstrong to move out of the road. He ignored her and continued talking to passengers in the rear of the taxi. Again Joyce asked him to leave the street. Armstrong turned, raised his hands in the air, and asked, "Why are you messing with me?"

"You're standing in the middle of the road," Joyce said, now joined by Sergeant J. Windt. Defiant, Armstrong stood in the middle of the road, refusing to move. With Armstrong posing a public-safety hazard to himself and others, Joyce approached and put her hand on his upper arm in hopes of guiding him out of the road. Armstrong knocked Joyce's hand away, struck her in the arm, and pushed her away. When Joyce reached to restrain him, Armstrong jerked away. Three other officers immediately surrounded him and attempted to take him into custody. But Armstrong continued to resist, causing Joyce to unholster her Taser. Ultimately, her fellow officers handcuffed Armstrong. He was booked on charges of battery against a police officer and resisting arrest. In December 2003 a judge dismissed the case against Armstrong after ruling that it could not be proven beyond a reasonable doubt that Armstrong intentionally struck the officer.

Verbal assaults and physical attacks on uniformed officers are a brazen example of how above the law some players believe they are. Profanity-laced tirades, physical assaults, and threats to punish officers who are merely trying to do their job by protecting public safety are hardly becoming of men who are promoted by the NBA as action heroes.

Yet team officials excuse this behavior, while the league largely ignores it. Shortly after losing to the Chicago Bulls in the Eastern Conference Finals in 1997, Miami Heat point guard Tim Hardaway, a first-team all-NBA All-Star, was speeding along the MacArthur Causeway between Miami Beach and Miami in his $200,000 Ferrari. Police pursued him at speeds in excess of 110 miles per hour, yet still couldn't catch up to Hardaway, who weaved in and out of traffic. Hardaway stopped only after encountering bumper-to-bumper traffic. When Miami Beach police finally approached his car, Hardaway accused them of stopping him because he is black. He had been driving 110 miles per hour in a 40-miles-per-hour zone.

Next Hardaway, according to the police report, threatened the officers. "I have friends in high places who can make it very unpleasant for you," Hardaway told the two arresting officers. "If he arrests me, I'll take him down." The report also indicated that Hardaway used vulgar language to refer to the officers. Hardaway was not arrested, but received a $500 fine for speeding.

The league bears a great deal of responsibility for this attitude. Not only does it do nothing to punish athletes who abuse police, it fosters an attitude of lawlessness on the basketball court. When players commit acts of abuse and defiance, such as berating referees, coaches, or fans, they are merely slapped on the wrist. Before Bonzi Wells berated a police officer, he verbally abused and physically struck NBA referee Tim Donaghy during a game in November 2000. Players had to restrain Wells from going further. The league's response? They suspended him one game and fined him $10,000.

The following season, Wells was ejected from a game in Portland. On his way off the floor he threw his gum into the stands and hit a fan in the head. He later issued an apology and gave the fan a jersey.

On November 9, 2002, in a game between the Blazers and the San Antonio Spurs, Wells approached Spurs player Danny Ferry during a time-out and spit in his face. "It is a shame when you have somebody who decides that the best way to compete is to spit on somebody else," Spurs head coach Gregg Popovich said after the game. "Bonzi showed a complete lack of class."

Wells denied spitting on Ferry. Blazers head coach Maurice Cheeks said he believed Wells. "He told me he didn't do it," Cheeks said. "All I can do is take his word." Actually, there was a lot more Cheeks could have done. But the *last* thing he should have done was take Wells at his word. Witnesses far more credible then Wells saw him spit on Ferry. Blazers broadcaster Steve Jones even mentioned it on the air. "Unfortunately, I saw it," Jones said after the game concluded. Ferry's teammate David Robinson saw it too. Robinson, who earned a reputation as the most clean-cut player in the league, said that as the players were walking toward the bench during a time-out he heard spitting action. He turned and saw saliva hanging off Ferry's face. Robinson's account prompted the NBA to suspend Wells for one game.

But Cheeks continued to make excuses for Wells. "I don't think a man's character should be decided by one incident," Cheeks told the press. "I believe Bonzi has been a very good-character guy."

One incident? A good-character guy? Ferry, who is white, claimed that the spitting was associated with racial epithets spewed at him by Wells. He said Wells had called him "honkie" repeatedly. Other players accused Wells of racist remarks, too. Golden State forward Troy Murphy, who is also white, said that Wells kept calling him "cracker" during an exhibition game in October 2002. And after a game in April 2002, Dallas Mavericks point guard Nick Van Exel, who is black, said that Wells called the Mavericks "a bunch of soft-assed white boys." Cheeks denied knowing anything about any of the alleged racial comments. "I am not aware of it," he said. The NBA's senior vice president for basketball operations, Stu Jackson, who oversees league discipline, played ignorant too.

It is no wonder that Wells continued to act out. In November 2003, Wells flipped his middle finger at a fan. "I was probably wrong. But I don't remember doing nothing like that. I black out sometimes." He was fined $10,000. It may as well have been ten cents. The Blazers paid Wells roughly $7 million in 2003; the fine amounted to one-tenth of 1 percent of his salary. Not surprisingly, days after the fine was levied, Wells flipped out on head coach Maurice Cheeks, cursing him for taking him out of a game. Not until Cheeks became the target of one of Wells's tirades did he take action. Cheeks suspended Wells for two games, stripped him of his co-captaincy status, and immediately began looking for a team to trade him to. On December 3, the Blazers traded Wells to the Memphis Grizzlies.

Officer Mark Friedman, who arrested Wells in Portland on the trespassing charge, said his respect for the NBA has faded with the endless train of offenses and no accountability. "I've given up on NBA basketball," said Friedman. "I don't watch them anymore. People tend to be extra forgiving in Portland because there's no other game in town. If there was, the team would really be feeling it in their pocketbooks. It's a sign of the times."

Meanwhile, Wells was given a king's welcome in Memphis. "We're very excited about the opportunity to acquire a player of the caliber of Bonzi Wells," Grizzlies president Jerry West said. West said this despite the fact that Wells had earlier told *Sports Illustrated*, regarding all the off-the-court things that went on in Portland: "We're not really worried about what the hell [the fans] think about us. They really don't matter to us. They can boo us every day, but they are still going to ask for our autographs if they see us on the street. That is why they are fans and we are NBA players."

SEVEN

PUT YOUR HANDS UP

A disrespect for the law and an attitude of absolute confidence that laws can be broken without consequence do not instantly develop in a player the moment he signs his first pro contract. It takes prior experiences—lots of them—to build up this level of arrogance and reach the point where a player can make a sport out of assaulting or verbally abusing law-enforcement officials. The worst of this behavior manifests itself at the pro level. But the seeds of lawlessness and the attitude of immunity from consequences are sewn in the minds of gifted athletes long before they become pros. High school and college are typically where athletes are taught by experience that they are above the law.

It was four-thirty in the morning on March 31, 1989, when the phone rang in Iowa State University head coach Johnny Orr's hotel room in Seattle, Washington. The call came from Iowa State's assistant athletic director, David Cox. His message stunned Orr. His best player, eighteen-year-old forward Sam Mack, along with an Iowa State football player, had just been arrested for armed robbery back in Iowa. Both players had been shot by police and were hospitalized under armed guard.

"What? Are you sure?" Orr said.

Orr instantly became sick to his stomach. He had gone to Seattle to celebrate, mingle with other coaches, and watch Michigan take on Duke, Seton Hall, and Illinois in the Final Four. Before taking over at Iowa State in 1980, Orr coached Michigan for twelve years. He twice led the Wolverines to Top Ten finishes and left as the most successful basketball coach in the school's history.

But none of that seemed important suddenly. One of Orr's players was lying in a hospital with bullets in his body and felony charges hanging over his head. The six-foot-seven-inch Mack was a graduate of Thornridge High School, where he was voted the most valuable player in his suburban Chicago conference. But his substandard high school transcript left him academically ineligible to play basketball his freshman year at Iowa State. The 1988–89 season had been his first season in uniform. He emerged as the most all-around talented player on Orr's roster and displayed rare skills that made him a likely candidate for the NBA. There were far more important issues to deal with now. Orr caught the first available flight back to Iowa.

When Sam Mack and football player Levin White checked out at Kmart in Ames, Iowa, on March 30, 1989, they made just one purchase: a box of bullets. Next they stopped at a convenience store and bought two forty-ounce bottles of beer. After drinking them, they waited for closing time to approach a Burger King. Just before eleven, Mack pulled his red Ford Escort into the Burger King parking lot at 209 Lincoln Way in Ames. Only two customers remained inside eating. White loaded the bullets into a rifle. Mack stepped out and urinated in the parking lot before pulling his gray sweatsuit up on his face and putting on a pair of dark sunglasses to disguise his identity. A basketball team poster hanging inside the restaurant prominently displayed Mack's face.

Donning a red cap, White pulled his turtleneck up over his face, leaving only his eyes exposed. He hid his loaded rifle under his blue jacket. Mack carried a large knife. Together, they headed toward the rear door leading into the dining room.

Her back to the cash registers, twenty-one-year-old Amy Konek, a college student and a three-year employee at the restaurant, looked forward to closing time. She ran water in the sink in preparation for cleaning the milk-shake machine. Then she heard a gunshot.

"Everybody down!" she heard an unfamiliar male voice yell.

Frightened, Konek peeked through an opening between the back kitchen area and the front counter. She saw a large man wearing a blue coat and holding a rifle. She could not see his face.

Konek immediately climbed out the drive-through window and darted into the street. She approached a car and begged two strangers to let her in. They drove her to the police station a few blocks away.

Inside the Burger King, after herding employees and two customers into the walk-in cooler, Mack cleaned the money out of the cash register. Meanwhile, White held the manager at gunpoint, directing him to turn over the money in the office safe. Within minutes they had grabbed over $1,600.

Police cars sped into the Burger King parking lot. Officers John Burnett and Edward Morton spotted an employee outside the front of the restaurant frantically pointing toward the back. The officers shined their car headlights in that direction. Mack and White were crouched down, making their way toward the double doors at the rear of the dining area. Officer Morton grabbed a shotgun, opened the squad car door, and took cover behind it. Burnett ran, with his revolver drawn, toward the corner of the building as Mack and White came through the first set of glass doors into the alcove.

"Police!" Morton shouted, taking aim. "Police! Drop the gun!"

White raised his rifle from underneath his coat. Morton repeatedly yelled at White to drop the gun while a third officer crossed the parking lot toward the rear of the building. When White raised his rifle to his shoulder and aimed toward the officers, Morton fired three shots into the alcove. Seeing that White still had not dropped his rifle, Officer Burnett fired six rounds. Glass shattered and White and Mack dropped, before scurrying back inside.

As officers closed in, cash, glass, a knife, and a .22-caliber ammo clip littered the alcove. The money bag, bursting with five-dollar bills, was wedged between the alcove doors. A trail of blood led back inside the restaurant. Burnett entered. White, hit in the foot, was on the ground, still holding the rifle. Burnett ordered him to drop it and place his hands behind his head. White surrendered.

Mack continued crawling toward the kitchen. After repeated demands to stop and drop his weapon, Mack finally put his hands on his head and stood slowly. With bullets lodged in his buttocks and the back of his thigh, blood ran down his leg and seeped through his pants. Burnett handcuffed Mack, patted him down, and called for an ambulance. Both athletes were rushed to the hospital.

At 1:08 A.M., Detective Mark Wheeler entered Sam Mack's hospital room, read him his rights, turned on a tape recorder, and started asking him questions. Mack described herding Burger King employees into the freezer. "I say, 'Come on, get in the freezer, get in the freezer,' and, um, they got in the freezer, and I closed it."

Next Mack described taking the manager toward the cash register area to retrieve money from the safe. "I walked with him up there to the front. I said, 'Where the money, where the money at?' and the dude said, 'This is it, right here.' The dude started showing it to me, and I started putting it in the Burger King sack."

Less than twenty-four hours after the robbery, Iowa State University suspended Mack and White and revoked their athletic privileges. Three days later, the university brought administrative charges against them for violating the school's student code of conduct. And then the county prosecutor added felony kidnapping and terrorism charges to the armed robbery charges. Both men faced fifty-five-year prison terms.

Johnny Orr didn't know what he was going to say. The prosecutor had given him permission to visit Mack in the hospital. Passing the two armed police officers stationed outside Mack's door, Orr entered. Before he could speak, Mack did.

"I didn't do it, coach," Mack said.

"Sam, how can you tell me you didn't do it when you got a bullet in your butt and a bullet in your leg?" Mack replied.

Mack said he would never do something like rob a restaurant. He blamed the incident on Levin White, insisting he was coerced into participating in the robbery.

Orr didn't know White. After talking to Mack, he decided to pay him a visit, too.

Levin White came from a broken home in the Greater Los Angeles area. His mother was unemployed. His father lived in Virginia. White had come to Ames, Iowa, for one reason: to play college football. He arrived with a beat-up old car and no money. He was not allowed to get a part-time job, as the NCAA forbids student-athletes from being employed while on scholarship. When White's car broke down and was towed shortly after he arrived in Iowa, he abandoned it, unable to pay the towing fee.

White brought something else with him to Iowa: a criminal history. Back in California he had been arrested twice for robbery. One case was dropped when witnesses could not identify him. In the second case he was convicted, but on the reduced charge of possessing a dangerous weapon—a sawed-off shotgun—for which he served ten days in jail. He also had a vehicle theft charge dismissed.

But none of this had been an obstacle to White getting football scholarship offers from top colleges and universities around the country. An exceptional high school athlete, White attended a junior college before signing a letter of intent to attend the University of Southern California. However, when USC later withdrew its scholarship offer, freeing up White to go elsewhere, Iowa State recruiters were quick to offer him a complete scholarship with room, board, and tuition. But he had been forced to sit out his first year at Iowa State in order to obtain his eligibility.

After White's arrest, Iowa State's football coaching staff wanted nothing to do with him. Unlike Mack, White, a nonstarting defensive back, was replaceable. In a sworn deposition, White testified that not one of his coaches or recruiters, or any school official, visited him the entire time he was hospitalized or incarcerated in the Story County Jail awaiting trial. Only Orr visited him. Unlike Mack, White confessed the obvious to Orr: they did the robbery and it was planned.

Levin White could not afford an attorney. Represented by a public defender, he pleaded guilty to armed robbery on April 28 and was sentenced to twenty-five years in state prison. And so, before playing a single down of football at Iowa State, his football career was over and his life behind bars was begun.

Less than twenty-four hours after Mack and White had been hospitalized on the night of the robbery (March 30), the phone rang in the Des Moines law office of Ray Rosenberg. The call came from Chicago attorney Barry Sheppard, whose secretary, Joyce Mack, is Sam's sister. As soon as she informed Sheppard of her brother Sam's circumstance, Sheppard telephoned Sam at the hospital. Next, as a member of the National Association of Criminal Defense Lawyers, Sheppard consulted the organization's directory and found Rosenberg, who was rated among the best lawyers in the vicinity of Ames, Iowa. Sheppard told Rosenberg what had happened and asked him to consider representing Mack.

After hearing the facts, Rosenberg didn't think Sam Mack's chances looked very promising. But after talking with Mack's family two days later and discussing the case with other lawyers in his office, Rosenberg agreed to defend him. Since the Macks were not in a position to afford his standard hourly rate, Rosenberg agreed to bill them at a reduced rate. The family rounded up a $5,000 retainer and agreed to make additional payments as the case proceeded. Three days after being contacted by Sheppard, Rosenberg and his firm began officially representing Sam Mack. The first thing he and his associate Paul Scott did was meet with Sam, who told them the same thing he told Orr: White had planned the robbery and forced him at gunpoint to participate.

Levin White told prosecutors a rather different story. In a sworn deposition, White told authorities that Mack planned the robbery and the motive was to obtain money to purchase cocaine.

The following is an excerpt from White's deposition:

Q: Had you ever heard that Sam Mack was buying or dealing
   or using cocaine?
A: *I heard that he sold cocaine.*
Q: You heard he sold cocaine?
A: *Yes.*
Q: Who told you?
A: *Sam told me.*
Q: Sam told you?
A: *Yes, sir.*

White said that Mack had told him that he had belonged to a
gang in Chicago, had used a gun before, and had previously sold
cocaine.

While admitting to having a criminal record, White had no
known history of either drug use or drug sales. He maintained
that he had no desire to buy, use, or sell cocaine, and he made
that clear to Mack. White's motivation for carrying out the robbery, he insisted, was his need for cash. He had no money to pay
the school the roughly $400 in late fees that were preventing him
from registering for classes and threatening his athletic eligibility.
That was the least of White's problems. In addition to his mother
being broke, White had fathered an out-of-wedlock baby just a
few months earlier in California. White's mother, White's new
baby son, and the baby's mother were all broke.

Prosecutors did not grant immunity to White when he testified
about Mack's alleged drug-related motives. Nor did White receive a
reduced sentence for his testimony. And all the while, he was subject
to prosecution for perjury if he made false statements under oath.

Ray Carreathers, another Iowa State athlete who knew both
White and Mack, had been present during some of their conversations, according to White. "He [Mack] also asked me to sell cocaine with him and he asked Carreathers," White testified. "He

was there, Carreathers, at the time. He asked Carreathers to sell cocaine with him."

In his sworn deposition, Carreathers confirmed that he had been present when cocaine and the robbery were discussed. When asked by Mack's lawyers who had talked about the cocaine, Carreathers replied: "We all did."

Carreathers then added: "It was talked about, the cocaine, [about how] the robbery will lead to the cocaine. So in other words, the money from a robbery would be used to get cocaine."

Under cross-examination by the prosecutor, Carreathers was asked about his understanding of what Mack intended to do with any money that was obtained in a robbery. "Well, intentions was cocaine," he testified. "That's what the intention was. The money was got, you know, to make more money, was going to be with cocaine."

"When you say to make more money with cocaine, what do you mean?"

"Can't snort it. Sell it."

The question for the jury would be whether Mack robbed to finance a cocaine transaction or whether he had been coerced to rob at gunpoint and followed through out of fear for his life.

In the meantime, Iowa State officials did not want Mack back on campus. Mack's defense lawyers knew it, and Orr knew it, too. When the school suspended Mack, the university's judicial affairs coordinator said in a formal notice, issued April 3, that the "alleged criminal charges constitute a potential danger to the health, safety and well being of the residents at RCA [the student housing area] and the University Community." On top of criminal charges, Sam Mack faced charges under the Iowa State student code of conduct.

Yet shortly after Levin White pleaded guilty, on May 23, the university inexplicably lifted Mack's suspension, enabling him to return to campus and begin using the school's athletic and academic facilities. Word of this change came in a confidential memorandum from the university's vice president for student affairs, Thomas B. Thielen, directly to Mack.

The decision flew in the face of the school's April 3 decision and contradicted a public statement issued by the university's president, Dr. Gordon Eaton, on March 31 that said, in part: "Pending a legal resolution of the case, their team memberships and athletic department privileges have been suspended."

But the case had not been legally resolved. Even the university charges had not been resolved. Nothing about Mack's legal situation had changed since the robbery. So why had the university changed its stance toward Mack?

"They reinstated him because they feared getting sued," Orr said. School officials were concerned that Mack might sue the university for denying him academic privileges when he had yet to be convicted of any criminal wrongdoing.

Colleges and universities are authorized to issue temporary suspensions to students who violate student honor codes. As a general rule, breaking state or federal laws constitutes a clear violation of a student honor code. Under such circumstances, most schools have a provision that enables suspended students to petition for reinstatement, following a hearing before the school's judiciary board, which in turn often follows the disposition of the criminal case.

The conundrum arises when schools suspend students on the basis of an arrest. Within the criminal justice system, individuals are afforded the presumption of innocence until proven guilty. But when the allegations involve violence, a university has a public-safety interest in suspending the accused in order to remove a potential risk of further harm or injury from the student body and greater campus community. Mack had used a weapon to rob a business and had taken two bullets from police officers. Students were among the employees who had been victimized in the robbery.

Nonetheless, a criminally accused student-athlete has a powerful incentive to push for reinstatement. The NCAA, of course, requires student-athletes to remain enrolled as a condition of sports participation. As a result of being shot and incarcerated, Mack had been forced to withdraw from the spring semester without completing any of his courses. In order to remain eligible to play in the upcoming season, Mack would have to be reinstated in his spring classes or take summer courses. Neither option was open to him as long as he was suspended.

For players like Sam Mack—and others like him who possess a better-than-average chance of graduating from the ranks of college sports to professional sports—a suspension can derail a career opportunity. For Mack, college athletics served as a stepping-stone, a vehicle to the professional ranks. Academics and grade-point averages were merely a means to more lucrative ends: an NBA contract. To deny Mack access to school on the basis of an arrest, he could argue, is akin to denying him his due-process rights.

Around the time that White pleaded guilty, Mack notified the university's Withdrawal Committee that he wanted to be reinstated. The committee, which consisted of the university's dean, Margaret A. Healy, and two Ph.D.s representing the Student Health Services and Student Counseling Services, scheduled a closed-door meeting with Mack on May 12. Yet arguably the most important person in the room was an observer, Reid Crawford, the university's legal counsel.

According to confidential internal memorandums, Mack reiterated his request that his suspension be lifted. The committee questioned him about his alleged role in the armed robbery.

Mack maintained his innocence. His criminal defense attorneys were not present, but they had offered no opposition to his answering questions.

Following the hearing, Dean Healy sent an internal memorandum to university vice president Thomas Thielen on May 19, recommending that the emergency suspension be removed. The dean said that the committee had "come to a consensus that Sam Mack does not pose an immediate danger to the health and well-being of other students, faculty, or staff."

A copy of this memorandum was sent to the university attorney.

Four days later, Vice President Thielen notified Mack by letter that he was welcome back on campus.

Weighing the risk of placing an accused armed robber back on campus versus the risk of a lawsuit by the accused robber, the university chose to invite Mack back. Thielen's notice informing Mack of the decision gave the impression that the decision was motivated by a desire to advance Mack's education. "This change in your status will allow you to utilize educational facilities and resources at Iowa State University," Thielen wrote to Mack in his decision letter. "I know I speak for the university community when I say I wish you much success in your future educational endeavors."

Educational endeavors? Mack's decision to attend Iowa State was not an "educational endeavor." It was a basketball endeavor. He arrived on campus under the NCAA's Proposition 48, a provision that allows academically ineligible athletes to take courses in an attempt to obtain eligibility. Mack's freshman course schedule was intended to boost his grade-point average. He took a high school algebra course (for which he received no credit), a one-credit Developmental Reading course, and two Library Instruction courses, both of which he failed. He also failed to complete his Introduction to Western Civilization class. His only two-credit course was Basketball Techniques, for which he received an A.

The second semester was not much better. Although he continued in high school algebra and Introduction to Western Civilization, and added a computer course, half of Mack's accredited classes were PE courses: Badminton (1 credit), Tennis (1 credit) and Weight Training (1 credit).

This course schedule enabled Mack to satisfy the NCAA's rules for eligibility, but it hardly advanced his education. Perhaps the biggest lesson that the NCAA rules taught Mack was that athletic eligibility trumps personal and social accountability. The system of college sports had already taught him that different rules apply for gifted athletes.

Now Iowa State was playing along. School officials were well aware that Mack's motive for returning to campus was to advance his athletic career. "I understand your interest in taking courses this summer to preserve your athletic eligibility for the coming year," Iowa State academic adviser Nancy Osborne wrote in a confidential memorandum to Mack on May 30. "I know that you are now quite motivated to do well in your class work at Iowa State and you have the strong support of your family behind you. These are great strengths indeed!"

Mack could only hope the criminal justice system would be as forgiving as the system of college athletics.

EIGHT

STAYING POWER

As Mack's trial date approached, Ray Rosenberg realized he and his law firm were not going to get paid. Mack did not have the money, and his family, despite a prior commitment to pay, came up empty-handed. Beyond the original $5,000 retainer, they had made just one additional payment of $1,000. They owed far more, and Rosenberg could have dropped the case for lack of payment. Yet if Mack were convicted at trial he would be facing over fifty years in prison. Rosenberg and his colleagues had started to think they had a chance of winning at trial. They planned to pit Mack's reputation and his version of being coerced against White's reputation and his version of Mack planning the robbery to raise drug money.

Rosenberg decided to proceed without payment. Besides the high stakes and high publicity surrounding the trial, there remained the outside chance that if Mack were acquitted and ended up in the NBA, the lawyers could recoup legal fees down the road. Ultimately, it was Mack's status as a talented basketball player that enabled him to hold on to the top legal talent in Des Moines. "There was a lot of interest in our practice in doing the case," Rosenberg said. "We had a couple lawyers who were basketball players and who were big basketball fans."

Rosenberg's assessment of Mack's image and how it would project at the trial proved correct. It was apparent the moment Mack stepped foot inside the courthouse, dressed in a conservative suit with a white shirt and tie. "During the trial whenever there was a break you could always find Sam in the sheriff's office right next to the courtroom schmoozing with the girls," Rosenberg recalled. "They all liked him. Even one of the policemen who was a formal witness against Sam said to him 'Good luck, Sam,' as he left the courtroom. Sam was well liked in the community."

Meanwhile, prosecutor Mark Cullen opened the state's case against Mack by telling the jury: "The whole purpose that Sam Mack was so intent on making money was because he wanted to buy a quarter-kilo of cocaine, turn around, sell it and make more money."

To support this claim, the prosecution called as its lead witness Levin White, who had to be transported from prison to testify. He reiterated his prior deposition testimony: Mack masterminded the robbery, the object of which was to obtain money to buy drugs for resale. The jury, which consisted of three Ph.D.s and a foreman who taught physics at Iowa State, had to balance this theory against the compelling question that Rosenberg raised in his opening statement: Why would Mack, a young man from a strong family and with no prior history of crime or drugs, risk a college scholarship and a shot at the NBA to rob a Burger King? This defied logic and common sense. Rather than erase the doubts raised by Rosenberg's contention, White's presence and his testimony only added to them.

"White's testimony played into our hands," said Rosenberg's associate Paul Scott. "He was a terrible witness."

Mack's lawyers countered with Coach Orr, who agreed to testify as a character witness on Mack's behalf. Orr met in consultation sessions with Mack's lawyers three times before he testified. When Orr took over as Iowa State's coach in 1980 the school had recorded a losing record in its five previous seasons and hadn't appeared in a postseason tournament in over forty years. Attendance at games averaged less than 6,500 spectators.

Orr changed all that. Under Orr the team recorded five twenty-win seasons and went to the NCAA tournament six times. The team won conference championships and churned out future NBA players Jeff Hornacek, Victor Alexander, and Jeff Grayer. Attendance at basketball games jumped 95 percent, and Iowa State started appearing on ESPN. Orr was so beloved by Iowa fans that before every game, when he ran onto the court, the pep band belted out the theme from Johnny Carson's *Tonight Show*. In a state with no professional sports franchises, the Iowa State Cyclones basketball program was as big as it gets, and Orr was the leader.

Having Orr as a character witness was like rolling out Iowa's most celebrated citizen. The day Orr testified the atmosphere in the courthouse resembled a sporting event. Outside Sam Mack signed autographs for young boys who showed up with pads and pens. Inside, a standing-room-only crowd packed the courtroom. Orr took the stand and told jurors that he never knew Mack to be involved in drug dealing. Orr added that Mack had a very strong relationship with his family, that he wasn't permitted to roam the streets in his neighborhood as a teenager, and that he was highly recruited out of high school. "He was a very good prospect," Orr testified. "There is no question about that."

The contrast between Orr and Levin White was profound: Mr. Basketball versus an incarcerated felon. "Coach Orr's testimony was devastating to the prosecution," one state's attorney conceded. "In walks one of the most popular, respected men in the state of Iowa and he vouches for Sam Mack."

The jury acquitted Mack. Prosecutors, police, and the victims inside Burger King on the night of the robbery were stunned. Mack had committed an armed robbery and had a bullet in his leg to prove it. Coach Orr was stunned too. "I was shocked when he got acquitted," Orr said. "Dammit. They robbed the Burger King."

Yet Mack was free. "I'm positive he got off because of me," Orr conceded. "At that time I was very popular in the state."

Despite his popularity, Orr said that after the trial he took tremendous criticism for having supported Mack. "Testifying was one of the toughest things I have ever done," Orr recalled. "Everyone said, 'Dammit, Orr, you got him off.' I had people threaten me. I went to bat for him because I felt so badly for his mother."

After the trial, jurors explained their verdict to the press. "We put a lot of weight on the fact that Mr. Mack had no previous incidents of trouble," one juror said.

But, unbeknownst to the jury, Mack did have a prior incident of trouble.

Almost a year earlier, on July 19, 1988, Mack had been arrested within miles of his home in Illinois and charged with unlawful use of a weapon. That night a dispatch went out over police radios indicating that an aggravated assault had taken place in Harvey, Illinois. Two black males were described fleeing the scene in a red Ford Escort, the same car Mack drove the night he and White robbed Burger King. A patrol officer in the vicinity of the incident spotted a car matching the description and being operated by two black males. The vehicle's license plate also matched the one provided in the dispatch. The officer pulled the car over and approached the driver's-side window. The driver was Sam Mack.

Looking inside the vehicle, the officer observed the barrel of a gun under Mack's seat. Mack was arrested and the gun was taken into evidence. It had been fashioned to resemble a .357 Magnum handgun. "The gun's not mine, it belongs to a friend," the report quotes Mack as saying. He subsequently told police: "My mom told me I would get in trouble for having that thing."

The case was treated as an armed robbery investigation with Mack as the central suspect. Again Mack's sister came to his rescue by calling on her boss, Barry Sheppard, to defend Sam. On August 30, 1988, Sheppard appeared with Mack in room 204 in Markham Court in Illinois to answer the weapons charges, just weeks before Mack began his sophomore season at Iowa State. Today Illinois treats unlawful possession of a firearm as a felony. But at that time, simple possession of a firearm was only a misdemeanor, as long as the firearm was not used to commit an offense. And misdemeanor offenders were eligible to undergo one year of court supervision, a form of probation. Mack was still under court supervision in the gun case in Illinois at the time of the robbery in Iowa. Had he been convicted in the robbery trial he would have been in violation of his probationary status in Illinois. Nonetheless, Sheppard had the gun case expunged from Mack's record two years after he completed his supervision requirements.

The jurors in Iowa never heard any of this. Nor did Orr. "If I had known that, we would have never had him back [on campus]," said Orr. "You can't take chances like that. If his lawyer knew he never told me that. When I was on the witness stand I never knew he had been in trouble."

The prosecutors and the defense attorneys knew about Mack's prior arrest. But since Mack had entered a pretrial supervision program, the case was not treated as a conviction and therefore was inadmissible as evidence in a criminal trial.

•   •   •

Outside the courtroom following the verdict, Mack rejoiced and signed more autographs. "The people at the Story County courthouse just loved him," recalled Paul Scott, one of Mack's defense attorneys at the trial. "He was the most charming guy, just a really nice man. He seemed to be the guy who made it out of a questionable background and basketball helped him."

Basketball did more than help him. It enabled him to retain and keep top-shelf legal representation. It brought him the best character witness in the state. And it gave him the benefit of the doubt in the eye of the jury and the public. A lead editorial in the *Ames Daily Tribune* opined: "Society will be better served by letting Sam Mack alone and allowing him to rebuild his life and his athletic career unencumbered by whatever mistakes he might have made."

Mack thought that his basketball career would resume at Iowa State. "Iowa State could not stop him from coming back," Orr said. Mack had a scholarship and he had been found not guilty by a jury. But Orr had other plans. He went to Illinois and met with Mack and his mother in their home and told them that Mack should not return to Iowa State.

Mack's mother didn't understand why not. Her son had been acquitted, she pointed out. Orr gingerly explained that Sam's return to campus and the team would generate adverse publicity both for Mack and Orr. "I think it is best for him to get a fresh start," Orr told Mack's mother. He suggested a school like the University of Tennessee at Chattanooga.

But Mack opted for Arizona State. Orr tried to discourage this, recommending a smaller school in a smaller city. But Orr's former assistant at Michigan, Bill Frieder, was the head coach at Arizona State and had heavily recruited Mack out of high school. Frieder talked with Orr and other people close to Mack to assess whether to offer him a scholarship. "We all believed as far as the criminal system went that Sam had a pretty good shot at becoming a pro," said his attorney, Paul Scott, "and that he was just not going to be involved in the criminal justice system again."

Frieder offered Mack a scholarship and Mack transferred to Arizona State. Frieder got his first look at Mack during the team's intersquad games that fall. After the scrimmages, Frieder called Orr. "Boy, that guy can flat-out play," Orr recalled Frieder saying about Mack. "He's better than anybody I got."

Two months later, Orr received another phone call from Arizona; this one from Mack. "Coach, I didn't rape that girl," Mack began. He had barely been at Arizona State two months and had yet to play in his first regular season basketball game when he was accused of raping an eighteen-year-old student on campus. His call to Orr and his denial of guilt sounded remarkably similar to the conversation Orr had with Mack in his hospital room after the robbery. Orr asked him what happened. Mack said that he had consensual sex with his accuser and that other men were present and had watched. "I got witnesses," Orr recalled him saying.

In fact, there were no witnesses. According to more than 200 pages of police documents, including transcripts of tape-recorded interviews with Mack and his accuser, on the evening of November 5, 1989, Mack visited the dorm room of two of his teammates. When he arrived, Jamie Gilbert and a couple other girls were present. At one point, one of Mack's teammates and the other girls at the dorm room left to pick up some other friends, leaving behind Mack, Gilbert, and another player, who had fallen asleep on his bed. The sleeping player had a sexual relationship with Gilbert that included Gilbert performing oral sex on him and engaging in sexual intercourse. Only days earlier, the player had shared this information with Mack, unbeknownst to Gilbert.

According to Gilbert's tape-recorded police statement, shortly after the room cleared out, Mack turned off the television, dimmed the lights, and pulled down his sweatpants. She saw that he had an erection and said she instantly became fearful, as she had heard stories about Mack being involved in an armed robbery in Iowa and thought he was likely to become violent. The dorm room is a box-shaped, fourteen-by-eighteen-foot room with two beds, two desks, a dresser, and a small refrigerator. Since the room contained no couches or comfortable chairs, Jamie was sitting on the other bed, her back against the wall, reading a magazine. She told police that Mack approached the bed and stood facing her. "He grabbed my head and made me put my mouth on his penis," she told investigators. "I kept pushing him away saying no, no, and I was crying." Mack, she said, kept saying in hushed tones: "Be cool. Be cool."

During this time, Mack's teammate was roughly ten feet away, sound asleep on his bed. The player later told police that he was not awakened by anything going on the room that night, but that he was a heavy sleeper.

Gilbert told police that after forcing her to briefly perform oral sex on him, Mack pushed her back on the bed and used his right hand to squeeze her wrists together while using his left hand to undo her blue jeans and force them down just below her knees. As soon as he let go of her hands, Jaime said she tried to pull her pants back up but that he "wiggled" his way between her legs. She said her attempts to squeeze her legs together were futile, too. "He undid my legs," Gilbert said, "and wiggled his way up so that I couldn't move my legs and then he went inside of me." Gilbert reported that he only stopped when he heard a car pull up outside the dorm room window. As he climbed off Gilbert to see who had arrived, Mack ejaculated on her panties, blue jeans, and the bedspread. When Mack realized that the group of students that had left a short while earlier to pick up friends had returned, he quickly gathered himself and turned the television back on. Jamie pulled her pants up and sat back up on the bed.

But she did a poor job masking her emotions. One of her girl-friends noticed tears in her eyes and quickly took her home. The following morning Gilbert reported the incident to the police and underwent a rape-kit exam at Tempe St. Luke's Hospital, where Dr. Mark Rogers took two vaginal smear slides, four vaginal swabs, a urine sample, a blood sample, and saliva samples. Jamie also gave investigators her panties and blue jeans, which contained a white crusty substance consistent with semen. Later that day, Detective Bennett Rowe of the Arizona State Police Department obtained a warrant to search the room where the incident occurred, as well as a warrant to take blood, saliva, and hair samples from Mack.

In the dorm room, police recovered the bedspread Gilbert described. It contained a white crusty substance similar to what was detected on Gilbert's panties and jeans. Detectives Rowe and his partner then located Mack in a study hall. With a tape recorder concealed in his pocket, Rowe displayed his badge and asked to speak with Mack. Cooperative and friendly, Mack immediately began talking freely about the Iowa robbery and his basketball stardom. Rowe read Mack his Miranda rights and served him a search warrant ordering him to provide blood, saliva, and hair samples. While escorting Mack to the hospital, Rowe asked Mack if he would apologize to the victim.

"I'm willing to do whatever," Mack said.

"She told you it was OK, didn't she?" Rowe then asked. Silent, Mack nodded his head up and down. Rowe asked if the victim asked for both oral sex and vaginal sex. "It wasn't, it wasn't uh uh uh . . . a basic, you know, ask. It was just, you know, I mean, you know, the lights was out and you know the things led to one another and she did this."

"What did she do exactly?"

"Oral sex," Mack said. "And you know."

When they reached Tempe St. Luke's Hospital, Rowe and his partner took Mack inside. While waiting to provide body samples, Mack told them he had a bullet in his leg. Then he told them how he got it. He said he had been a customer at a Burger King when a man with a rifle with a thirty-round banana clip entered, pointed the gun at Mack, and robbed the place. Mack said he ran from the restaurant to escape the gunman and was shot by police, who mistook him for a robber. This was not only a lie, it conflicted with the testimony Mack had delivered under oath at his trial in Iowa, all of which Rowe and Wilson were briefed about by Iowa authorities.

Then Dr. Mark Rogers, who had previously examined Gilbert, drew two vials of blood from Mack's arm, a saliva sample from his mouth, and removed hair samples from his head and pubic area. During this process, a court officer arrived and served Mack with an injunction signed by a local judge. It ordered him to have no further contact with the victim and to refrain from harassing her. It listed Mack as a defendant. Shaken up by the whole experience, Mack returned to the police car for his escort ride back to his apartment.

"Can you tell me how it really happened so we can clear this whole thing up?" Rowe asked.

"All right, all right," Mack said. "I mean, I'm willing to make an apology and I'm willing to tell you guys what happened." Seated in the backseat while a tape-recording device was running on the front seat, Mack told the officers that the victim was "really inebriated" and had been sitting on a bed inside his teammate's dorm room when he sat down next to her. "I think she liked me," Mack said. "And um, we were just sitting over there talking and one thing led to another. You know, like she just . . .

well, I think I must of asked . . . You know . . . it just happened. You know she didn't say no or nothing."

"Who made the first sex move?" Rowe asked.

"Um, she grabbed me and she tried to kiss me. Yeah, that's what it was."

"How many dates have you been out with her?"

"None," Mack said. "You see it's like, with athletes you know, it's kinda like you're considered a star. And you know, some girls they see you have a good game or something and they want to go home with you."

Mack's response reflected the view of many celebrated athletes: I'm a star and as a result some girls want to have sex with me. And *some girls* is defined as any girl who crosses the athlete's path.

Under further questioning, Mack admitted that the victim never took her pants off. Instead, they were halfway down her legs at the time he penetrated her. The image of blue jeans restricting the movement of a woman's lower legs is hardly consistent with a woman consenting to sexual intercourse. "Do you think if she was interested in making love she would take her pants all the way off?" Rowe asked.

"Well, it all depends . . . on you know," Mack said, hesitating. "If it's a, you know . . . it all depends." Mack never answered the question. Rowe pointed out that the victim's pants were also ripped inside the crotch area. "Do you know how they might have gotten ripped?"

"No," Mack said. "Like I said, she didn't have them all the way down."

Rowe asked if there had been any discussion about birth control before sex took place. "Naw," said Mack, who also said he did not use a condom. Rowe asked why the eighteen-year-old college freshman would risk getting pregnant. Again, Mack had no answer.

The scenario Mack described suggested a girl who barely knew him, yet was so eager to make love to him that she didn't bother taking her pants off or taking precautions to protect herself from possible pregnancy—all this because she wanted to go to bed with a celebrated athlete. Trying to characterize his victim as a groupie presented a problem—besides the fact that groupies remove their pants before sex. Groupies also brag about their conquests, the same way athletes do. But when asked if he or his accuser had told anyone about their encounter, Mack said they had not. "We didn't want nobody to know what we had did," Mack said.

Once again, Mack called attorney Barry Sheppard in Chicago, who referred him to a very good criminal defense attorney in Tempe. Three days after the alleged rape, news of the investigation appeared in the *Arizona State Press,* along with a report that Coach Frieder had telephoned the police department in an attempt to persuade investigators that the case was a basketball matter, not a police matter. Frieder immediately held a news conference to announce that he had suspended Mack from the basketball team indefinitely. "I'm not passing judgment at all," Frieder said. "But Arizona State University and myself cannot tolerate this kind of behavior or situation that would take my attention away from the team. We can't have you people [the media] out there worrying about Sam Mack's situation and having that [be] detrimental to the team."

Frieder's decision had an immediate public-relations impact, but little practical impact. Mack was already ineligible to play basketball in the upcoming season anyway, as NCAA rules require transfer students to sit out one year. And since Frieder did not strip Mack of his scholarship, the only thing that changed was the fact that Mack could no longer practice with the team until the rape case was resolved. As to whether the rape investigation caused Frieder to have second thoughts about granting a scholarship to a player who had just stood trial for armed robbery, Frieder adamantly defended his decision. "The bottom line is that he was acquitted and we gave him a chance," Frieder said. "I would do that in a minute again. This is the United States of America."

He closed the press conference by criticizing the police for rebuffing his request for information about the investigation. "They were not very cooperative with me," Frieder said. "They were not very nice. If there is a police matter which involves a basketball student-athlete, then it becomes a basketball matter as well." He said that contrary to a published report, he did not try to influence the outcome of the investigation in any way. "I'm going to challenge all of you to find out who in that police department made that statement," Frieder said. "And I challenge you to find out who it was so we can fire his ass."

Frieder managed to denigrate police officers, to trivialize the importance of a criminal investigation by implying that basketball is just as important, and to threaten to have a law-enforcement officer fired. It is any wonder that players develop a sense of superiority over police officers? Coaches, particularly at the college level, can be powerful influences on their players.

On November 16, the police completed their investigation and forwarded the case to the Maricopa County Attorney's Office for review, recommending that Mack be charged with kidnapping and two felony counts of sexual assault. But four days later the state declined to prosecute the case, citing "no reasonable likelihood of conviction." When contacted in connection with this book and asked to explain why the case was dropped, Maricopa County Attorney spokesman William FitzGerald provided a written statement: "The issue for us in this case was consent. With someone in the room who heard nothing, the question is did she object? Or did she give consent? The testimony that would have been admitted at trial would have covered the victim's association with other athletes and why nobody heard her protest."

After the case was dropped, Frieder permitted Mack to remain on scholarship. Four months later, Mack was arrested for using a stolen American Express card to purchase $1,400 in gold jewelry in Phoenix, Arizona. He was charged with theft and forgery. This time Frieder didn't hesitate. He kicked Mack off the team for good.

So much for due process. There were no hearings, no formal adjudication, no hearing of evidence. Frieder simply got rid of him.

Mack eventually entered a plea and received probation in the fraud case. But before the case was resolved, Mack transferred to Tyler Junior College in Texas. Tyler's head coach Roy Thomas called Orr for a recommendation. Orr told Thomas that Mack was a tremendous talent but needed a constant eye. In his one season at Tyler, Mack dominated, averaging over twenty-four points per game. He was the MVP of his conference. "He [Thomas] brought me in there and let me play my game without any distractions," Mack said.

Following Mack's year at Tyler, Thomas helped convince University of Houston coach Pat Foster to let Mack play his final season at Houston. The transfer was key to giving Mack a stage to showcase his talents to NBA scouts. Once again, Houston's head coach Pat Foster called Orr for a scouting report. Once again Orr praised Mack's skills but warned about his problems. Foster signed Mack. "Houston looked at it as, 'Everybody makes mistakes,'" Mack said. "I'm just doing the right thing now. I'm just trying to show my skills and trying to make it to the next level."

Mack delivered for Foster immediately. In his first game he

scored 23 points in 23 minutes against Villanova. Then he scored 32 points in 34 minutes against North Carolina, and 31 points in 34 minutes against North Texas.

Foster called Orr again to tell him that he couldn't get over the talent Mack displayed on the court.

Mack finished the season with Houston averaging nearly eighteen points a game. Less than two months later, the University of Houston Police Department arrested Mack and charged him with criminal mischief. According to the police report, Mack was transported to the Harris County jail after attempting to enter someone else's dorm room and breaking out a thirty-six-inch-square glass window. A week later the charge was dropped.

By the time Mack finished up at the University of Houston, in the spring of 1992, he had attended four different colleges in five years. Like a hotel guest, he checked in, played ball, and checked out when trouble arose. During five years of college basketball he had been investigated for a felony sexual assault, arrested four times, and charged with four felonies and three misdemeanors, shot by police officers, tried and acquitted for armed robbery, and convicted of theft and forgery. Despite all this, he reached the NBA unscathed. A few months after leaving college, on September 25, 1992, Mack signed a free-agent contract with the San Antonio Spurs.

NINE

CRIMINALS ON SCHOLARSHIP

Once Mack started earning his NBA salary, his Iowa defense attorney, Ray Rosenberg, requested that Mack pay his long-standing legal bills. Billing records from the Rosenberg Law Firm indicate that Mack racked up over $37,000 in fees and expenses associated with his defense in the robbery case. But he had paid only $6,000, leaving an unpaid balance in excess of $31,000. The payment did not come, however. So Rosenberg and his colleagues sued Mack in 1993 in an attempt to collect payment. But in 1994, within two years of making the NBA, Mack filed for bankruptcy. After Mack joined the Houston Rockets in 1996, Rosenberg worked out an arrangement with that team by which a small amount of money from Mack's paychecks was withheld. These withholdings were paid to Rosenberg's firm. But Rosenberg never came close to recovering the full amount of money owed. And Mack made no more payments after he left the Rockets in 1997. Later that year, Mack signed a $1-million contract with Vancouver. At that point Rosenberg abandoned his pursuit of payment and wrote it off as a loss. Just as he avoided paying any penalty for his role in the Iowa robbery, Mack avoided paying a penalty for failing to pay for the legal services that secured his acquittal.

Mack's refusal to pay attorneys who saved him from prison

and secured his passage to the NBA is stunning. It is also another symptom of the sense of invincibility and unaccountability that goes with the wealth and success that come to gifted athletes. "People learn from their experience," said Rosenberg. "But they don't always learn the right thing. When he [Mack] was acquitted, it may have created a sense of invulnerability."

Sam Mack's odyssey to the NBA is not unique. There are many players who enter college with substandard academic records, have run-ins with the law while in their adolescence, and emerge from college with a rap sheet instead of a diploma. And they go on to play in the NBA and make millions, because diplomas and a clean criminal history are not prerequisites to joining the league. Consider the following examples:

Kansas City native Anthony Peeler is one of the best basketball players ever to attend the University of Missouri. From 1988 to 1992 he dominated his opponents and earned the Big Eight Conference Player of the Year honor during his senior year. But criminal matters and academic problems plagued his college days. After his freshman season he reportedly entered a substance-abuse facility. He missed part of his junior season when he was declared academically ineligible. Like Mack, these problems did not deter him from returning to the basketball court.

But during his senior year, on May 30, 1992, right after the basketball season ended, police in Columbia, Missouri, were called to College Park Apartments, near the university campus, where two female students waited. One of them, twenty-year-old Angela Link, was crying and shaking. She had bite marks on her face, shoulder, and abdomen. Officer Steven Brown asked who had inflicted the wounds. "Peeler," she said. Brown asked her to be more specific. "Anthony Peeler, the basketball player," she said.

According to police records, Link was in bed wearing a night-shirt and underwear when Peeler telephoned her at two A.M. and

said he was on his way over. Peeler let himself in through an un-
locked door, appeared at Link's bed, and expressed anger that she
had been out without his knowledge. Link told police that Peeler
put his hands around her neck, held her down, and bit her about
the body. "Ms. Link did exhibit what appeared to be human bite
marks in these positions," Officer Brown noted. A forensics officer also photographed Link's injuries. There was more. Link told
police that Peeler held a gun to her head. She provided a physical
description of the weapon.

Link's screams during the attack awakened April Marks,
whose dorm room is directly across the hall from Link's. Marks
ran across the hall to help Link. Instead she ran into Peeler as he
exited the room. Marks told police he looked "wild." She also revealed that she had previously dated Peeler and that "he had
abused her and choked her around as well."

Officer Brown encouraged Link to press charges against
Peeler. But she said she feared intimidation and retaliation. According to her statement, she had been assaulted by Peeler previously. One incident that she reported involved Peeler choking her
inside her apartment until he "cut off her breath." In the interim,
Brown sought an arrest warrant for Peeler. Roughly six hours
later, at 9:10 A.M., police from the University of Missouri Police
Department, aware that Peeler was wanted on assault charges,
pulled him over as he drove a Nissan Maxima through campus.
The campus police cited him for driving with an expired license
and radioed Columbia Police for backup assistance. When
Columbia officer Chester Heyer arrived at the scene, Peeler was
on his cell phone, talking to his criminal defense attorney, Wally
Bley. Peeler was removed from the vehicle and read his Miranda
rights. A subsequent search of his vehicle turned up a .45-caliber
semiautomatic Glock handgun hidden beneath a floor mat. It
was black and metallic and matched the description provided by

Link. Beside it, police found a clip containing nine live rounds of ammunition. Peeler was charged with assault and carrying a concealed weapon.

With his senior season behind him and Peeler projected to be a first-round pick in the upcoming NBA draft, the timing could not have been worse. After his arrest, Peeler told the press that Link's allegations were made up. "That's the way people are," he said. "They just try to bring you down." Yet Peeler pleaded guilty on June 16 to a felony weapons charge and two misdemeanors related to the assault on Link. He received five years' probation. The next day he was honored by the Big Eight Conference as Male Athlete of the Year. (In 1998, a jury in federal court in St. Louis awarded Angela Link $300,000 in damages and $2.1 million in punitive damages after she sued Peeler and testified that he pinned her down and held a gun to her head.)

But two days before the NBA draft, Peeler was arrested again on assault charges. This time the complaint originated in Kansas City, where a nineteen-year-old woman claimed that Peeler punched her in the face. If convicted, Peeler would face jail time for violating probation on his felony weapons conviction.

Within forty-eight hours, however, the Kansas City Prosecutor's Office dropped the case without explaining why. Peeler's Kansas City–based lawyer, Wally Bley, told the press that Peeler's accuser had recanted her statement. The day after the charges were dropped against Peeler, the Los Angeles Lakers made him their number one draft choice.

The NBA is littered with stories like these. Roughly one-third of the NBA players with an arrest record already had been in trouble with the law before leaving college. Put another way, one out of every three players in the NBA with an arrest record had been charged with a criminal offense while on scholarship. The league and its teams like to argue that players from troubled backgrounds deserve a second chance and that basketball affords them that chance. One example of this is the experience of Gary Trent, who played this past season alongside Kevin Garnett for the Minnesota Timberwolves. It marked Trent's ninth season in the NBA.

Trent was an eighth grader when his father, thirty-one-year-old Dexter Trent, became the first person to receive a life sentence on a federal drug conviction in Columbus, Ohio. (He was released from prison after serving six years and seven months.) He had been convicted for possessing crack cocaine with intent to distribute.

By age thirteen, Gary was selling cocaine himself, making $300 a day. He witnessed a drive-by shooting that killed his friend. He saw relatives incarcerated and killed in crime-related incidents. "Jail was just part of my life," Trent said. "It's like my whole family was mobsters and gangsters."

How does a guy with these credentials obtain a scholarship? By the time Trent reached his senior year of high school, he stood six-foot-seven and averaged thirty-two points per game and sixteen rebounds. He set a U.S. high school record for field-goal accuracy. And he received a scholarship to attend Ohio University.

In college his strength and athleticism made him virtually impossible to stop and garnered comparisons to Charles Barkley, Karl Malone, and Shaquille O'Neal. Trent could bench-press 390 pounds and had a forty-five-inch vertical leap. He was voted the most valuable player in his conference.

All of this catapulted him from the ghetto of Columbus, Ohio, to multimillion-dollar earnings in the NBA. But after signing with the Portland Trail Blazers, he was arrested in January 1997 on domestic-violence charges. The victim, his pregnant girlfriend, told police that Trent struck her in the face and kicked her in the ribs. Trent's girlfriend did not want to cooperate with prosecutors, however, and Trent pleaded guilty to a misdemeanor, for which he was placed on probation and required to undergo therapy.

Three days after the sentence was imposed, Trent was accused of assaulting a man in a Portland bar. The man required stitches to his head and ear. Trent called his actions self-defense. A grand jury declined to indict him.

Then Trent was charged with choking and punching another man. This charge was dropped after Trent reached an out-of-court settlement with the victim. But this constituted a violation of his probation in the 1977 domestic-violence case and landed Trent in jail for five days.

Through it all, his pro sports career has gone uninterrupted.

All of this raises a couple of questions: Is it really in the best interest of athletes who have run-ins with the law to be afforded scholarships and shepherded through college solely so they can land a million-dollar salary in the NBA? And what happens to them after their basketball careers end?

The argument in favor of giving scholarships to troubled players is that basketball may be their ticket out of trouble. "Without basketball, I don't know how Sam would have ended up," said Mack's Iowa attorney Paul Scott. "But I have to believe that athletics helped him. Whether he would have become a neighborhood thug or drug dealer had he not gone through the athletic system, I don't know."

But a drug dealer and a neighborhood thug is precisely what Sam Mack ended up being called by the state of Illinois at the close of his NBA career.

After being released by the Golden State Warriors in 2000, Mack moved back home with his mother, into the same house he lived in as a high school senior when Johnny Orr visited him on a recruiting trip.

On the evening of July 11, 2000, Mack ran a stop sign six blocks from his house. Police sergeant Derek Guess and his duty partner Vernon Mitchell observed the violation and attempted to pull Mack over. Instead, Mack fled, speeding over 70 miles per hour. The police gave chase. Mack stopped when he reached his mother's driveway. As police approached and got Mack out of the vehicle, they recognized him immediately. These same officers previously had multiple run-ins with Mack over a period of months leading up to the chase. Each of the prior incidents had taken place while police were conducting drug investigations. While Mack was not the subject of the investigations, he had surfaced repeatedly at scenes where officers were questioning suspected drug dealers or users. Each time Mack had verbal confrontations with officers, though he was never charged in any of those incidents.

This time he was, however. Guess and Mitchell observed a rock of cocaine on the floor of Mack's vehicle. With probable cause to search the vehicle, they probed further. Inside they found nineteen bags of marijuana, a digital scale, and nearly $3,000 in cash. Mack was charged with felony drug possession. "When everything comes out, I wonder what people will say then," Mack told a television station after his arrest. "I know they smeared my name real bad. But you know I'm not ashamed because I didn't do anything and I'm innocent."

Again Mack turned to Chicago lawyer Barry Sheppard, who helped Mack enter into a plea agreement that resulted in a Cook County judge ordering him to attend a drug-treatment program and complete certain terms of probation.

Then on April 21, 2001, he was charged with criminal mischief in Houston, Texas. In August 2001 he entered a plea and received probation and paid a $300 fine. One month later he made a final attempt to reenter the NBA. Pat Riley and the Miami Heat signed him on September 14, 2001. Neither his convictions in Illinois or Texas, nor his probationary status, nor the NBA's highly touted drug policy, which prohibits the use of marijuana, never mind possession of cocaine, stopped him. But his return proved short-lived. He played just twelve games and averaged three points before Miami released him in December 2001. Mack was thirty-one years old.

Seven months later, he filed for bankruptcy for the second time. Out of the NBA and out of money, Mack continued to live with his mother. Then he was accused of the most serious crime of his life. A grand jury in Cook County, Illinois, indicted him for attempted first-degree murder in August 2003. According to court documents, on July 29, 2003, Mack "intentionally and without legal justification caused great bodily harm" to another man. The victim sustained a broken jaw, a broken orbital to both eyes, and a broken nose.

"It really is a tragedy," said Paul Scott, who defended him in the armed robbery case. "It happens because of the world they [athletes] are in and the amount of money they have. They are always being taken care of. I don't know whether life skills would help these guys. That is the problem with athletics. Players go from nothing to everything."

The coddling of these players begins in college, where universities continued to give players like Mack scholarships after repeated run-ins with the law. And the NCAA simply looks the other way. Mack's on-court performance entertained the student body and the booster club members at those universities. He helped his coaches earn fat salaries. And he made revenue for those schools by helping them win basketball games. In exchange for that, he got not a second chance on life but a repeated free pass for poor academic performance and habitual encounters with law enforcement. As long as Mack scored on the court, nobody cared if he was hauled off in handcuffs for things that endangered the safety of others, even tuition-paying students. But when his playing days ended, his problems became the burden of society at large. No college and no NBA teams were standing by to clean up—or cover up—his mess. Instead, it was left to police officers, prosecutors, and judges.

The NBA surely bears some responsibility for aiding and abetting this problem. But the NCAA and its member institutions are where it begins.

So is basketball a good thing for players like Sam Mack?

"On balance I'd say yes, basketball was a good thing for Sam," said Ray Rosenberg. "On the other hand, if he didn't have basketball and hadn't got a scholarship and hadn't gone up to school at Ames he would have ended up the same way and maybe sooner."

On November 20, 2003, Sam Mack entered the Cook County Courthouse, the same courthouse that handled his very first arrest for unlawful use of a weapon after his freshman year at Iowa State. Passing through metal detectors, Mack stood out amidst a mass of humanity filing in for arraignments and bond hearings. Standing six-foot-seven and dressed in stylish clothes, he still looked the part of an NBA player.

But he wasn't. Nobody asked for his autograph. Only his mother stood by his side. Together they ducked into a small courtroom and Mack read the sports page of a local newspaper while waiting for his attorney, Barry Sheppard, to arrive. Mack and Sheppard's reunion in the same courtroom that they had appeared in fifteen years earlier to respond to charges that Mack had unlawfully possessed a firearm seemed to bring his career, and his interaction with law enforcement, full circle.

"If Sam Mack were an impoverished kid from the ghetto and had no basketball ability," said Sheppard, who has been a Chicago Bulls season ticket holder for twenty-five years, "his life would have been a lot worse. He is somebody that would have gotten ground up in the criminal justice system. If he didn't know me or Ray Rosenberg and the other top defense attorneys I've referred him to, he could have been an unfortunate statistic."

Postscript: I attended Sam Mack's pretrial hearing in connection with the attempted murder charge. When I introduced myself to Mack and his mother outside the courtroom, he was every bit as pleasant, polite, and affable as his lawyers and coaches describe him. We discussed this book, and when I told him my desire to formally interview him for it, he gave me his phone number and indicated a willingness to be interviewed. But he never responded to more than a dozen phone calls placed to his home, a certified letter sent to his home, or a written request sent through his attorney. At the time this book went to press, Mack was playing in the Continental Basketball Association (CBA) and awaiting trial for attempted murder. Levin White was released from a state penitentiary in Iowa on July 7, 1995, after serving six years for armed robbery. His whereabouts today are unknown. Mack's former coach at Iowa State, Johnny Orr, has retired. Though he still maintains a residence in Iowa, he spends half the year living in Florida, where he golfs and enjoys retirement with his wife.

PART III

BAD HEROES

TEN

INDULGE ME

In a culture that heaps wildly disproportionate rewards on the athletically gifted, fame can become confused with such true hallmarks of heroism as courage, loyalty, and self-restraint. NBA players are ordained heroes merely on the basis of physical and athletic prowess. The bigger the player's star quality, the more likely his image will appear on posters hanging from children's bedrooms or grace the front of a cereal box. Far more than NFL players, NBA players are selected as spokesman and pitchmen for every kind of consumer product advertised on television, from fast food to computer equipment.

Why do companies and advertisers prefer NBA players over NFL players? NBA players are far more recognizable to consumers. NFL players perform behind pads and helmets that obscure their identity. NBA players wear nothing but tank tops and shorts. NFL teams play just sixteen games a year in large outdoor stadiums, where fans and television cameras are far removed from them. NBA players play between eighty-two and ninety games a year in more intimate arenas, where fans and television cameras are right on top of them.

Basketball players' hyperexposure before the general public through television makes them very attractive as pitchmen for companies that advertise on television. This hyperexposure also creates a false sense of familiarity with them on the part of fans. Seeing so much of NBA players through television, we think we know them. This greatly inhibits our ability to picture them as rapists or wife beaters when our only point of reference is seeing them hit a game-winning shot or hefting a cheeseburger on television on behalf of a fast-food restaurant.

In reality, we don't know these players at all. A closer look at the men behind the images of some of the NBA's most successful stars reveals a very ugly picture of infidelity, domestic strife, illegitimate children, and violence. It is bitter irony that the men held up to market family-friendly products—from hamburgers to breakfast cereals—are often presiding over families that are a mess of neglect, abuse, and violence.

The public has a hard time understanding why players who seem to have everything choose to commit crimes that put their careers in jeopardy. Whether Kobe Bryant committed rape (as charged) or adultery (as he claims), one thing is clear: he took an enormous risk the night he invited his accuser into his hotel room. Conventional wisdom begs the question: Why do so many players jeopardize public reputation, endorsement contracts, and criminal prosecution?

The reason, more often than not, is much like the reason an informed adult continues to smoke cigarettes despite overwhelming evidence that it causes cancer: habit. Sexual gratification becomes so routine to some ballplayers that the quest to obtain it is as normal as lighting up is to a smoker. Some players like to point out that there is nothing illegal about being entertained by exotic dancers or having sex with willing partners, no matter how often. But when a player's exposure to women becomes limited almost exclusively to those whose role is a sexual one, it is not difficult to see how some players begin to view all women in the same context: as means to his sexual gratification. So while it may be legal in most cases for a player to take advantage of the wealth of opportunities for sex with various partners, it doesn't take a road map to see where such indulgence will lead.

The constant satisfaction of one's urges does not instill discipline and self-control. Rather, a man—be he a star athlete or otherwise—who is always told yes may find himself in uncharted territory when he's told no. The players who see life in the NBA as a license for indiscriminate sexual encounters are the same players who end up scratching their heads, trying to figure out why they so often get accused of committing sex crimes or mistreating women.

Miami Heat forward Anthony Mason had barely finished playing a summer league game in the Jersey Shore Basketball League on the evening of July 9, 2001, when he started looking for a girl to have sex with. He used his cell phone to call twenty-nine-year-old Olivia Tamika in Brooklyn, New York. Mason barely knew Tamika, a flight attendant for USAir and a bartender. They had met one month earlier at a Manhattan nightclub, where they exchanged phone numbers. They had not seen each other since.

When Tamika answered her phone, Mason offered to have a limousine pick her up within an hour and transport her to New Jersey to party and hang out with him for the evening. It was nearly eleven P.M. She asked if she could bring along her roommate, a male friend. Mason said no. Tamika hesitated then opted to go. She hung up and put on a pink, strapless halter top over a red strapless, seamless bra, blue jeans, and a pair of black high-heel sandals. Scheduled to bartend the next day, she threw some work clothes—black cargo pants and a black T-shirt—into an overnight bag, along with a pair of shorts, a T-shirt, a change of underwear, lotion, body wash, deodorant, and a toothbrush.

Within an hour, Mason's driver, Shadi Khader, arrived outside Tamika's apartment in a Lincoln Navigator. She got inside and asked Shadi where he was taking her. He said he wasn't sure. His instructions were simply to deliver her to exit 105 off the Garden State Parkway in Jersey.

At one-thirty in the morning, Shadi pulled into the parking lot of the Holiday Inn in Tinton Falls. Mason soon arrived in a separate limousine. He got out, embraced Tamika, and then she accompanied him inside the hotel, where Mason had reserved a room for himself and three other rooms for his teammates. Shadi returned to New York City. Three hours later he got an unexpected return call from Mason, telling him to come back and get the girl and take her home to Brooklyn.

Shadi did as directed. Later that morning, Tamika telephoned the 88th Police Precinct in Brooklyn and reported she had been raped by Mason and two of his teammates. She told the police that she thought they were going to Atlantic City for the evening and that as soon as she stepped inside room number 221 at the Holiday Inn, Mason began pinching her nipples and then fondling her breasts and vaginal area. "I was like pushing him away, I'm like, no," she told police. "And he's like why did you come out here if you didn't want to be bothered?"

Tamika told police that when she asked if they could just talk, Mason said: "Why the f— would I ask you to come out here if I just wanted to talk to you?" She reported that he then pulled at her jeans and panties until he removed them, then opened her thighs. "Then he put his face in between my thighs," she told police, adding that he then tried to have intercourse with her. Tamika told police that she warned Mason that she was not on birth control and asked him to use a condom and he refused.

At that point two men knocked on the hotel room door, yelling, "Mase, Mase, open the door." Both said they could hear commotion coming from the room. Both men entered the room. Tamika did not know their names and did not get a good look at their faces. But she said that both men tried to have intercourse with her from behind. "They all grabbed me and laid me down, facedown into the mattress," she reported. "Someone was holding my neck and someone came up behind me and tried to insert their penis inside my rectum. I was squirming. . . . They were screaming obscenities at me."

After talking to the victim, the police transported her to Brooklyn Hospital, where she spent five hours undergoing a rape-kit exam and doing more interviews with medical personnel and criminal investigators. Meanwhile, the NYPD notified the police in Tinton Falls, New Jersey, who immediately dispatched officers to the Holiday Inn, where they obtained registration forms confirming that Anthony Mason had rented room number 221. The room had still not been cleaned. Inside, the police recovered a condom wrapper and a box of eaten fried chicken. The condom wrapper was sent to a fingerprint lab for analysis. They also took photographs and collected the bedsheets and pillowcases for evidence.

The rape-kit results from Brooklyn Hospital were turned over to the Tinton Falls Police. And on July 12 Tamika returned to New Jersey, where she gave a detailed statement to a detective from the Monmouth County Prosecutor's Office and a sergeant from the Tinton Falls Police Department.

Mason's criminal defense attorney, Franklin Rothman, was not surprised when he received word that Mason was under investigation. "I've dealt with athletes and hip-hop guys," Rothman said. "It's the same stuff all the time. Limelight people and groupie-type women. The women do things and then they're asked to leave the room. The player says: 'See you later. Nice knowing you.' The girl feels taken advantage of. Next thing you know, there's a rape complaint."

The Tinton Falls case wasn't the first time Rothman had to defend Mason against rape charges. Mason and his cousin William Duggins were charged by police in Queens, New York, with statutory rape, sexual abuse, and endangering the welfare of a child on February 8, 1998. Two girls, ages fourteen and fifteen, told police they were picked up in Mason's limousine and taken to Duggins's Queens apartment, where they had sex with Mason and Duggins during the NBA All-Star Game break. Police recovered semen from one of the girls' clothing. Rothman said that DNA analysis of the sperm excluded Mason as the donor. Prosecutors dropped the felony statutory rape charge and Mason pleaded guilty to two counts of endangering a child. He performed 200 hours of community service. Duggins pleaded guilty to one count of statutory rape and to endangering the welfare of a child, and was sentenced to five years' probation and 800 hours of community service.

One year later, on January 8, 1999, Mason was at his home in Charlotte, North Carolina, when he telephoned a twenty-year-old woman in Chicago. She had met him once before. When Mason offered to fly her down to Charlotte, she went. But the same day she flew back home, where she contacted the Chicago police and reported she had been raped. Chicago authorities referred the case to police in Charlotte, just like the scenario in Tinton Falls. Mason's accuser told Charlotte investigators that shortly after arriving at Mason's North Carolina home she had consensual sex with him. But she said the following morning he engaged in another act of sexual intercourse by force. She also alleged that Mason refused to wear a condom, and that he invited a second unidentified man to perform sex acts on her, too.

After a three-month investigation, Charlotte-Mecklenburg prosecutors dismissed the case. "There was insufficient evidence to show that any sexual act engaged in between Mr. Mason and this young woman was by force and against her will," prosecutor David Wallace said.

The Tinton Falls complaint marked the third criminal rape complaint filed against Mason in three years. In each instance Mason made contact with a woman, arranged for her transportation, and a woman willfully accompanied him to a room with a bed in it. And each time that woman complained that he became abusive.

"I've known Anthony for five years," Rothman said. "He is abrasive. Yet women make themselves available to him. He's flashy with money and jewelry. Women see a big jackpot at the end of it. But there's that night, and that's the end of the line."

Rothman accompanied Mason to the Monmouth County Prosecutor's Office in Freehold, New Jersey, on August 10, 2001. There Mason was confronted with a recording device operated by Detective Natalie Jones from the prosecutor's office and Detective Michael Jelinski of the Tinton Falls Police Department. "Please tell us in your own words what knowledge you have of this incident," Jones said.

Mason gave them an earful. He corroborated that he called Tamika, rejected her request to bring a male friend along, and sent a limo driver to bring her to the Holiday Inn. From that point on, his version differed greatly from hers. He said that shortly after she arrived at his room he ordered fried chicken. While waiting for the delivery, they had consensual sex, which was interrupted only by the deliveryman showing up at the door with the food. "After we finished eating, I started trying to kiss her again," Mason said. "She was like, no. She didn't want to continue. And I said I'm not going to be like the Tyson case and I just stopped. I asked what the f— did she come down here for."

"When you said you had sex, do you mean that you vaginally penetrated her with your penis?" the detective asked.

"Yes."

"Did the two of you engage in any other sexual activity?"

"Oral sex, I did to her."

"How long were you having sex before the food arrived?"

"About ten or fifteen minutes."

"Did she ever scream or fight you in any way while the two of you were having sex?"

"No."

"Did you force her in any way to have sexual intercourse with you?"

"No."

"While you and her were having sex, did you use a condom?"

"No."

"Did you ejaculate?"

"Nope."

"Did you have a condom with you . . . and just didn't use it?"

"I think I had one or two in my bag."

After the interview, Rothman figured Mason would not be indicted. "He was abrasive and hostile and all that stuff," Rothman said. "He was Anthony. But it was clear that whatever he had was consensual."

But investigators were not convinced. Prosecutor Robert Honecker acknowledged that there were some problems with the accuser's version of events and some inconsistencies in her account of what transpired at the hotel. Despite these problems, Honecker and his office remained fully prepared to press the case against Mason. "In a lot of cases there are inconsistencies and problems," Honecker said. "We were willing to move forward even though those problems existed."

However, soon after Mason came in for questioning, Tamika

left New York and moved back to Chicago. Despite cooperating fully at the outset of the investigation, once she returned to Chicago, Tamika failed to return prosecutors' calls. When it became clear that Tamika would no longer assist investigators, prosecutors dropped the case. "We were convinced in the end that she did not want to cooperate."

When asked in an interview for this book if they thought the allegations against Anthony Mason were false, prosecutors in New Jersey pointed out that the alleged victim in that case went to the police precinct in New York and made a formal complaint, submitted to a rape-kit exam at a hospital, and followed through with a formal complaint to the Monmouth County investigators in New Jersey. Furthermore, law-enforcement agents conducted a comprehensive criminal investigation that lasted months and used up lots of resources and man-hours. Taken together, all of these points support a belief on the part of law enforcement that the charge was not fabricated. "The primary reason why a charge was not brought is that the victim in this case became less and less cooperative over time," Monmouth prosecutor Robert Honecker said. "Ultimately she refused to be found. That resulted in the case being closed."

While maintaining that Mason did nothing to merit criminal charges, Rothman did concede that Mason's quest to meet women for sex provided fertile ground for complaints to be filed against him. "These guys can afford anything," Rothman said, referring to NBA players and professional athletes in general. "If they're just looking for sex, and a lot of them are, they should just call an escort service."

Why don't Mason and players with a similar mind-set do that? "There's no chase involved in that," Rothman explained. "He likes the chase that every guy likes. This is what he has always done. He doesn't think about it as another disaster. Instead it's, 'I don't have to pay to get laid.'"

ELEVEN

SLEEPING WITH THE ENEMY

Like sex crimes, domestic violence is one of the crimes that challenge the public perception of athletes as paragons of heroism and strength. There is nothing manly about beating a woman, especially when she is a foot or two shorter and over one hundred pounds lighter. Yet there is a connection between players who sexually exploit women and those who abuse spouses or girlfriends. One of the most common triggers in domestic-violence incidents involving NBA players is disputes over fidelity. While players want the freedom to be sexually active outside marriage, they often demand rigid fidelity from wives and girlfriends. When players suspect disloyalty, the consequences can be lethal, another symptom of the inferior role women often play in the lives of celebrated athletes.

"I'm going to come over there and whoop your ass. Don't you worry. I'll be out there."

According to court documents, that's the last thing Milwaukee Bucks All-Star forward Glenn Robinson told his ex-fiancée, Jonta French, before he hung up with her around seven P.M. on July 19, 2002. He suspected she had been with another man.

French, who has a three-year-old daughter with Robinson, lived in one of Robinson's homes, a large colonial in an upscale residential section of Chicago Heights, Illinois.

In police reports and court filings, French provided a chilling account. Around 3:45 A.M., Robinson showed up at the front door. French and the toddler were asleep inside. There was no other man around. After using his cell phone to call and wake her up, Robinson, who was intoxicated, accused French of being with another man, then began beating on the door, demanding to be let inside. When French refused, he tried to enter through a back sliding glass door. But it was locked.

Next Robinson pleaded with French to let him, saying he could not drive because he had been drinking. He threatened that if she forced him to sleep outside he would be mad as hell in the morning. Still, French refused. But Robinson persisted, promising he would stay on the couch downstairs if she would let him in. Reluctant, she finally opened the door.

"You know you have f—ed up now, don't you?" said Robinson, grabbing her by the hair. Fearful, French, who is five-foot-six and weighs 140 pounds, began to cry. According to court documents and police records, Robinson, who is six-seven and weighs 240 pounds, dragged her through the home, slamming her head against a wall and banging her body into a counter and other objects before forcing her upstairs, where he pinned her to a bed. After striking her repeatedly, Robinson grabbed her face and banged the side of her head against the bedpost, then ripped her pajama top. "You are going to do what the f— I say."

"F— this," Robinson screamed. "F— this. Where's my gun? F— this. I am ready to die. You are going with me. You, me, both of us, we are going."

Robinson left the room and headed to the master bedroom to find his gun. One week earlier he had brought a Glock semiautomatic 9-millimeter handgun to the residence and left it on the master bedroom dresser. French later hid it out of reach of their three-year-old. Terrified that Robinson would find it, French didn't dare flee the house and leave the toddler alone with Robinson. Minutes later he stormed back into the bedroom with his shirt removed and a plastic planter in his hand. "I should knock you out with this so you don't know what the f— is happening," he said.

"Please don't take away my baby," French pleaded.

Robinson grabbed French and threw her down on the bed. He demanded to know where she had put the gun. "In the bedroom," she said, referring to the master bedroom. He ordered her not to leave the room while he searched for the gun. Fearing she might not get out alive if she hesitated, French waited only until he was out of sight before bolting down the stairs and out the front door. She reached the street before Robinson caught her from behind. She pleaded for her life. "Get your ass back in the house," Robinson said.

French, a kickboxing instructor who teaches fitness courses, broke free and ran, screaming for help, toward her neighbor's house. Robinson retreated into his house. When French's neighbor did not answer, she ran to the next house in the cul-de-sac. Forty-one-year-old Sandra Finley, the president of the nonprofit League of Black Women, heard French coming and opened her door. Once inside, French called the police.

Officers arrived just in time. The three-year-old was recovered safely from the home. In the master bedroom police found Robinson's gun. It was loaded with twelve rounds of ammunition. Robinson was arrested and charged with domestic battery, assault, and unlawful possession of a firearm.

Domestic violence. A gun. One of the NBA's most high-profile players in handcuffs. Normally this combination would guarantee national headlines and a full-court press by the NBA's public-relations damage-control team. But the press wrote little of Robinson's arrest and the NBA said even less. Both the media and the NBA were consumed with an even bigger NBA star facing gun charges stemming from domestic strife.

Three days before Robinson's arrest in Chicago Heights, police in Philadelphia arrested the NBA's Most Valuable Player, Allen Iverson, after receiving a 911 call from twenty-one-year-old Charles Jones, who told authorities that Iverson had thrown his twenty-six-year-old wife, Tawanna, out of their $2.4-million home in the Gladwyne section of Philadelphia naked, causing her to flee the residence and go into hiding. (In a published press report, Tawanna later denied that she had been naked.) Jones also reported that later the same evening, Iverson burst into his Philadelphia apartment, displayed a gun tucked inside the waist of his pants, and threatened to harm Jones if he didn't lead Iverson to his wife.

After an almost two-week joint investigation by police and prosecutors, Iverson was charged with a fourteen-count indictment that included four felonies, including false imprisonment, criminal trespass, conspiracy, making terroristic threats, and various gun offenses. The gravity of the charges against Iverson, combined with the fact that he was the league's top scorer and MVP, generated a wave of controversy and press coverage. Fans and throngs of reporters converged on the courthouse when Iverson was arraigned.

The spectacle completely overshadowed the equally serious charges filed against Robinson. All the focus was on Iverson. Yet the criminal case against Iverson quickly disintegrated following a pretrial hearing in which the prosecution's two primary witnessed testified. Seventeen-year-old Hakim Casey, who was present in Jones's apartment the night Iverson entered, said that he did not see Iverson brandish a gun. Nor did the police ever recover one in connection with the case. Casey also testified that Jones told him to back up Jones's story about Iverson having a gun.

When Jones took the stand, he denied telling Casey what to say to the police. But his credibility was dismantled by Iverson's lawyer, who demonstrated that Jones waited until the following day to place his 911 call. And phone records indicated that the 911 call was placed only moments after Jones had called a civil-liability lawyer. After hearing the evidence, the judge dismissed twelve of the fourteen charges against Iverson.

Prosecutors subsequently dropped the two remaining charges—misdemeanor counts for making terroristic threats—when District Attorney Lynne Abraham announced that Casey and Jones no longer wanted to pursue the case. Abraham said she could have compelled the two men to testify, but both men had left the state. "I don't think the taxpayers want to spend that kind of money on this kind of case," Abraham said.

With the media and the public's attention diverted by the Iverson case, the league faced almost no questions about Robinson's domestic-violence and gun case, which the league surely didn't mind. If there's one conversation the NBA doesn't want to have, it is one involving domestic violence or guns.

DOMESTIC VIOLENCE

Research conducted for this book turned up thirty-three criminal complaints of domestic violence against NBA players who played during the 2001–02 season. This is probably the tip of the iceberg. Nationally, domestic violence competes with child abuse and rape as the most underreported crime in our society. Fear, embarrassment, and the fact that the victim typically lives with

the perpetrator all contribute to low reporting rates. Those factors are magnified for victims whose abuser is an NBA player—or
any professional athlete or high-profile person, for that matter. A
review of court and police records, as well as interviews with domestic-violence investigators and victims, indicates that much
domestic violence on the part of NBA players goes unreported.
The reasons why women are reluctant to report players vary.

Buried deep in the Glenn Robinson police file is a document
in which investigators ask Jonta French whether she had ever
been abused previously. She indicated that she had. Similarly, the
Ruben Patterson domestic-violence arrest in Portland led to information indicating that it had not been the first time, either. It
rarely is.

Yet Mrs. Patterson, after finally calling 911 and making a
criminal complaint, essentially recanted her complaint, prompting prosecutors to drop the case. It was as if the broken glass,
blood on her hand, and the shouting hadn't happened. This is
not unusual behavior on the part of women abused by famous
athletes, basketball players or otherwise. Probably the most convincing illustration of this involves the domestic-violence case
brought against NFL superstar Warren Moon.

On July 18, 1995, police in Missouri City, Texas, responded to
the Moon residence after their eight-year-old son called 911, crying, and reported: "My daddy gonna hit my mommy. Please
hurry." When police arrived they found Felicia Moon with blood
on her face and scratch marks and abrasions on her neck. "He
[Warren] beat the shit out of me," Felicia told police. She also
told police that Warren had slapped her about the head and
choked her to the point that she couldn't talk or breathe.

Investigators discovered that Felicia had previously obtained
a restraining order against Warren for allegedly threatening her.
And court records indicated that Warren had physically attacked

his wife on at least three prior occasions during their marriage. But each of those complaints was dismissed, citing "lack of prosecution." Warren insisted the allegations were not true.

But this time prosecutors did indict him on domestic-violence charges and made clear they intended to bring him to trial. Felicia, a past board member of the Fort Bend County Women's Center, which runs a shelter for battered women in Texas, generated national headlines when she tried to convince prosecutors to drop the case against her husband. Prosecutors refused. So Felicia refused to testify at trial. Relying on a Texas law that enabled prosecutors to compel victims of domestic violence to testify, the state threatened to cite Felicia with contempt and jail her. Ultimately, she took the witness stand and took the blame for the incident, denying that she knew how she received the bruises and injuries graphically displayed in police photographs. "They might have been self-inflicted," she told the jury. On February 22, 1996, the jury acquitted Warren Moon.

Why are women who are beaten by prominent athletes so reluctant to press charges against them? For many of the same reasons that any other domestic-violence victim does not want to cooperate with law enforcement—principally fear. Fear of retaliation. Fear of being unable to support young children if their dad is incarcerated. Fear of friends and family finding out.

But there is one additional fear that is unique to victims of domestic violence at the hands of athletes and other high-profile men: fear of publicity. Victims know that if they come forward there will be an immense amount of media coverage.

Normally, the press pays little attention to all-too-common instances of domestic violence, even those most extreme examples of abuse that leave women maimed. But anytime an athlete is reported in a domestic-violence case, no matter the degree of seriousness, headlines are a virtual guarantee. Accused athletes cry foul, complaining their cases receive undue scrutiny merely on account of their fame. They are right. But in the long run this works to an abusive athlete's advantage. The guarantee of publicity prevents women from reporting cases. And it causes those who do report to try to convince police and prosecutors not to file formal charges. Take the domestic-violence case brought against NBA star Jason Richardson by his ex-girlfriend.

After leaving Michigan State following his sophomore season, the twenty-year-old Richardson became the fifth pick overall in the 2001 NBA draft when he was selected by the Golden State Warriors. He won the league's slam-dunk competition at the All-Star Game and was named to the league's rookie All-Star Team.

According to police records, on April 29, 2003, Richardson returned to his hometown of Saginaw, Michigan. That evening he visited the apartment of his former girlfriend, Roshonda Jacqmain, who is the mother of Richardson's three-year-old daughter. Jacqmain left Richardson alone to spend time with his daughter. When she returned to her apartment a couple hours later, Richardson had rifled through her belongings and found pictures of Jacqmain with her new boyfriend. "What is this?" he demanded, throwing the pictures at her.

Jacqmain asked Richardson to leave. "F— you!" he said. "You stupid bitch. I am not going anywhere."

Jacqmain said that her new boyfriend would never speak to her that way. Richardson then charged at her and pushed Jacqmain back into their daughter's bedroom. The force of the blow knocked Jacqmain down and her head went through the wall. Richardson stepped over Jacqmain and lifted their daughter out of bed. On his way out of the room with the child, he kicked Jacqmain while she was still on the ground. "Move the f— out of the way."

After Richardson left the apartment with his daughter, Jacqmain got up, removed pieces of drywall from her hair, and waited two hours before calling 911. When police arrived, they observed the head-size hole in the child's bedroom and photographed it for evidence. Jacqmain stressed she did not want to file charges against Richardson. She practically begged the police not to arrest him. She only wanted the incident documented. Why? According to the police report she knew the arrest would be a magnet for publicity and that she would be hounded by reporters.

The police located Richardson at his mother's home, where they questioned him. His explanation of events differed. He said that Jacqmain had "stumbled and fell back, hitting her head on the wall." With regard to Jacqmain's accusation that he had kicked her in the side as she lay on the floor, Richardson said he "brushed by Jacqmain with his foot, but didn't kick her."

Police arrested Richardson and transported him to jail. As soon as the arrest became public, Jacqmain's fears became reality. Reporters camped outside her residence and dogged her for interviews. The case received front-page treatment in Saginaw. Strangely, this complaint would have received much less publicity but for Richardson's decision to insist on a jury trial. Having handled scores of domestic-violence cases that received no press, Saginaw County prosecutor Michael Thomas recognized the excessive media scrutiny this case would generate. He also knew that Richardson had no prior criminal record involving domestic violence. So Thomas offered Richardson deferred adjudication if he agreed to plead guilty. In essence, in exchange for pleading guilty, the state would recommend he be placed on probation for one year. If after the year there were no violations of the probation, his record would be wiped clean. If he accepted this offer, the case would have quickly faded from the headlines.

But Richardson rejected the offer. His lawyers told prosecutors that the NBA had an unwritten policy that in cases of domestic violence, if substantiated, players are required to miss games and forfeit salary. Prosecutors asked to see this in writing. Richardson's lawyers never provided it.

At the end of August 2003, the case went to trial. Richardson testified in his own defense. He admitted grabbing and pushing Jacqmain, but insisted it was an act of self-defense. Richardson is six-six and weighs 220 pounds; his ex-girlfriend is five feet three inches tall. On August 28, 2003, the jury found Richardson guilty of domestic violence. The judge sentenced him to one year's probation and ordered him to perform forty hours of community service and complete batterer-intervention treatment.

The fact that Richardson went to trial is extremely unusual; only three out of thirty-three domestic-violence cases reviewed for this book went to trial. But the fact that Richardson was convicted is not so unusual. Sixteen—essentially half—of the players reported to police for domestic violence were either convicted or took advantage of deferred adjudication and were placed on probation. Unlike the situation with sex crimes, domestic violence is one crime for which NBA players actually get convicted with some degree of regularity. The difference is largely attributable to the fact that domestic violence produces bruises, broken bones, bleeding, and damaged property, all of which makes compelling evidence in front of a jury, not to mention terrible public relations. Moreover, with domestic violence it is tough for players to argue that the victims—spouses and girlfriends—are groupies who asked for it, as is the standard tactic in sex crimes cases. Hence, players are far more likely to plea-bargain in order to quickly extinguish the case.

GUNS

Roughly twenty criminal complaints alleging illegal use or possession of guns by NBA players were examined for this book. By itself, this number does not indicate an acute problem with respect to gun crimes. But this number is by no means a good gauge of how many players are armed. It is merely a snapshot of those who have been caught by law enforcement doing something illegal with a gun.

Mounting anecdotal evidence suggests that gun ownership is considerable among NBA players, and rising. Both the *Chicago Tribune* and the *New York Times* have reached this conclusion in separate investigations published in 2003. But it is near impossible to determine through records checks the number of NBA players who own handguns. Some players who carry guns don't register them, a fact borne out in the number of arrests related to players carrying unregistered guns. Glenn Robinson, for example, had not registered his gun in Illinois.

Records verifying how many players have lawfully registered a gun are hard to get at. States and cities have varying gun-registration requirements, and often the records of these registrations are not available to the public. The result is that there is little reliable information on how many NBA players are armed, illegally or otherwise.

One clue to how commonplace gun ownership has become among NBA players is evident in the arrest of the Golden State Warriors' Byron Houston. He was stopped in the Oakland International Airport when he tried to carry an unlicensed and loaded .25-caliber semiautomatic pistol through a metal detector. He was carrying the gun in a small brown cloth purse. He told the police that he forgot he had the gun on him. *Forgot that he was carrying a loaded gun in an airport?* To reach a point where carrying a loaded weapon is so easily forgettable, the practice of having a loaded gun with you has to be pretty commonplace.

NBA players have increasingly been outspoken about needing guns for protection. After Chicago police arrested Bulls star Scottie Pippen for illegally possessing a handgun in his car, he said: "Because of what's happening in the world of sports today . . . you have to protect yourself."

Another Bulls player, Jalen Rose, strongly advocates that NBA players arm themselves. In September 2002, a carjacker tried to stop Rose's car in Los Angeles by pulling a gun. When Rose sped off, the man fired eight shots at the car. One shot hit Rose's passenger.

Another player who has been the victim of gun violence is Anfernee "Penny" Hardaway. Before entering the NBA, Hardaway was shot when four men attempted to rob him and a friend.

Yet it is hard to find a single example of an NBA player preventing or escaping danger by possessing, much less using, a gun. One thing that is clear, however, is that in the few documented cases where players have been charged with illegally using a gun in the commission of a crime—as opposed to merely illegally carrying or concealing one—all of the victims were women. Hardaway is a player who claims to own a gun for the purpose of protection, yet he has been charged with using a gun in a domestic-violence incident.

On November 18, 2000, Latarsha McCray, the mother of Hardaway's eight-year-old daughter, flew from Memphis to visit Hardaway at his home in Paradise Valley, a suburb of Phoenix, Arizona. According to a statement she later gave to police, the following events transpired after she arrived at Hardaway's home. An argument ensued between them over sex. (Hardaway wanted to have it; she didn't.) Hardaway told her to get her things and proceeded to drive her back to the airport. But after talking, they turned around and returned to the residence. At this point it was well after midnight. To avoid further conflict, McCray decided to sleep in Hardaway's SUV. She told police that Hardaway went into the house and returned ten minutes later with a gun. "Get the f— out of the truck," she reported him saying.

Scared, McCray complied. Following McCray through the house, Hardaway, according to the report, said: "I'm sick of you. You just don't know how good you have it. You are so f—ing stupid." As they walked, McCray could hear Hardaway clicking the gun. She didn't dare turn around to see what he was doing to make the gun click. The couple then went to sleep without further incident. A day later she was scheduled to return to Memphis. While at the airport she telephoned her father and informed him about the incident with Hardaway and the gun. Her father told her to file a police report before flying out of Phoenix.

Following her father's advice, McCray drove from the airport to the Paradise Valley police station, where she made a complaint. Prosecutor Andrew Miller reviewed the case and on December 14 filed a formal complaint against Hardaway for threatening and intimidating in a domestic-violence incident.

A few weeks later, Miller's office also handled the domestic-violence case against Hardaway's teammate and fellow All-Star Jason Kidd. Kidd's case did not involve a gun and after his arrest he quickly acknowledged responsibility for his actions and volunteered to undergo counseling. Prosecutors offered him deferred prosecution as a first-time offender. Following a one-year probation, the charge would be removed from his record.

By contrast with Kidd's case, Hardaway fought the charges against him. "I am very disappointed by the decision by the Paradise Valley City Attorney to move forward with this case," he said. "I have done absolutely nothing wrong. There are two sides to this story. In this case, the allegations surrounding my actions have been misrepresented."

Prosecutors were preparing to try Hardaway on the domestic-violence charge but ultimately dropped the case against him in January 2001. "I always said I did nothing wrong," Hardaway told the press after learning the charges had been dropped. But prosecutor Andy Miller said the decision to drop the case was based on McCray's decision to no longer cooperate against Hardaway. She was living in Memphis and, despite cooperation early on, informed prosecutors that she would not show up for the trial. "We have no power to compel her to come across state lines," Miller said. "We sought for a couple weeks assurances that she would come. But we never heard back. But based upon the facts we were prepared to go to trial."

Illinois authorities charged Robinson with multiple offenses in connection with his attack on his ex-fiancée, Jonta French, in July 2002. It wasn't the first time the Bucks star had been in trouble with the law. On June 28, 1999, Robinson was arrested in Miami Beach, Florida, after being denied entrance to a nightclub. While Robinson verbally berated a doorman, a uniformed police officer attempted to calm Robinson down. "I ain't talking to you," Robinson shouted at the officer. The officer reported that Robinson's aggression then escalated to an intense level and he appeared on the verge of physical violence. When the officer tried to convince Robinson to calm down, Robinson shouted: "I don't have shit to say to you." A crowd gathered. Robinson started threatening the officer. Robinson's friends tried to restrain him but he overpowered them. "Fearing for my personal safety due to [Robinson's] large physical size," the officer wrote in his report, he arrested Robinson for disorderly intoxication and transported him to the police station for booking. (One year after filing charges against Robinson, Florida authorities declined to prosecute him on August 22, 2000.)

This was not Robinson's first incident involving police officers. Milwaukee police cited Robinson for disorderly conduct and obstructing the issuance of a citation in December 1997. The incident also took place outside a nightclub. Robinson was ordered to pay a fine.

In September 1995, Gary, Indiana, police investigated Robinson after a female gas-station attendant reported that Robinson took a swing at her and scratched her. The Lake County Prosecutor's Office declined to indict him.

But after the domestic-violence arrest, the Milwaukee Bucks traded the nine-time All-Star to the Atlanta Hawks on August 2, 2002. He played through the season, and his lawyers managed to delay the disposition of his case until after the 2002–03 season. Cook County prosecutor Tammy Connors was surprised that Robinson opted to go to trial rather than enter a plea. Robinson did not testify in his own defense. Instead he issued a statement that was read to the jury. "I wanted her to shoot me," he said. "I told Jonta to shoot because I was tired of life. I felt that if she wanted me to die, then she should pull the trigger herself."

Connors reminded jurors that there was a three-year-old child in the house while Robinson was beating French and searching frantically for his loaded gun. On May 15, 2003, jurors deliberated for less than three hours before returning a guilty verdict on the domestic battery and assault charge. He was sentenced to one year of probation, five days of community service, and ordered to complete an anger-management program.

When NBA players are charged with serious crimes, such as domestic violence and gun-related offenses, the league and its teams take a standard wait-and-see approach. Glenn Robinson and Jason Richardson no longer enjoyed that luxury of American jurisprudence after jurors found them guilty of domestic violence. So what was the NBA's penalty? Both received three-game suspensions. Under the NBA's collective-bargaining agreement, players face a minimum ten-game suspension if convicted of a violent felony. Robinson and Richardson committed violent misdemeanors. Fortunately for abusive NBA players, domestic violence is typically treated as a misdemeanor in most states, unless there are aggravating circumstances, such as the use of a weapon. In Robinson's case he didn't actually use the gun; he only attempted to.

For a league that places such a premium on convictions as a basis for taking disciplinary action against players who abuse women, all of this legal hair-splitting only serves to water down the seriousness of the consequences. The three-game suspension was particularly light for Glenn Robinson, whose offense involved a gun, a child, and a greater degree of violence.

The NBA's public hand-slapping of Robinson may have helped him gloss over his criminal conviction. But privately, Robinson had a lot more to worry about than missing three games. Right after his arrest on domestic-violence charges, Robinson had been hit with a restraining order to avoid any physical contact with Jonta French. She also filed a petition for sole custody of their three-year-old daughter, as well as a petition for child support. Under Illinois law, a minor child is entitled to a standard of living that she would have enjoyed if her parents were married. Robinson's annual salary at that time exceeded $9 million. On an interim basis, the Domestic Relations Division of the Cook County Court ordered Robinson to pay $6,000 per month in support, a $10,000 payment for rent and moving expenses for French and the child (whom Robinson had ordered out of his home), and $20,000 in legal fees for French. But lingering disputes over the final disposition of child-support payments and property division caused the case to languish in the courts even after the jury convicted Robinson in the domestic-violence case.

One month after the criminal trial, French filed a civil suit against Robinson on June 19, 2003, over the assault.

Then on July 23, the Hawks traded Robinson to the Philadelphia 76ers. The trade made big headlines in the basketball world, as it paired Robinson with Allen Iverson. But their on-court debut was delayed while Robinson sat out the first three games of the season on account of his domestic-violence conviction. "I certainly hate that I have to miss three games for it," Robinson said at the time. "But we've got more games left after that."

TWELVE

POUND OF FLESH

The long-standing logo of the NBA is a red, white, and blue silhouette of a basketball player dribbling a ball. The image symbolizes Americana and the beauty of pure skill. But there is nothing admirable or beautiful about the emerging image of today's NBA player: diamond-studded ears, flesh plastered with offensive body tattoos, and nicknames like "The Answer" and "Big Dog." Instead of a place to showcase teamwork, courageous play, and selfless passing, individual NBA players are converting the hardwood into a stage for hedonists to thumb their noses at the rules, laws, and social norms accepted by a large segment of the NBA's traditional fan base.

The NBA can wring its hands all it wants and say that today's players simply mirror the culture of the day. That's like the NFL inviting MTV to produce its Super Bowl halftime show and then acting surprised when the game becomes overshadowed by the embarrassing, crude actions of the performers. The NBA may not mind fooling itself when it comes to downplaying the image being promoted by its players. But unless the league wants to reduce its audience to a fan base of teenagers, it should think twice about the perception its players are creating with the public.

• • •

Man enough to pull a gun, be man enough to squeeze it. Those are the
words of Allen Iverson. Not Allen Iverson the NBA player, Allen
Iverson the rapper, as performed on his CD, which contained a
song that concluded with a murder scene and the sound of a gun
being cocked.

The problem is that there is only one Allen Iverson. The NBA
would love to distinguish between the things he does on the
court and the things he says and does off of it. Even Iverson tries
to confuse fiction with reality. "I don't feel like being real is picking up a gun to shoot somebody," he said after recording the CD
that glorified violence and riches and referred to women as
bitches. "Or smoking weed, or hanging with your boys all
night, or messing around with a bunch of women. That ain't
real to me."

Here's what is real: Iverson's image sells. After authorities announced a fourteen-count criminal charge against Iverson in
Philadelphia, sales of his official NBA jersey soared. After all
charges were dropped, Reebok extended his $50-million shoe en-
dorsement contract indefinitely. "Someone like Iverson has an
edgy street reputation, and that's an incredible asset to the NBA
and his endorsers with anyone under the age of twenty-five," said
Rick Burton, executive director of the sports marketing center at
the University of Oregon.

These are the kinds of things the NBA hates to admit. But it
is getting harder for the league to deny that it contributes to the
increasingly interchangeable image that melds some of its biggest
stars, like Iverson, with the gangster image celebrated in rap
music. In 2003, the NBA's official website promoted a joint ad
campaign, with Reebok, that featured Allen Iverson and rapper
50 Cent, whose CD *Get Rich or Die Tryin'* was named hip-hop

album of the year in 2003. Like Iverson, 50 Cent endorses footwear for Reebok, sports tattoos about his body, and is surrounded in controversy. He has been shot nine times and has feuded with other rap icons. But this brash approach has vaulted his records to bestseller status and established him as arguably the most popular rapper.

Reebok officially formed the Iverson–50 Cent duo in a marketing campaign that included billboards in New York, Atlanta, Baltimore, Boston, Chicago, Detroit, Houston, Miami, Philadelphia, and Washington, D.C. This is the ad campaign the NBA hyped on its website.

Marketing experts confirm that Iverson's bad public image is good for profits. "It might even help sales," Alan T. Brown, the president of a sports marketing firm, said at the time. "Yes, it's the bad-boy image, but the bad-boy image unfortunately right now is what sells, and he's the best bad boy out there."

The idea that a bad-boy image is good for advertising is not new. Iverson's brushes with the law have only enhanced his bad-boy image. Iverson was convicted for his part in a 1993 brawl that left a man maimed. Iverson spent four months in a Virginia prison until Governor Douglas Wilder granted him clemency, enabling him to enter Georgetown University on a basketball scholarship. After his freshman year his conviction was overturned on appeal.

In 1997, just weeks after being named NBA Rookie of the Year, Iverson was a passenger in his own brand-new Mercedes when police near Richmond, Virginia, clocked the car going 93 miles per hour in a 65-miles-per-hour zone. At the time of the stop, police found marijuana in the car. Iverson also had a gun. Though he claimed that it was in plain view, the officer saw it differently and charged him with carrying a concealed weapon and possession of marijuana. He pleaded no contest to carrying a concealed weapon. The marijuana-possession charge was dropped after Iverson completed three years of probation, and submitted to drug testing for two years, and was ordered to perform one hundred hours of community service.

In 1998, Iverson's car was stopped again, this time in Norfolk, Virginia. This time Iverson was not in the vehicle. The two occupants, both of whom were friends of Iverson's, had his permission to use his car. They were arrested after completing a drug deal. One was charged with possession of marijuana. The other was charged with possession of cocaine with intent to distribute. He had previously been convicted of cocaine possession. This same individual had been in Iverson's Mercedes in 1996 when shots were fired at the car in Hampton, Virginia. After the drug arrest in Norfolk, the police impounded Iverson's car.

The NBA's silence in all this may say something about the league's perception of its changing fan base. It is hard to imagine fans from the era of Bill Russell, Bill Bradley, and Oscar Robertson warming up to these players had they been getting arrested on weapons and violence charges, while promoting the same values through music and advertising.

Regardless, as the public face of the NBA's stars becomes less and less distinguishable from the likes of gangster rappers, the NBA has a lot more to worry about than losing some of its longstanding fans. It runs the real risk of losing a star or two. The risks today's NBA players take, the crowds they run with, and the establishments they frequent have threatened the life of more than one player of late.

No example illustrates this more chillingly than the case of Celtics star Paul Pierce, who came within an inch of being murdered in a violent altercation with a thuggish rap group. Boston authorities received the following call on September 25, 2000:

"9-1-1. This line is recorded. What is your emergency?"

"Hi, it's New England Medical Center Emergency Room. And I'd like to call to report a stabbing."

(911) "A stabbing?"

(hosp.) "Someone was stabbed and they were brought in."

(911) "Okay, did they walk in or drive in?"

(hosp.) "They were brought in by someone."

(911) "You got a name?"

(hosp.) "No. Male patient, multiple stab wounds."

(911) "Okay, was he black, white, Hispanic, or Asian?"

(hosp.) "Black."

(911) "What is your name?"

(hosp.) "Lisa."

(911) "Lisa, are you a nurse or a supervisor?"

"Secretary."

Stripped, bleeding, and strapped to a gurney, Paul Pierce wanted to ask a question as medics raced him toward the Intensive Care Unit. But speaking was a chore. A knife had ripped through his chest, puncturing his lung and stopping less than one inch from his heart. Breathing had never been so hard. "Am I going to be okay?" he finally uttered. "Am I going to be okay?"

A doctor told him he had to undergo surgery at once. The collapsed lung was only the beginning of his problems. He had multiple stab wounds to the torso; five more stab wounds dotted his neck and back; and a gash ripped across his right temple and tore away his eyebrow. He had lost a lot of blood.

Inside the operating room somebody shoved a surgery-consent and liability-release form in front of Pierce to sign. Fearing he would die, Pierce stared up at the ceiling lights as an anesthesiologist slipped a mask over his face.

When Pierce woke up from surgery hours later, he had tubes going through his arm, his chest, and his nose. He felt groggy. He worried that he might never play basketball again. Two detectives were waiting to interview him. They wanted to know what he re-membered from the night before.

The following account comes from confidential grand jury transcripts, internal police records, crime-scene photographs, court records, and press reports, as well as interviews conducted for this book.

Paul Pierce had just returned to Boston from an off-season stay in Los Angeles when he hooked up with teammate Tony Battie and Battie's brother Derrick around midnight on Septem-ber 25, 2000. They headed to Backstage, a Boston nightclub. But the place was quiet. A friend at the club—Big Ken—informed them that a private hip-hop party was taking place at the Buzz Club. Pierce and the Battie brothers didn't have an invite. But they had money. Big Ken said with money he could get them in.

It was a few minutes before one A.M. when the three men parked their Cadillac Escalade on Stuart Street and approached a drab gray building with a weathered blue canopy across the front that read BUZZ CLUB. It sat next to a pawnshop on the corner of Stuart and Tremont Streets in Boston's Theater District. Tony Battie paid a sixty-dollar cover charge for the three of them, after which they were frisked for weapons, then let inside. The interior made the exterior look plush. A dingy stairwell led to the second-floor club, where a ratty, multicolored industrial rug covered the floor. Rectangular metal garbage cans heaping with litter and plastic beverage cups dotted the room. Banged-up pool tables surrounded by brown, imitation-leather sofas sat off to the side of a tiny wooden dance floor. Nearly three hundred people were packed inside. It was dark, loud, and smelled of sweat and alco-hol—hardly the kind of place one would expect to find a man worth nearly $100 million, the approximate value of Pierce's NBA salary and other endorsement contracts.

Wearing a leather jacket over a stylish button-down, short-sleeve Polo shirt, Pierce stood out. Many of the men in the crowd were wearing Timberland boots, dark jeans, denim jackets, and bandannas or do-rags. Pierce's and the Batties' height distinguished them, too. Paul is six-foot-six; Tony and his brother are six-eleven and six-ten respectively.

While Tony ducked into the men's room, Pierce went straight to the dance floor. One of his favorite songs pulsated through the sound system. He danced alone.

Minutes later the song ended, and Pierce spotted a woman making eye contact with him. Standing near the pool tables, she wore a zebra-print top that revealed her hard-to-turn-away-from figure. "Hi," she said as Pierce got close enough to touch her. She never asked his name and Pierce didn't offer it. He was used to meeting attractive women in public places, especially clubs. "What are you drinking?" he asked.

Pierce was flirting with her when a second woman leaned over and whispered something in the ear of the woman with the animal-print top. Pierce flashed a smile. "What did you say?" Pierce asked her.

"She didn't say anything," interjected William "Roscoe" Ragland, an imposing, husky man who stood nearly six feet tall. "You know, that's my sister."

Pierce stared down at Ragland, who had a goatee and was wearing a dark denim outfit and a bandanna on his head. "There was no disrespect," Pierce said.

Ragland glared at Pierce. Pierce stared back. He had no idea that he was looking into the eyes of a career felon. At age fourteen Ragland shot and killed a man. In all, the Ragland record included sixteen criminal convictions, among them robbery and multiple assaults. He had been released from jail only weeks earlier and was awaiting trial on charges of illegal possession of a firearm and ammunition. His $25,000 bond in that case had been paid in cash by Ray "Benzino" Scott, the leader of Boston's gangster-rap group Made Men, which was notorious for violence. The Boston Police Union threatened to sue after the band released "One in the Chamba," a song that, police said, inspired fans to take up arms against law-enforcement officers. Ray Scott had been charged with assault and battery on a police officer.

Ragland was at the club with Scott, whose group always traveled with a posse, a group of current and former gang members hired to provide security and dish out intimidation. Ragland belonged to the posse.

Ragland knew who Pierce was: the pride of the Boston Celtics. Pierce had everything Ragland craved: wealth, power, and fame. He despised how Pierce got those things, by excelling in a game revered on the same streets that Ragland had dominated as a thug. Pierce and his teammates might rule the artificial world beneath the spotlights of Boston's Fleet Center. But Pierce was on Ragland's turf now, the dark side of Boston's streets, where violence was real. And he was hitting on a woman surrounded by members of the Made Men posse.

Ragland, armed with a knife, challenged Pierce. Trained as a player to never back down from a challenge on the court, Pierce exchanged words with him. This was no gym with bright boundary lines and referees to enforce rules. Ragland enforced his words by hacking into Pierce's body with the knife, sending him staggering backward. More then ten men emerged from the dark shadows of the dance floor and pounced on Pierce. A flurry of fists and blades fueled by hatred pummeled Pierce's body. As Pierce spun to defend himself, someone broke a bottle over Pierce's temple. Blood streamed into his eye, obstructing his vision. Another man used a pair of brass knuckles with a knife attached to it to punch Pierce about the side of his body, while another man with a knife clutched Pierce's throat. Pierce dropped to the floor. A man with blood on his hands repeatedly kicked Pierce as he struggled to get off the floor.

"F— Paul Pierce!" Ragland gloated as thirty-six-year-old club bouncer Michael Nunes, carrying a radio and wearing an earpiece and microphone, rushed to Pierce, who was in a bloody heap on the floor. His leather jacket had been hacked off of him. His shoes were removed. His Polo shirt was drenched in his own sweat and blood.

Other security guards streamed into the area, sending patrons scrambling. Pierce's attackers fled. Nunes used bar towels to try to stop Pierce's bleeding and whisked him to a nearby stairwell. Another few seconds and Pierce, one of the NBA's top players, could have died alone at the bottom of a heap on the floor of an old hip-hop club, just minutes from the Fleet Center, where he performed for thousands.

Derrick and Tony Battie were at the bar, ordering drinks, when they saw the security guards running in one direction and a bunch of people running in the opposite direction. "Where's Paul?" Tony asked. Derrick hadn't seen him since they entered the club.

Derrick grabbed his brother by the arm and started pushing his way through the crowd. Suddenly they spotted Pierce, blood gushing down his face.

"What happened, man? What happened?" Tony said.

"They jumped me," Pierce told them, stuttering.

"Who was it?" Tony asked.

It was the Made Men guys, security guard Michael Nunes explained.

Only Pierce's undershirt remained on him. It was soaked and stuck to Pierce's torso. Derrick lifted Pierce's undershirt. Blood oozed from incisions, one in his stomach and two near his heart. Something white and fleshy hung from his abdomen area.

"We got to get him to the hospital," Tony said.

Pierce started to droop. Leaving Pierce with the security guard, Tony and Derrick ran to get the SUV and bring it to the rear exit. In the parking lot they saw three or four men with bandannas on their heads climbing into a gray Mercedes with shiny chrome wheels. One of them smirked at the Batties.

Tony pulled the truck out of the parking lot. Derrick ran back inside to get Pierce. Reaching his arms around Pierce's waist and neck to support him, Derrick felt blood all over his hands. He paused and pulled back Pierce's T-shirt from the back, exposing multiple stab wounds to his neck, all of which were bleeding. "Man, did you even know that you were stabbed in the back?" Battie asked.

Pierce just wanted to get to the hospital. Derrick put him in the backseat, where Pierce, panicking, leaned over and clutched his stomach. Tony drove one block to the hospital and parked at the wrong entrance. Pierce got out and staggered toward the emergency room doors. A man with a wheelchair observed Pierce and rushed toward him, caught him, and then wheeled him inside.

Medics stripped him naked, observing at least ten separate wounds from his stomach to his head, some of them life threatening. "We'll take it from here, guys," one of the medics said to Tony and Derrick, instructing them that they were not permitted to go any farther in the ER.

The Batties were angry and on edge. Derrick dialed 911 from the hospital. He wanted to be sure police had been sent to the club to find Pierce's attackers.

"Boston police. This line is recorded. Do you have an emergency?"

"I'm trying to see if an emergency unit has been dispatched to the Club Eurora," Battie said, mispronouncing the Buzz Club's prior name, Club Europa.

"Where?"

"Eurora . . . on Kneeland Street."

"Hold on. Let me check."

"I'm talking about a police unit."

"Hold on, hold on. What's going on over there?"

"Ah, just a guy got stabbed up real bad."

"So you need the police?"

"I need several police. It's one of our local celebrities, please."

"Give me the address of the club."

"Kneeland and . . . damn it, the same street the Roxy is on. I can't think of the street."

"Hold on. Hold on."

"I'm trying to make sure they get the right motherf—er to get the information," Battie shouted in frustration. "'Cause you know I saw the cat. I know he can say, hey, this is the one who did it."

"And who is the celebrity? You know?"

"I can't give you that information, I'm sorry."

"You want to leave your name?"

"Nope, I don't. I'm just a very concerned person. We're looking for the Made Men, who's a rap group here."

"Made Men?"

"In Boston. Some of their lead singers."

Hanging up the phone, Derrick turned to Tony. "Yo, come on. Now we need to be locating them immediately."

As the Batties left the ER, Boston police officer William Toner and his partner arrived there. ER staff explained that Pierce had been stabbed up to ten times in the back, neck, face, and torso. The injuries were life threatening, and Pierce had been rushed into surgery in the Intensive Care Unit; he might not survive. Toner radioed for the Boston Police Homicide Unit to respond to the Buzz Club at once.

The Batties got back to the scene first and immediately began searching for witnesses. But nobody dared talk, not even the security guards. "You guys don't live here," one of them told the Batties. "We got to live here year-round with these guys. We don't want to get involved. Man, I make fifty dollars a night at this club."

Derrick pulled out a one-hundred-dollar bill and handed it to the guard. "Was it the Made Men who attacked Pierce?" he asked. The guard nodded his head affirmatively.

Tony pulled out another hundred. "Give me a name. Give me a name."

No one would. Tony Battie was getting a taste of what police officers experience when they investigate crimes committed by NBA players. They often have great difficulty getting witnesses to come forward. Battie himself had been arrested by Boston police on April 17, 1999, after being told several times to move his Lincoln Navigator from in front of another Boston nightclub at two-thirty in the morning. Officer Ray D'Oyley said that Battie refused to identify himself and started to drive away to avoid arrest. D'Oyley, whose arm was trapped in Battie's driver's-side window, got dragged down the street. Battie stopped, according to D'Oyley, only after the officer drew his gun. Battie pleaded no contest and his record was wiped clean after completing a year of probation.

Now Tony Battie was getting stonewalled in his attempt to track down his teammate's attackers.

When Paul Pierce woke up from surgery, Detectives Thomas Leahy and Andrew Creed were waiting to interview him in the ICU. They wanted to know if Pierce recognized anyone at the club. Pierce didn't. "I don't know people in Boston," he told them.

When asked if he had any friend in Boston besides his teammates, Pierce did not provide a single name. Amazingly, the biggest star in the city was all alone.

Later that day police returned with a photo lineup containing a mug shot of one of his attackers. Pierce could not pick him out.

With little help from Pierce, authorities arrested Tony Hurston and Trevor Watson on September 27, 2000, and charged them in connection with the stabbing. Both men had ties to Made Men. And both were known to law enforcement.

Hurston, a hulking 340-pound bodyguard for Made Men, who also coached youth football, previously belonged to a notorious Boston-area street gang called the Corbet Street Crew, according to published reports citing Boston police records.

Watson had just been released from prison, where he served five years for felony possession of a firearm. Prior to that, he received a twenty-year suspended sentence for armed robbery.

William Ragland was taken into custody shortly after Hurston and Watson. All three were indicted for attempting to murder Pierce.

The same day their arrests were announced, Celtics coach Rick Pitino warned his players to "be careful." To call this a naive approach would be putting it mildly. It is either dishonest or a profound misunderstanding of the risks that today's NBA players take and the dangerous circles in which they routinely run. For many of today's players, early morning is bedtime, not wake-up time. And clubs—strip clubs, topless bars, and hip-hop joints—are their nightlife venues of choice. Pierce is hardly the first player to be involved in a violent altercation in one of these venues.

In fact, Pierce's teammate Walter McCarty is fortunate that he did not become a victim along with him. McCarty, whom Rick Pitino coached at Kentucky, was inside the club at the same time Pierce and Battie were. McCarty, who owns Ice Storm Productions, a music production company, had just cut his own CD.

Only hours before heading to the club he had finished shooting his own music video in the Boston area. He had been put on the VIP list to the hip-hop party at the club. The police were unaware that McCarty had been there and therefore never questioned him during the initial investigation. But McCarty saw things that night that played a key role in the authorities' ability to catch and convict Pierce's attackers. McCarty revealed these things in secret grand jury testimony. The account below comes from a transcript of McCarty's testimony.

One of the first people McCarty saw when he arrived at the club around eleven-thirty was Ray Benzino, the leader of the group Made Men. McCarty knew him. They said hello and talked just briefly.

Dressed in a fancy cream-colored suit and expensive shoes, McCarty immediately felt out of place. Sensing the potential for a conflict, McCarty went up to the third floor, a more secluded area away from the dance floor, pool tables, and bar.

He remained up there until around one A.M., when three bouncers ran up and grabbed him. "I need to get you out of here," one of them told McCarty, informing him that his teammate Paul Pierce had just been stabbed. McCarty had no idea Pierce had been in the club. Fearing for his own safety, McCarty followed security, which led him down the back steps, over broken glass and past the bloody towels left behind by Pierce.

Once outside, McCarty hustled to his car and tried to quickly exit the side parking lot. Pulling out, he encountered a gray Mercedes pulling in. McCarty stopped and put down his window. The driver of the Mercedes did, too; it was Ray Benzino. In the backseat McCarty saw Trevor Watson and Tony Hurston. McCarty recognized Watson right away as a bodyguard for Made Men. McCarty had seen Watson plenty of times in nightclubs, wearing a bandanna and tank tops.

"What happened?" McCarty asked Benzino. "What's going on?"

"You guys just need to stay away, stay away from these clubs," Benzino told McCarty.

By "you guys," he meant, specifically, NBA players. In grand jury testimony taken during the Pierce investigation, Benzino prided himself on the fact that when he entered places like the Buzz Club, everyone knew him and everyone showed their respect. Only the appearance of someone like Paul Pierce or Walter McCarty could upstage him. In a club like the Buzz Club, only NBA players are richer and more famous than the rappers who rule there.

Miraculously, Paul Pierce recovered fully from his attack and was in the Celtics lineup on opening night, just weeks after the stabbing. He was named co-captain and played all eighty-two games that year, turning in his best season. He averaged over twenty-five points per game and logged more than 3,000 minutes of play. The following year, Ragland, Watson, and Hurston stood trial for attempted murder. Happy to be alive, Pierce hardly seemed eager to see justice done. "The past is what the past is," he told the Boston media after he testified at the trial. "This court stuff, I'll be happy when it's all over with so I can just mainly concentrate on basketball."

After the jury acquitted all three men on attempted murder charges but found Ragland and Watson guilty on the lesser charge of assault, Pierce issued a public statement through the Celtics PR office. "I'm happy this case has come to an end," it read. "It was an unfortunate incident for all involved and I'm looking forward to putting it behind me and focusing my attention on the upcoming season."

Unfortunate incident? For all involved? Minus Pierce, "all involved" were a pack of armed men who left him for dead in a heap of his own carved-up flesh and blood on the floor of a dark nightclub. Most of the men involved were never charged. One of the three who was charged went free. The other two got off with mere assault convictions. The only thing more bizarre than Pierce's indifference was Tony Hurston's statement. After being acquitted, Hurston hugged his shackled codefendant Trevor Watson. Then he complimented Pierce. "Paul's a good dude," Hurston told the press. "He got us caught up in a situation we had nothing to do with. He's a victim as much as us."

THIRTEEN

SEE NO EVIL

On October 8, 1997, shortly before four A.M., security guards at the Walt Disney World Institute—a complex of villas and bungalows—received a complaint about a loud party in room 35. The room was registered to Indiana Pacers forward Dale Davis and was one in a series of rooms occupied by members of the Pacers team, which was holding its preseason training camp at a Disney sports complex. When security responded to the room they discovered a group of people standing outside in an adjacent parking lot, surrounding a woman who was crying and bleeding badly from the facial area. As security started asking questions, the group disbanded, largely refusing to talk. Security called for an ambulance and police assistance.

Sergeant Kevin Stenger was on duty when a radio dispatch came into the Orange County Sheriff's Office, reporting a possible domestic-violence incident at the Disney Institute. Less then fifteen minutes later, Stenger and his partner arrived on the scene. Disney security guards told them that the incident apparently happened outside the bungalows and that the victim had already been rushed to Sandlake Hospital for emergency treatment. The suspect was nowhere to be found and the only information available on him was his first name: "Tyrone."

Stenger and his partner went directly to the hospital. Inside they found nineteen-year-old Shala Miller. Stenger had trouble looking at her; one side of her jaw was higher than the other, and a small piece of bone had pierced through her cheek. Doctors confirmed Miller's jaw had been broken in more than one place. Her jaw would have to be wired in place.

Stenger asked Miller if the person who did this to her was her husband or boyfriend. Miller turned her head side to side, indicating that he was not. Stenger asked her if the man's name was Tyrone. She nodded her head up and down. He asked her if she knew Tyrone's last name. She turned her head from side to side.

Stenger asked Miller if she could write down her vital information. But she was in too much pain to write. Instead, she offered Stenger her driver's license. Stenger left his card and asked the nurses to call him as soon as Miller was able to at least write, if not speak.

In hopes of confirming the identity of the suspect and determining his whereabouts, Detectives Bill Reynolds and Frank Delguercio Sr. returned to the Disney property, where they learned that room 35 had been cleaned by housekeeping and contained no signs of a violent incident. But Disney produced three members of the housekeeping crew who revealed that when they had entered room 35 earlier that morning they found blood in the kitchen sink, on the kitchen floor, on the coffeepot, and splattered against an air-conditioning vent and on the wall around the vent. Detective Reynolds wanted to talk to Larry Bird, the Pacers' head coach.

Immediately after being notified that a detective wanted to see him, Bird arrived at the office and met privately with Reynolds, who advised him of the situation. Bird promised to cooperate fully with the investigation and provide access to any players the police wanted to question. Reynolds asked to speak

with Pacers center Rik Smits, who was staying next door to room
35, in room 36. Bird produced Smits, who confirmed hearing a
loud party next door the night before. But Smits had never left
his room and saw nothing.

Next Reynolds asked to speak with Dale Davis. He admitted
being inside the room playing cards at the time of the incident.
But he insisted he did not see anyone get hit. Nor did he see any
blood. This puzzled Reynolds. The living room and kitchen area
were all part of one large open room. The victim's injuries and
the location of blood evidence around the room indicated that
the blow she sustained had been delivered with tremendous
force. In addition to such a blow surely eliciting a loud cry or reaction from the victim, her blood remained present until housekeeping cleaned it up. Yet Davis heard and saw nothing?

Even more puzzling was the smirk on Davis's face during the
questioning. His strange smile said more than Davis's words. Finally, Reynolds asked Davis if he knew the identity of the suspect.
Davis said he had no idea who the suspect was or where he lived.

While Reynolds interviewed Davis, Detective Delguercio went
to room 35 to interview the other two men staying there: Davis's
brother, Maurice Davis, and his friend Tommy Harper. When
Delguercio arrived, Harper hid to avoid detection. But Delguercio
found him. Neither he nor Maurice Davis would cooperate. Davis
admitted knowing the suspect and witnessing him strike Miller
before fleeing the scene. But he refused to identify his friend.

Harper also admitted knowing the suspect and witnessing
the assault. But he too refused to identify him. Hotel registration
records indicated that the fourth man staying in room 35 with
the Davis brothers and Harper was Dan Daniels, who listed a
Georgia address and phone number. Airline records at Orlando
airport revealed that Daniels, Davis, and Harper flew in together
on a flight from Atlanta, and the three had tickets to return to-

gether. Detective Reynolds contacted an officer at the airport to determine whether Daniels had left the area by air. Just three hours after the assault, Daniels boarded a 7:00 A.M. flight bound for Atlanta. He paid for his ticket in cash, leaving no other identification besides his name.

Reynolds requested authorities in Georgia to do a records check on Daniels. His name did not show up in Georgia's criminal records. And the address that Daniels listed when he checked into the Disney hotel turned out not to exist. The phone number he provided was false as well. The authorities were stymied. They were particularly irked by Dale Davis's attitude, as well as that of his brother and friend. "The investigators didn't think highly of Mr. Davis's cooperation," said Orange County Sheriff's Office commander Steve Jones. "They said he was smiling like he didn't care. Usually, if you have somebody around who's that seriously hurt, you would show some kind of concern." A spokesman for the Pacers declined to comment on the incident, saying only: "We're comfortable that Dale was not involved in the incident."

The detectives hoped that when Shala Miller was able to talk she could shed more light on what triggered the assault. After leaving the Disney property, Reynolds and Delguercio went to see her at the hospital, only to discover that she had been transferred to the Orlando Regional Medical Center for oral surgery. After she recovered from surgery, Miller signed a sworn statement indicating that she and two female friends had attended a party in Davis's room. At one point, the suspect used a derogatory name to refer to one of her female friends, prompting Miller to criticize him for his comments. In response, the man wound up and punched Miller in the mouth with a closed fist, breaking her jaw in two places.

On November 7, when detectives called Miller to follow up, they discovered that her telephone number had been disconnected. No forwarding number was available. A letter to the victim went unreturned as well. With no cooperation from anyone involved, investigators inactivated the case on November 14, 1997.

"Larry Bird was very cooperative," said one of the investigators who worked this case. "But we're talking to people and everybody tells us, 'I don't know anything.' Somebody had to know. I'm not saying everybody knew. But the player who the bungalow belonged to was supposedly playing cards at that time. You couldn't have missed this."

Davis's behavior is consistent with the see-no-evil approach that is pervasive throughout the NBA when it comes to the crimes and other misdeeds of its players. Examples abound. It is evident in Bonzi Wells using racially derogatory language to demean opponents and spitting in the face of opponent Danny Ferry, actions that would provoke outrage in almost any venue outside the NBA hardwood. Yet, with saliva hanging from Ferry's face, Wells's coach Maurice Cheeks took the position that he couldn't do anything because he didn't see or hear any of this behavior for himself. Yet witnesses did see and hear, and said as much.

It is evident in the reaction—or lack of action—on the part of league and union officials after Damon Stoudamire got caught with pounds of marijuana in his home. The league and the union seemed to find solace in the fact that the judge threw out the evidence on grounds that the seizure had been improper. No one disputes that the drugs were there. That fact, and not the legal technicality that saved Stoudamire from prosecution, is what should matter to the league and the players union.

It is evident in former Boston Celtics head coach Rick Pitino declaring he found no evidence that his players were involved in anything stemming from a rape complaint, when the press and police reports clearly demonstrate something did happen and that his players were directly involved. The only issue was whether what happened was consensual.

It is evident in Portland Trail Blazers owner, Paul Allen, on one hand, approving a $33-million contract to a registered sex offender, while on the other hand telling the press that "unacceptable conduct will not be condoned," and that the team is "prepared to suspend players, levy heavy fines, and trade or release players" who run afoul of the law.

It is evident in a woman getting her face busted up so violently that a bone pierced her skin and the Pacers team taking comfort that its player Dale Davis didn't deliver the blow. That's comforting? What about Davis's clear mockery of the legal process?

Suffice it to say that examples of this attitude are evident at every level, from team owners to coaches to lawyers to agents. While writing this book, I telephoned or wrote certified letters to the agents representing most of the players profiled here. My general method of introduction was to say that I was writing a book about the NBA and crime. I then requested an interview with the respective agent's client. Some agents were quick to admit that there were plenty of players in the NBA who are thugs and criminals. But in the next breath the same agent would also insist that *his* client was no such person.

My conversation with Anthony Mason's agent, Don Cronson, was somewhat typical. I requested an interview with Mason in order to discuss the fact that within less than a four-year span he had been investigated by authorities in three different states for allegedly raping three different women. I hardly got past my introduction when Cronson unloaded.

"That Anthony Mason is the main part of your chapter involving crime flies in the face of all reality," Cronson said. "There are guys in the NBA who have done a lot more serious things than he has. And the public record is rife with examples of those cases. Now, was he involved with situations? There is no doubt. But, I mean—talk about selective reporting and unbalanced journalism."

Selective reporting? Actually, I had not planned on reporting on the litany of run-ins Mason has had with law enforcement since entering the NBA. But since Cronson brought up the public record, let's take a look:

On June 21, 1989, in his rookie year, Mason was arrested in New York and charged with a felony, unlawful possession of a loaded firearm. He pled guilty and received five years' probation and was required to perform community service.

In July 1996, New York City police officers arrested Mason and charged him with felony assault, menacing, resisting arrest, and disorderly conduct after an altercation with police officers outside a Manhattan restaurant. According to published reports, it took ten police officers to place Mason under arrest, and three officers were injured. "It is our position that there was no incident," one of Mason's lawyers said after the arrest. "But if there was an incident it was provoked by the police." Mason later pled guilty to disorderly conduct and was sentenced to community service and paid a fine.

In 1998, he pled guilty to two counts of endangering the welfare of children after he was arrested for statutory rape in Queens, New York.

In February 2000, Mason was arrested and charged with assault after a melee outside a Manhattan nightclub. The charges were later dropped.

In July 2000, Mason was arrested again, this time for inciting a riot, assaulting police, and resisting arrest on Bourbon Street in New Orleans. Mason was sprayed with pepper after he allegedly hit an officer and rallied the crowd. Six months later the charges were dropped when the prosecuting attorney for the city of New Orleans announced the city was uncertain it could sustain its burden of proof at trial.

Besides being the subject of three sexual-assault investigations, Mason has also been sued numerous times for alleged acts of violence. For the NBA's sake, let's hope Cronson is wrong when he says there are guys in the NBA who have done a lot more serious things than Mason has.

It should not be surprising that so many NBA players are being arrested these days. We should be surprised that players aren't being arrested even more. After all, they are, by and large, adolescents who are excessively paid and overhyped to play a boy's game while living in a cocoon where they are pampered, protected, and never told no. When they are accused of breaking the law, handlers and the best lawyers money can buy rush to their side. Excuses are made, exceptions to rules are demanded, and quick and dirty forgiveness is expected through lawyerly denials, public apologies, and an occasional hand-slapping in the form of a one- or two-game suspension and a small fine.

There is no shortage of losers in this brutal game. This book is full of examples of real people, all sorts of people—children, parents, a nanny, girlfriends, wives, law-enforcement officials—who have been on the receiving end of crimes committed by NBA players. So who are the winners? Lawyers and agents. The criminal troubles of NBA players are keeping a lot of lawyers gainfully employed. Young, naive to the workings of the legal system, and supremely rich, criminally accused players get superior legal representation—and pay a premium price for it.

Even in misdemeanor cases, lawyers representing players sometimes act as if they are handling the crime of the century.

Consider the Damon Stoudamire situation. His arrests for walking through an airport security checkpoint in Tucson with marijuana and for possession of marijuana in a vehicle traveling on a Washington State freeway are probably the two least serious crimes chronicled in this book. Yet two years of legal wrangling, hearings, appeals, motions, and negotiations have been carried out by Stoudamire's legal team. As this book went to press, neither of these misdemeanor cases had been resolved. Officials in Lewis County, Washington, were waiting to charge Stoudamire with violating probation for his arrest in Arizona. But officials in Arizona have been deterred from completing the prosecution of Stoudamire in the airport offense on account of repeated appeals and motions by Stoudamire's lawyers that are aimed at getting the marijuana evidence dismissed.

Lewis County prosecutor Jeremy Randolph has been frustrated and amazed at the amount of time and effort expended by Stoudamire's lawyers to fight this simple marijuana-possession charge. Randolph said that one of Stoudamire's lawyers even drove all the way from Portland to his Washington office simply to discuss a proposal to have the charge dropped in exchange for Stoudamire's making appearances in Washington State public schools to talk about the evils and dangers of drug use. "He drove up all the way up here from Portland to talk to me," Randolph said. "We're two hours away. Those are billable hours. He also flew down to Arizona to talk to the Pima County officials. Tens of thousands of dollars have gone into this defense. Athletes with limited education are being taken advantage of."

Randolph wondered if Stoudamire's lawyers had told Stoudamire that the state of Washington was willing to only impose a two-day jail term if he would simply drop his appeals in Arizona and admit guilt. Through his agent, Stoudamire declined to comment.

• • •

Who's to blame for the problems detailed in this book? It would be easy to simply point the finger at the NBA. But the NBA is what it is: an entertainment business driven by the bottom line. The NBA is not in business to solve society's ills, nor is it equipped to reform players who are both a product of those ills and on another level a contributor to them.

But institutions of higher learning, on the other hand, are not bottom line–driven business enterprises whose mission is merely to entertain (at least they are not supposed to be). And they do have a responsibility to train and educate young minds to address and improve the world's social ills and problems. They certainly should not be in league with a system that shepherds gifted yet criminally troubled and academically inept athletes through schools, only so they can remain eligible long enough to make their way into the NBA draft. Of course, not all players coming out of college and entering the NBA are criminals or academically deficient. But the ones who end up in handcuffs as pros often are.

There's a more pernicious problem here. For every college basketball player who makes the NBA, there are roughly one hundred college players who don't in any given year; there are so few openings in the NBA and so many aspiring players. Each year thousands of sports scholarships are offered to basketball and football players—many of whom are minorities—to attend the country's top schools. But let's be candid: these student-athletes are brought there primarily to be athletes and entertainers, not scholars. Forty-four of the sixty-five teams in the 2004 NCAA men's basketball tournament had a graduation rate below 50 percent.

Certainly institutions of higher learning have an obligation not to exploit these athletes for four years—enabling schools to fill stadiums and arenas, or pay fat salaries to coaches who earn more than professors and college presidents—only to turn these student-athletes out without a diploma when their athletic eligibility expires.

How bad have things become? In February 2004, the NCAA received 1,500 pages of documents from the University of Georgia, which is being investigated by the NCAA for academic fraud. After the allegations surfaced, Georgia's head basketball coach, Jim Harrick, and his son, assistant coach Jim Harrick Jr., were forced to resign. The NCAA concluded that Harrick Jr. "fraudulently awarded grades of A to three men's basketball students." The three players were enrolled in a course taught by Herrick, titled "Coaching Principles and Strategies of Basketball." Students in the class were given one exam during the semester, which formed the basis for the course grades. The multiple-choice exam included the following questions:

How many goals are on a basketball court?

How many halves are in a college basketball game?

How many quarters are in a high school basketball game?

How many points does a 3-point field goal account for in a
. basketball game?

I put these questions to my seven-year-old son, who does not play basketball and knows next to nothing about the game or the way it is played. Yet even he would have earned an A in this course, as he answered all four questions correctly.

When college presidents and the NCAA fail to put a stop to this mockery, who can be surprised that the NBA hasn't stepped up and exhibited leadership in this area?

No doubt the NBA has some responsibility for the players who wear uniforms bearing the league's logo. And while it would be admirable and appropriate for the league to do more to snuff out the lawlessness within the ranks of its players, such hopes are not realistic. Money more than moral obligations will dictate the league's course of action in this area. As long as corporate sponsors continue to advertise around the league and as long as fans continue to pay the price of admission, little will change.

So, what to do? Typically, this is the point in a book like this where solutions and policy suggestions are laid out. One obvious improvement would be for colleges and universities in this country to start acting the part and put a stop to the business of letting its campuses act as a minor league for the NBA by demanding that academic standards be met and criminally convicted players be denied scholarships.

But it seems somewhat pointless to offer additional suggestions that might ultimately rescue the NBA's credibility when the league is unwilling and seemingly unconcerned with saving itself. As I neared completion of this manuscript, Major League Baseball was in the grips of a national scandal over steroids. Even President Bush made reference to it in his State of the Union address. Yet compare steroid abuse to the problem plaguing the NBA. In the first week of March 2004, while some of baseball's most prominent stars were making public denials about using performance-enhancing substances, former NBA star Jayson Williams was on trial for aggravated manslaughter in a New Jersey courtroom, charged with killing his limousine driver with a shotgun. During the same period, lawyers for Kobe Bryant were in court in Colorado, demolishing his accuser's credibility—and the State of Colorado's rape-shield law—by trying to convince a judge that dragging the victim's sexual history into public view was essential to afford Bryant a fair defense.

Baseball is dealing with steroids. Basketball is dealing with aggravated manslaughter and felony rape. In terms of seriousness, Major League Baseball's problems hardly seem to compare with the NBA's problems. If the views of countless law-enforcement officials, lawyers, and other individuals interviewed for this book count for anything, they indicate that there is a growing tide of disgust and anger toward the league's approach to crime by its players. Sure, this kind of interviewing is anecdotal and skewed. But one thing's certain: the off-the-court conduct of its players has brought the NBA to a crossroads with its fans, putting the league in a position where it is going to have to choose whether it wants to be perceived as a league of selfish, shameless thugs, or return to the highly respected team sport it once was.

NOTES

Over 12,000 primary source documents (police records, court records, grand jury minutes and transcripts, and trial transcripts) were obtained or viewed for this book. They include depositions, affidavits, arrest and search warrants, evidence logs, police narratives, grand jury notes, indictments, arrest reports, incident reports, conviction and sentencing orders, and probation orders. Also, crime-scene photographs, police drawings, and video surveillance tapes were obtained and used to help describe some of the scenes detailed in the book. Finally, more than 400 interviews were conducted with individuals who were directly or indirectly involved with the cases featured herein.

Secondary sources included over 1,000 press reports, primarily in the form of newspaper and magazine articles. Those relied upon for text are identified in the bibliography that follows, as are a limited number of books that were used for reference.

Under each chapter heading I have identified the primary source documents, along with their corresponding case names and numbers. Where appropriate, I have also identified sources who were interviewed. When press reports were used, I identify them.

INTRODUCTION: EVERY WOMAN'S FEAR

7 *Pleasure Island tonight* "Statement," Orange County Sheriff's Office, Case No. 98-079912, October 13, 1998.

7 *Where are your friends?* Ibid.

7 *Be my guest* Ibid.

7 *Can't you take a joke?* "Incident Report," Case No. 98-079912.

8 *going up against* Interview with Shannon Baruch.
8 *he represented O'Neal* "Investigative Report," Case No. 98-079912.
9 *Again, Kirkconnell declined* Ibid.
9 *forwarded the case* "Investigative Report.".
9 *victim is going to say* Interview with prosecutor Bill Vose.
10 *defense to provide information* Ibid.
10 *were going up against* Interview with Baruch.
11 *I'm not most defense attorneys* Conversation with Kirk Kirkconnell.
12 *Second-class reserve officer* *Houston Chronicle*, "Shaq Takes Shot at Law Enforcement," July 13, 2002.

PROLOGUE: UNDER ARREST

Primary sources for this chapter consisted of police and court records from the Pima County Sheriff's Office and the Tucson International Airport Police, including a copy of a video surveillance tape depicting what transpired at an airport security checkpoint; police and court records from the Pima County Prosecutor's Office; police documents from the Washington State Highway Patrol; court documents from the Lewis County Prosecutor's Office; records from the Eagle County Sheriff's Office in Colorado; and multiple reports and case files from the Portland Police Bureau.

Interviews were also conducted with officials from the Pima County Attorney's Office, the Lewis County Prosecuting Attorney's Office, and the Multnomah County District Attorney's Office, as well as the Portland Police Department.

PAGE

13 *flight to New Orleans* Airport video surveillance tape, obtained by the author.
13 *needed to return to the terminal* "Detail Incident Report," Tucson International Airport Police, Case No. A03070064, July 29, 2003. Also, the "Incident Report" filed by the Pima County Sheriff's Department on July 3, 2003.
14 *Keith Kramer arrived* "Narrative," Tucson International Airport Police, Case No. A03070064, July 29, 2003.
14 *What's inside?* "Supplemental Narrative," Tucson International Airport Police, Case No. A03070064, July 29, 2003.
14 *into a private room* "Incident Report," Pima County Sheriff's Department, Incident No. A03070064, July 3, 2003.

15 *Granger had just signed* "Warrant for Arrest" (dated July 3, 2003), *Colorado vs. Kobe Bean Bryant,* Case No. 03CR204.

15 *surrendered to Lieutenant* "Appearance Bond," dated July 4, 2003.

15 *for further court proceedings* "Consent of Surety," dated July 5, 2003.

15 *Pippen had harassed* "Investigation Report," Portland Police Bureau, Case No. 03-4-443, April 29, 2003.

15 *After being heckled* "Special Report," Portland Police Bureau.

15 *kick your ass* "Non-connect, special report" (28 pages), Portland Police Bureau. Also "Property/Evidence Receipt" and supplemental four-page "Investigation Report." Case No. 03-4-443, April 29, 2003.

16 *contacted Pippen's lawyer* Interview with Multnomah County Deputy District Attorney James Hayden, January 9, 2004.

16 *Lakers guard Gary Payton* *Toronto Star,* "Three Bucks Charged in Assault at Strip Club," April 20, 2003.

16 *an altercation outside* Robbins, "Bucks Had Court Woes Extending Beyond Nets," April 21, 2003.

16 *authorities upped the charges* *Los Angeles Times,* "Charge Added Against Payton," July 20, 2003.

16 *Court officials will meet* Wells, "Cassell Enjoying All-Star Season," February 3, 2004.

16 *Prosecutors in Houston* Associated Press, "Rockets' Griffin Arrested on Drug Charges," April 8, 2003.

16 *assaulting a woman* United Press International, "Houston's Eddie Griffin Accused of Assault," October 25, 2003.

16 *signed by the New Jersey Nets* *Boston Globe,* "Nets Forward Griffin Stays Behind Bars," February 3, 2004.

16 *convicted on the marijuana-possession charge* Youngmisuk, "Griffin Guilty in Post Case." January 21, 2004.

16 *jailed in Houston* Associated Press, "Nets Forward Griffin Stays Behind Bars," February 3, 2004.

16 *indicted on felony charges* Associated Press, "Griffin Indicted, TV Report Says," February 13, 2004.

16 *world with the Nets* *Boston Globe,* "Nets Forward Griffin Stays Behind Bars.".

16 *Betty Ford Center* Ibid.

17 *a jury convicted Richardson* "Press Release," Saginaw County Prosecuting Attorney's Office, October 22, 2003.

17 *jury in Cook County, Illinois* "Court Order," Circuit Court of Cook County (Illinois), *Illinois vs. Robinson,* Case No. 02MC6014105.

17 *forward Chris Webber* "Indictment," *U.S. vs. Webber*, filed in U.S. District Court, Eastern District of Michigan, Southern Division.

17 *guilty of criminal contempt* Nish, "Webber Avoids Jail, Pleading Guilty on a Contempt Charge," July 15, 2003.

17 *Armstrong was arrested* "Charging Affidavit," Orlando Police Department, Case No. 2003-252723, July 7, 2003.

17 *Stackhouse was arrested* Associated Press, "Another Player in Trouble," July 15, 2003.

17 *Armstrong was dismissed* *Washington Post*, "Trail Blazers' Randolph is Charged With DUI," December 3, 2003.

17 *out-of-court settlement* Wyche, "Wizards' Brown Arrested for DUI," August 20, 2003.

17 *Authorities in Chapel Hill* *Greensboro News*, "Forte Set to Receive Warrant for Assault," May 14, 2003.

17 *settlement with the victim* Allen, "Forte Settles Assault Case," August 19, 2003.

17 *lifted the driver's license* Associated Press, "Portland Swingman Qyntel Woods Cited," September 30, 2003.

17 *for possession of marijuana* "Custody Report," Portland Police Bureau, Case No. 03-29940, March 29, 2003.

18 *driving without a license* "Traffic Violation Tow Report," Portland Police Bureau, March 29, 2003.

18 *no contest to the marijuana charge* Associated Press, "Qyntel Woods Pleads No Contest to Marijuana Charge," January 14, 2004.

18 *Grand American Hotel* Sandoval, "Wizards' White Won't Face Charges," May 28, 2003.

18 *insufficient evidence to indict White* Ibid.

23 *at this time they will decline an interview* Conversation with Aaron Goodwin's assistant.

23 *was going off at Stoudamire's house* "Police Log Entry," City of Lake Oswego Police Department," February 23, 2003.

23 *inadmissible as evidence* Hinkelman, "Stoudamire, Prosecutors Agree to Settle," March 20, 2003.

24 *marijuana in his vehicle* "Incident Report," Washington State Patrol, Case No. 02-012-908, November 21, 2002.

24 *cigarette rolling papers* "Additional Narrative," Washington State Patrol, Case No. 02-012-908, November 21, 2002.

24 *play it this way* "Citation," Trooper I. Brian Dorsey, Washington State Patrol, November 21, 2002.

25 *We smoked it all* Ibid.

25 *on the floorboard* "Marijuana Evidence Report," Washington State Patrol, Test No. 02-482/483, December 5, 2002 (date of test).

25 *in the glove box* "Crime Laboratory Report," Washington State Patrol, Laboratory No. 503-000010, January 28, 2003.

25 *Wallace were arrested* "Criminal Citation #C0336303," November 21, 2002.

25 *Randolph agreed to place* Interview with Lewis County Prosecutor Jeremy Randolph.

25 *for a one-year period* Ibid.

25 *his probation in Washington* Ibid.

25 *get the marijuana suppressed* "Minutes" from hearings held at the Justice Court in Pima County, Arizona, before Judge Paul Simon on September 29, 2003, and October 14, 2003 (Case No. CR03-313350).

25 *he may uncover* Ibid.

25 *authorities in Arizona* Interview with Pima County Assistant Prosecutor Bruce Chalk.

26 *fined Stoudamire $250,000* Associated Press, "Blazers fine Stoudamire $250,000," July 7, 2003.

26 *child-education program* Associated Press, "Stoudamire Reinstated with Team, Fine Cleared," October 1, 2003.

CHAPTER ONE: GROSS FELONY

The primary source for the sexual assault crime and the events leading up to it is 221 pages of reports, transcripts, and other documents, including diagrams, obtained from the Bellevue Police Department, which include more than a dozen transcripts of tape-recorded interviews with the principals involved in the case. The Office of the Prosecuting Attorney in King County, Washington, provided copies of the indictment, Patterson's plea agreement, and a copy of his sex offender registration papers. A transcript of Ruben Patterson's plea and sentencing hearing was obtained from the court reporter assigned to the presiding judge in this case.

Additionally, over 50 interviews were conducted with individuals associated with this case, as well as with others closely associated with Patterson and the victim.

Information about Patterson's previous contact with police authorities in Cleveland, Ohio, was provided by the Cleveland Police Department, which supplied printouts of incident reports pertaining to events described in the chapter.

To avoid repeatedly referring to individuals' transcribed interviews with the police or the police reports, I've limited my sourcing below to other documents. If a statement or fact is not sourced, it came from the victim's statement to police or interviews conducted by the author, which are noted in the text.

PAGE

31 *nasty attitude*   Lindy's 2003–2004 Pro Basketball.

31 *doesn't back down*   Ibid.

32 *held up at gunpoint*   "Incident Report," Cleveland Police Department, Case No. 1994-00021734, April 4, 1994.

32 *I'll get all you*   "Incident Report," Cleveland Police Department, Case No. 1997-00025209, March 3, 1997.

32 *fell to the ground*   "Incident Report," Cleveland Police Department, Case No. 1997-00025654, March 31, 1997.

36 *the account that Jenny told*   "Case Report," Bellevue Police Department, Case No. 00B-11121, September 30, 2000. The victim provided a tape-recorded statement on October 4, 2000 (49 transcribed pages) and a follow-up tape-recorded statement on November 6, 2000 (31 transcribed pages).

36 *flew home to Cleveland*   "Indictment," *Ohio vs. Ruben Patterson*, Case No. CR396453, June 11, 2000.

37 *Lewis suffered bruises*   "Incident Report," Cleveland Police Department, Case No. 2000-00277278, July 19, 2000.

38 *I'm going to be mad, aren't I?*   Transcript of police interview with Susie Sanders. October 18, 2000.

43 *Shannon, get over here*   Transcript of police interview with Mr. Stevens, October 31, 2000.

CHAPTER TWO: THE PROBLEM SOLVERS

The primary sources for Patterson arrest and conviction in Ohio on assault charges are police reports and summaries from the Cleveland Police Department, documents obtained from the Cuyahoga County Prosecutor's office, and documents obtained from the Cuyahoga County Court of Common Pleas. Interviews were also conducted with Cuyahoga County Prosecutor's Office and the Cuyahoga County Sheriff's Office.

PAGE

45 *She's full of shit*   Transcript of police interview with Rebecca Vidmore, October 23, 2000.

45 *receiving prohibited payments*   Sullivan, "Too harsh a penalty? Hardly," December 3, 1997.

46 *kicked an unconscious teammate*   McCallum, "'I know he's gone off before.'".

46 *marijuana to an undercover*   Associated Press, "Trouble Continues for Former Cincinnati Star," June 12, 1997.

46 *assaulting his girlfriend*   Ibid.

46 *walked up and whacked*   Cour, "Art Long Works to Overcome Famous Temper," February 2, 2002.

46 *with police in Georgia*   Wolff, "Breaking Through.".

46 *1996 cover story*   Ibid.

47 *repeatedly changed his story*   Shelman, "Patterson Suspension: 14 Games," December 3, 1997.

48 *Dan Fegan was graduated*   News Release, by CCN Matthews, December 6, 2000.

49 *six-month suspended jail*   "Plea Note," Cuyahoga County Court of Common Pleas, Case No. 396453, January 29, 2001.

49 *acquitted Melvin Scott*   Interview with Cuyahoga County prosecutor Brendan Sheehan.

49 *After this case*   Ibid.

50 *about this anymore*   Transcript of police interview with Vidmore, October 23, 2000.

51 *dollar to just go away*   Interview with Rebecca Vidmore.

54 *accused Lowry of fondling*   Simon and Postman, "Settlement Carries a Price," July 15, 1995.

54 *former aid $97,500*   Paulson and George, "Harassment Claim Costs Lowry $97,500," July 15, 1995.

54 *molesting another*   Kelley, "Gale Gilbert Resurrects Life," January 23, 1991.

54 *spare Gilbert any jail time*   Interview with John Wolfe.

55 *she had been assaulted*   Henderson, "Warrior Star Mullin Questioned by Police," April 4, 1994.

55 *Whelan and his female partner*   Interview with Lieutenant Dan Whelan.

55 *Pollak introduced himself*   Ibid.

57 *eight-page internal screening*   These documents were viewed at the City Attorney's Office in Seattle, Washington, on January 14, 2004.

57 *retired sex crimes detective*   See *www.redunn.com*.

58　*role in the surveillance*　Interview with John Wolfe.

60　*sufficient facts for a jury*　"Information," Superior Court of Washington for King County, Case No. 01-1-04295-1, May 1, 2001.

CHAPTER THREE: HUSH MONEY

The primary sources for the information about the sexual assault lawsuits filed against Michael Olowokandi and Elden Campbell were court documents and interviews. I obtained the complete court files from: *Salcido vs. Campbell*, Case No. YC-030310, California Superior Court, County of Los Angeles, November 5, 1997, and from: *Jane Doe vs. Michael Olowokandi*, Case No. CV007824, San Joaquin County Superior Court, June 1, 1999. Additionally, I conducted on-the-record interviews with each of the attorneys involved in those two cases. I also spoke to Elden Campbell's agent Richard Howell on more than one occasion.

The primary sources for the Ruben Patterson domestic-violence arrest were police documents from the City of Tualatin Police Department in Oregon, as well as roughly a dozen interviews with individuals who were associated or had knowledge of the case, which included Tim McGee, who represents Patterson.

PAGE

63　*got a zillion dollars*　Transcript of police interview with Isaac Vicknair, November 6, 2000.

63　*the Westside Church*　See *www.westsidechurch.com*.

63　*longtime friend*　Conversation with Richard Vicknair.

64　*what it was about*　Interview with Jenny Stevens.

65　*Wolfe issued a statement*　Ith and Demasio, "Sonics' Patterson Faces Rape Charge," May 8, 2001.

66　*treated very seriously*　Demasio, "Patterson Plea May Also Bring Penalty," May 9, 2001.

66　*a painful lesson*　Hearing Transcript (Court Reporter: Pam Weekley), Case No. 01-1-04295-1, May 15, 2001.

66　*out between us*　Ibid.

67　*around the league*　Ibid.

67　*were going to get*　Ibid.

68　*responsible for his actions*　Ibid.

68　*live with the negatives*　Ibid.

69　*third-richest man in America*　*Forbes*, Special Issue, 2003 Edition.

70 *I'm a great guy* Hall, "Blazers Sign Ex-Sonics Patterson," August 2, 2001.

70 *a registered sex offender* "Sex and Kidnapping Offender Registration," Appendix J in the "Judgment and Sentence," Case No. 01-0-04295-1.

71 *a half a million dollars* Interview with Larry Feldman.

72 *millions of dollars* Thomas, "Jackson Challenges $60 Million Lawsuit," June 12, 1996.

72 *sued after Pebbles Salcido* "Complaint," *Salcido vs. Campbell,* Case No. YC-030310, California Superior Court, County of Los Angeles, November 5, 1997.

72 *police complaint against* Interview with Redondo Beach Police Department.

72 *Campbell denied the charge* "Answer," *Salcido vs. Campbell,* December 23, 1997.

72 *sexual assault suit* "Complaint," *Jane Doe vs. Michael Olowokandi,* Case No. CV007824, San Joaquin County Superior Court, June 1, 1999.

73 *$15-million contract* "NBA Notes," *Washington Post,* January 30, 1999.

73 *a matter of business* Interview with Daniel Sullivan.

73 *things are involved* Interview with Stewart Tabak.

73 *supervised settlement conference* "Status Conference Minute Order," April 24, 2000.

74 *I heard the tape* Interview with Tabak.

74 *the light of day* Ibid.

74 *arrested by Manhattan Beach* "Incident Report," Manhattan Beach Police Department, Booking No. 94711, December 1, 2001.

74 *these false allegations* "NBA Notes," San Antonio Express-News, December 4, 2001.

75 *rob herself of property* *Toronto Star,* "Clipper's Not in the Clear Yet," December 6, 2001.

75 *we are not prosecuting* Associated Press, "No Charges Filed Against LA Center," December 14, 2001.

76 *needed proper guidance* Interview with Tim McGee.

76 *blood was dripping* "Incident Report," City of Tualatin Police Department, Case No. 02-3647, November 25, 2002.

77 *abuse her again* Statement of Shannon Patterson, contained in a "Continuation Report," City of Tualatin Police Department, November 25, 2002.

77 *I was called* Interview with John Wolfe.

78 *contact toward her* Interview with Tim McGee.

78 *did not assault me* Associated Press, "Ruben Patterson Was Arrested for Assault," November 26, 2002.

78 *one of those situations* Statement by District Attorney Bob Hermann, December 2, 2002.

78 *guilty in everything* Interview with Tim McGee.

79 *a business advisor* Ibid.

CHAPTER FOUR: SOMETHING BAD HAPPENED

The primary source for the events surrounding the sexual assault allegations made against Celtics players was court documents filed in *Jane Doe vs. Ronald Mercer et al.,* Case No. 98-10649RGS, U.S. District Court, District of Massachusetts, April 15, 1998. Initially, all of these documents were filed under seal. But by the time I did my reporting, the seal had been lifted and I was given complete access to the lengthy court file, which included multiple filings and answers by the Celtics players. I also spoke with lawyers representing the players and lawyers representing the alleged victim. I also had contact with the Middlesex County District Attorney's Office and the Waltham Police Department.

PAGE

84 *the Celtics released Webb* For a complete account of the Marcus Webb case, see Benedict, *Public Heroes, Private Felons: Athletes and Crimes Against Women.*

85 *Something bad happened* "Complaint," *Jane Doe vs. Ronald Mercer et al.,* Case No. 98-10649RGS, U.S. District Court, District of Massachusetts, April 15, 1998.

85 *a subsequent civil complaint* "Answer," (filed by Billups and Mercer), *Doe vs. Mercer,* Case No. 98-10649RGS, filed March 18, 1999.

86 *the night in question* "Answer" (filed by Walker), *Doe vs. Mercer,* November 16, 1999.

86 *anyonebody else from the Celtics* Weber, "Woman Claims She Was Assaulted," December 4, 1997.

87 *with the trade* Interview with Dennis Kelly.

87 *Mercer and Billups paid* Associated Press, "Ex-Celtics Settle Lawsuit with Woman," January 12, 2000.

87 *Walker subsequently reached* Murphy, "Celtic Walker Settles With Accuser," March 7, 2000.

88 *laced with a drug* "Complaint," *Salcido vs Campbell,* Case No. YC-

030310, California Superior Court, County of Los Angeles, November 5, 1997.

88 *like a cheap suit* Interview with Larry Feldman.

88 *those cases any day* Interview with Joe Hopkins.

89 *hires a civil lawyer* Interview with Bill Vose.

89 *and left the country* Ibid.

89 *Barkley pled no contest* Associated Press, "Barkley fined," June 26, 1998.

90 *no charges against Coleman* *Washington Post,* "No Charges Against Coleman," July 27, 1994.

90 *Howard sued Melissa Reed* "Complaint," *Juwan Howard vs. Melissa Reed,* Case No. 188604, Circuit Court for Montgomery County (Maryland), June 28, 1996.

90 *pay Howard $100,000* "Order of Default," *Howard vs. Reed,* September 29, 1998.

91 *a fourteen-year-old girl* See Benedict and Yaeger, *Pros & Cons: The Criminals Who Play in the NFL.*

CHAPTER FIVE: NO STRINGS ATTACHED

All quotes and descriptions of what transpired inside the Gold Club were obtained from trial transcripts, which I ordered and received for a fee from the federal court reporter assigned to the presiding judge at the trial. I also obtained a copy of the government's indictment. Interviews were also conducted with former Gold Club dancer and government witness Jana Pelnis, as well as her criminal defense attorney, Barbara Moon.

PAGE

94 *Ewing took a seat* Trial Transcript (Court Reporter: Nancy Smith-Wells), *U.S. vs. Steven Kaplan et al.,* Docket No. 1:99-CR-609, testimony of Jana Pelnis, July 23, 2001.

95 *Take care of Mr. Ewing* Ibid.

95 *racketeering indictment* "Indictment," *U.S. vs. Steven Kaplan et al.,* Case No. 1:99-CR-609, superseding September 1, 2000.

98 *the truth only* Interview with Barbara Moon.

99 *women are very vulnerable* Ibid.

100 *morning sickness so severe* Interview with Barbara Moon.

100 *Pelnis pleaded guilty* Associated Press, "Gold Club Stripper Admits Prostitution," August 22, 2000.

101 *sitting beside me* Trial Transcript (Court Reporter: Nancy Smith-

Wells), *U.S. vs. Steven Kaplan et al.,* Docket No. 1:99-CR-609, testimony of Patrick Ewing, July 23, 2001.

103 *Pelnis was sequestered* Interview with Jana Pelnis.

103 *I was sent up to his room* Trial Transcript (Court Reporter: Nancy Smith-Wells), *U.S. vs. Steven Kaplan et al.,* Docket No. 1:99-CR-609, testimony of Jana Pelnis, July 23, 2001.

105 *get on that plane* Interview with Barbara Moon.

105 *no criminal record* Ibid.

105 *Kaplan pleaded guilty* CNN.com, "Strip Club Boss Cops Plea," August 3, 2001.

106 *his life to Christ* CNN.com, "Sex, Sports, and the Mob," June 15, 2001.

106 *$50-million defamation suit* "Case Summary," *Davis vs. Sicignano,* U.S. District Court, Eastern District of New York (Brooklyn), Case No. 1:01 cv-04057-RJD-CLP, June 13, 2001.

106 *case was dismissed* Ibid. (Order signed by Judge Raymond Dearie on July 24, 2001.

106 *What's the big deal?* *Toronto Star,* "Oakley Got Freebies at Strip Club," December 8, 1999.

107 *Oakley struck Saronda* "Arrest Citation," Atlanta Police Department, Complaint No. 126-H-5546, August 26, 1991.

107 *in a three-way* Interview with Detective Rick Chambers.

107 *Oakley was charged* "Accusation," State Court of Fulton County Georgia, Acusation No. 219122, May 30, 2000.

107 *court dismissed the case* Ibid.

107 *Pelnis is the mother* Interview with Jana Pelnis.

107 *Rita Williams-Ewing* Singleton, "Unlike Knicks, Ewing's Wife Does Fine," February 14, 1998.

107 *Knicks City Dancer* Rush and Molloy, "Divorce Fight?" May 8, 1998.

107 *divorce was finalized* Conversation with Raoul Felder's office.

107 *write a novel* Sutton, "Hoop Skirts," September 4, 1998.

CHAPTER SIX: DO YOU KNOW WHO I AM?

The primary sources for this chapter are documents obtained from the Portland Police Bureau pertaining to Bonzi Wells and Cliff Robinson. I also conducted interviews with Portland Police Department officials and with former Blazers player Erick Barkley.

PAGE

112 *to start today*   Smith, "Wells' Focus Self-image," *Journal Gazette,* July 31, 2003.

112–13 *Leave the area!*   "Investigation Report," Portland Police Bureau, Case No. 01-84125, September 6, 2001.

113 *it's time to go*   "Narrative," Portland Police Bureau, September 6, 2001.

114 *the worst verbal abuse*   Interview with Officer Mark Friedman.

114 *Player of the Year*   Associated Press, "What's Left for Bonzi Wells," January 16, 1998.

114 *marks were visible*   "Arrest Report," Ball State University, Case No. 960-4077, March 28, 1996.

114 *Wells was jailed*   "Booking Photograph" and correspondence from Delaware County Sheriff's office, Muncie, Indiana.

115 *knew who I was*   Interview with Erick Barkley.

115 *I'd be mad, too*   Ibid.

115 *it went away*   Ibid.

116 *case is dropped*   Interview with officer Mark Friedman.

117 *striking a female police officer*   "Incident Report," Portland Police Bureau, Case No. 90-36868, April 29, 1990.

117 *the hit worthwhile*   Ibid.

117–18 *pled guilty to assault*   *New York Times,* "Guilty Plea for Blazer," May 30, 1990.

118 *Hummer waiving guns*   "Custody Report," Portland Police Bureau, Case No. 97078629, July 30, 1997.

118 *pleaded guilty to possession*   *Seattle Times,* "Still No Answers," July 11, 2002.

118 *messing with me?*   "Charging Affidavit," Orlando Police Department, Case No. 2003-252723, July 7, 2003.

119 *judge dismissed the case*   *Washington Post,* "Trail Blazers' Randolph is Charged With DUI," December 3, 2003.

119 *110 miles per hour*   D'Angelo, *Palm Beach Post,* June 24, 1997.

119 *I'll take him down*   *Chicago Sun-Times,* "Heat's Hardaway in Trouble," June 24, 1997.

120 *struck NBA referee*   Eggers, "Spit Didn't Exactly Polish," November 22, 2003.

120 *fined him $10,000*   Ibid.

120 *threw his gum*   Ibid.

120 *spit in his face*   Ibid.

121 *Robinson's account prompted*   Ibid.

121 *soft-assed white boys*   Ibid.

121 *I am not aware of it* Ibid.
121 *stripped him of his* USA Today, "Trail Blazers sit Wells," November 19, 2003.
121 *Blazers traded Wells* USA Today, "Trail Blazers Make Statement," December 4, 2003.
122 *a sign of the times* Interview with Friedman, September 23, 2003.
122 *caliber of Bonzi Wells* NBA.com, "Bonzi on the Move," December 3, 2003.
122 *we are NBA players* Sports Illustrated, "They Said It," November 17, 2003.

CHAPTER SEVEN: PUT YOUR HANDS UP

The primary sources for the armed robbery incident and the events leading up to it are first, hundreds of pages of documents from the Story County Attorney's Office, including transcripts of depositions with the witnesses, evidence reports, and the indictment. Second, I obtained dozens of documents from the Ames Police Department, which included incident reports, narratives, and summaries of interviews with witnesses, including a transcribed copy of a tape-recorded interview that investigators conducted with Sam Mack at Mary Greeley Hospital. Finally, I conducted over 25 interviews with prosecutors, police officers, witnesses, defense lawyers, and university officials. (I did not have access to trial transcripts, as they were destroyed under the court's document retention policy. The court reporter prepared the transcripts was also contacted, but neither he nor the presiding judge had maintained trial transcripts.)

For this chapter I also relied on confidential "Interoffice Communications" from Iowa State University, documents from Sam Mack's "Disciplinary File" at the university, Mack's grade transcripts, and billing records from the Rosenberg Law Firm. The law-firm billing records were obtained through a public records request filed with Arizona State University's police department, which seized the records from Mack's apartment while executing a search warrant in connection with a rape investigation involving Mack during his brief tenure at the university.

PAGE
124 *Are you sure?* Interview with coach Johnny Orr.
124 *in the school's history* Information about Orr obtained from a document titled: "Iowa State Head Men's Basketball Coach Johhny

Orr," provided by Iowa State University's Athletic Media Relations Department.

124 *a box of bullets* Prosecutor's files.

125 *she heard a gunshot* "Deposition of Amy Konek," (taken May 17, 1898), *Iowa vs. Sam Mack*, Case No. 14599.

125 *she could not see* Ibid.

125 *grabbed over $1,600* "Incident Report," Ames Police Department, Case No. 8901370-V, March 30, 1989.

126 *Police! Drop the gun!* "Detail," and "Supplement," Ames PD, March 30, 1989.

126 *Mack continued crawling* Ibid.

126 *I closed it* Transcript of police interview with Sam Mack, conducted March 31, 1989 at Mary Greeley Hospital.

127 *The Burger King sack* Ibid.

127 *I didn't do it, coach* Interview with Orr.

127 *his mother was unemployed* "Deposition of Levin White" (taken May 17, 1989).

128 *the towing fee* Ibid.

128 *theft charge dismissed* White's criminal history was documented in prosecutorial files viewed by the author. Also see, Fowler and Witosky, "ISU's White Arrested for Robbery," April 4, 1989.

128 *guilty to armed robbery* Hemphill, "White Enters Guilty Plea," April 29, 1989.

129 *office of Ray Rosenberg* Interview with attorney Ray Rosenberg.

129 *Sheppard telephoned Sam* Interview with attorney Barry Sheppard.

129 *a $5,000 retainer* Billing records from the Rosenberg Law Firm.

129 *gunpoint to participate* Interview with attorney Paul Scott, November 24, 2003.

130 *or using cocaine?* "Deposition of Levin White" (taken May 17, 1989).

130 *out-of-wedlock baby* Ibid.

130 *did not grant immunity* Interview with former prosecutor Mark Cullen.

131 *We all did* "Deposition of Ray Carreathers" (taken July 6, 1989).

131 *to get cocaine* Ibid.

131 *Can't snort it* Ibid.

131 *the University Community* "Administrative Hearing Notice," Dean of Students Office, Iowa State University, April 3, 1989.

132 *a confidential memorandum* Letter from university vice president Thomas Thielen to Sam Mack, dated May 23, 1989.

132 *privileges have been suspended*   Text of statement by president Gordon Eaton, March 31, 1989.
132 *feared getting sued*   Interview with Orr.
133 *Mack notified the university*   Memorandum from Dr. Margaret Healey to Vice President Thomas Thielen, dated May 19, 1989.
134 *suspension be removed*   Ibid.
134 *Thielen notified Mack*   Letter dated May 23, 1989.
134 *future educational endeavors*   Ibid.
135 *this course schedule*   Grade and course transcripts, Iowa State University.
135 *great strengths indeed!*   Letter dated May 30, 1989.

CHAPTER EIGHT: STAYING POWER

The primary source for the reporting on the rape investigation involving Sam Mack at Arizona State University was over 200 pages of documents obtained from the Arizona State University Department of Public Safety, including police reports, search warrants, custody reports, medical and forensic reports, and transcripts of tape-recorded interviews with Mack, his accuser and various witnesses, including members of the Arizona State basketball team. Interviews were also conducted with lawyers and individuals who spoke to Mack about this incident.

For the gun-related arrest in Harvey, Illinois, I obtained a copy of the Harvey Police Department incident report and obtained information from the records clerk at the Cook County courthouse where this case was adjudicated.

PAGE
137 *Rosenberg decided to proceed*   Interview with Rosenberg.
137 *big basketball fans*   Ibid.
138 *liked in the community*   Ibid.
138 *make more money*   Burkhead, "White Refuses to Testify," July 13, 1989.
138 *a terrible witness*   Interview with Paul Scott.
138–39 *met in consultation sessions*   Rosenberg Law Firm billing records.
139 *Orr was the leader*   Information about Orr obtained from a document titled: "Iowa State Head Men's Basketball Coach Johhny Orr," provided by Iowa State University's Athletic Media Relations Department.

139 *Mack signed autographs* Photograph obtained from the *Ames Daily Tribune* (Iowa).

139 *no question about that* Barnes, "Mack Testifies," July 18, 1989.

140 *robbed the Burger King* Interview with Orr.

140 *badly for his mother* Ibid.

140 *incidents of trouble* Burkhead, "Jury Explains Mack Verdict," July 21, 1989.

141 *The gun's not mine* "Incident Report," Harvey Police Department (Illinois), Case No. 9599C-88, July 19, 1988.

141 *the gun case expunged* Interview with Sheppard. Also, interview with clerk at the Cook County records office.

141 *You can't take chances* Interview with Orr.

142 *basketball helped him* Interview with Scott.

142 *he might have made* Editorial in *Ames Daily Tribune* (Iowa), July 21, 1989.

143 *justice system again* Interview with Scott.

143 *anybody I got.'* Interview with Orr.

143 *didn't rape that girl* Ibid.

143 *tape-recorded police statement* Transcript of police interview with victim, November 7, 1989.

144 *room is a box-shaped* Diagram from the police file.

144 *I was crying* "Incident Report," Arizona State University Police Department, Case No. 89-3133, November 5, 1989.

144 *"wiggled" his way* Transcript of police interview.

145 *rape-kit exam* "Chain of Custody Form," Tempe St. Lukes Hospital, No. 89-3133, November 7, 1989.

145 *two vaginal smears* "Scientific Examination Report," Arizona Department of Public Safety," November 16, 1989.

145 *consistent with semen* "Agency Request for Scientific Examination," Arizona Department of Public Safety.

145 *warrant to take blood* "Order" to obtain body fluids," Arizona State University Police Department, November 7, 1989.

145 *I'm willing to do whatever* Transcript of police interview with Sam Mack, November 8, 1989.

146 *Gilbert, drew two vials* "Supplemental Report," Arizona State University Police Department, November 8, 1989.

147 *the first sex move?* Transcript of police interview with Mack.

147 *all the way down* Ibid.

148 *Mack called attorney Barry* Interview with Sheppard.

148 *detrimental to the team* Burgess, "Mack Suspended Over Assault Probe," November 9, 1989.

149 *This is the United States* Somers, "Mack Linked to Sexual Assault," November 9, 1989.

149 *can fire his ass* Burgess, November 9, 1989.

149 *felony counts of sexual assault* "Charges Submitted" document, dated November 16, 1989.

149 *no reasonable likelihood* Burgess, "County Attorney Declines," November 21, 1989.

150 *heard her protest* Email from FitzGerald to the author, February 3, 2004.

150 *American Express card* Associated Press, "Sports News," March 13, 1990.

150 *kicked Mack off the team* *Houston Chronicle,* February 12, 1992.

151 *with criminal mischief* "Incident Report," University of Houston Police Department, Case No. 92-35290, May 1, 1992.

151 *charge was dropped* "Case Information," District Clerk's Office, Houston, TX.

CHAPTER NINE: CRIMINALS ON SCHOLARSHIP

The primary sources for the arrests of Anthony Peeler in Missouri are documents obtained from the Columbia Police Department in Columbia, Missouri; documents obtained through the Cole County clerk of courts, and prior reporting done by the *St. Louis Post-Dispatch,* the *Kansas City Star,* and articles obtained through the Columbia Missourian Newspaper Library.

All information reported on Gary Trent was obtained from prior published reports.

Primary sources for reporting on Sam Mack's drug case are court documents from *Illinois vs. Samuel Mack* (Case No. OOMC6011644), obtained from the Markham Courthouse in Cook County, Illinois, as well as police records from the Phoenix (Illinois) Police Department, which made the arrest. Interviews were also conducted with police and with Mack's criminal defense attorney.

Primary sources for reporting on Sam Mack's attempted murder case are documents from *Illinois vs. Samuel Mack* (Case No. 03601452601), obtained from the Markham Courthouse in Cook County, Illinois, as well as interviews with the State's Attorney's Office in Cook County and Mack's criminal defense attorney.

PAGE

153 *had only paid $6,000*   Rosenberg Law Firm billing records.

153 *Rosenberg sued Mack*   *Houston Chronicle,* "NBA Notes," February 2, 1993.

153 *withholdings were paid*   Interview with Rosenberg.

154 *sense of invulnerability*   Ibid.

154 *substance-abuse facility*   Gregorian, "Peeler Arrested Again," June 23, 1992.

154 *bite marks*   "Incident Report," Columbia Police Department, Case No. 92011138, June 3, 1992.

155 *cut off her breath*   "Supplementary Report," Columbia Police Department, June 9, 1992.

155 *campus police cited him*   "Supplementary Report," Columbia Police Department, May 30, 1992.

156 *Peeler pleaded guilty*   "Criminal Docket," Cole County Court, Missouri, Case No. CR192-0071F.

156 *honored by the Big Eight*   Gregorian, "Mizzou's Peeler Is Named," June 18, 1992.

156 *$2.1 million in punitive*   Bondy, *New York Daily News,* September 1, 1998.

156 *Peeler was arrested again*   Gregorian, "Peeler Arrested Again," June 23, 1992.

156 *dropped the case*   Gregorian, "KC Prosecutor Drops Charge," June 24, 1992.

157 *a life sentence*   Schmaltz, "Trent Steered Clear of Trouble," March 9, 1993.

157 *Gary was selling cocaine*   Blauvelt, "Shooting for a Better Life," November 30, 1994.

157 *mobsters and gangsters*   Ibid.

157 *domestic-violence charges*   Clarkson, "Trent Brings Plenty of Baggage," February 14, 1998.

158 *Trent pleaded guilty*   Ibid.

158 *grand jury declined to indict*   Voisin, "Pro Basketball: NBA Western Conference," March 30, 1997.

158 *I don't know*   Interview with Scott.

159 *run-ins with Mack*   Interview with Derek Guess.

159 *felony drug possession*   "Complaint," *Illinois vs. Mack,* Circuit Court of Cook County, Illinois, (Case No. OOMC6011644). Also see Vivanco, "Ex-NBA Star Faces Drug Charges," July 12, 2000.

159 *and I'm innocent*   Associated Press, "Former NBA player Says He's Innocent," August 2, 2000.

159 *terms of probation* "Order," *Illinois vs. Mack*, September 27, 2000.

159 *criminal mischief in Houston* "Case Information," District Clerk's Office, Houston, Texas,.

160 *great bodily harm* "Grand Jury" notice, *Illinois vs. Mack*, Circuit Court of Cook County, Illinois (Case No. 03601452601), August 2003.

160 *nothing to everything* Interview with Scott.

161 *and maybe sooner* Interview with Rosenberg.

162 *an unfortunate statistic* Interview with Sheppard.

CHAPTER TEN: INDULGE ME

The primary sources for the Anthony Mason sexual assault cases are: first, hundreds of pages of documents from Monmouth County Prosecutor's Office in Freehold, New Jersey (Prosecutor's Case No. 0002274-01); second, police records from the Tinton Falls Police Department in Tinton Falls, New Jersey (Case No. 2001-36-2678); third, records from the Brooklyn Hospital (New York); fourth, police records from the City of New York Police Department (Complaint No. 2001-088-004090); fourth, interviews with prosecutors and law-enforcement officials in New Jersey and North Carolina, as well as lawyers representing Anthony Mason.

PAGE

167 *deodorant, and a toothbrush* This and all information preceding it about Tamika and her ride to New Jersey come from police records based on tape-recorded interviews with her and other witnesses.

168 *Shadi did as directed* "Statement, Shadi Khader," taken and recorded by Monmouth County prosecutors on July 14, 2001.

168 *want to be bothered* "Investigative Report," Monmouth County Prosecutor's Office, Case No. 0002274-01.

168 *between my thighs* Ibid.

168 *Mase, open the door* Ibid.

169 *pillowcases for evidence* "Supplementary Investigation Report," Tinton Falls Police Department, July 11–14, 2001.

169 *a detailed statement to* "Statement," taken and recorded by Monmouth County prosecutors on July 12, 2001.

169 *there's a rape complaint* Interview with Franklin Rothman.

170 *with statutory rape* "Investigation Report," New York City Police Department.

170 *sperm excluded Mason* Interview with Franklin Rothman.

170 *Mason pleaded guilty*   United Press International, "Felony Charges Dropped Against Mason," June 25, 1998. Also, see *New York Times,* "Mason Is Guilty of 2 Misdemeanors," June 26, 1998.

170 *Mason offered to fly*   Interview with Mecklenburg prosecutor David Wallace.

170 *refused to wear a condom*   Associated Press, "Prosecutors decline to bring," April 13, 1999.

171 *against her will*   Interview with Wallace.

171 *end of the line*   Interview with Rothman.

171 *what knowledge you have*   "Statement," Anthony Mason, taken and recorded by Monmouth County prosecutors on August 10, 2001.

171 *come down here for*   Ibid.

172 *two in my bag*   Ibid.

172 *Honecker acknowledged*   Interview with Robert Honecker.

172 *those problems existed*   Ibid.

173 *prosecutors dropped*   "Screening Memorandum," Monmouth County Prosecutor's Office, Case No. 02-01076, signed October 7, 2002.

173 *want to cooperate*   Interview with Honecker.

173 *the case being closed*   Ibid.

173 *an escort service*   Interview with Rothman.

173 *pay to get laid.*   Ibid.

CHAPTER ELEVEN: SLEEPING WITH THE ENEMY

Primary sources for the Glenn Robinson domestic-violence case are: first, court documents from *Illinois vs. Robinson,* Case No. 02MC6014105, filed in Cook County, Illinois; second, documents obtained from the City of Chicago Heights Department of Police (Event No.01-02-025973); third, documents obtained from the Office of the State's Attorney in Cook County, Illinois; fourth, court documents from the civil case *French vs. Robinson,* Case No. 2003-L-007427, filed in the Law Division of the Circuit Court of Cook County, Illinois; fifth, documents from the "Petition for Custody" filed against Glenn Robinson in Cook County Circuit Court by Jonta French on July 22, 2002. I also conducted person interviews with lawyers, police officers, prosecutors and witnesses.

Information about the Robinson home where the domestic-violence incident occurred was obtained from real estate and property records in Cook County, Illinois.

Sources for Robinson's arrest in Miami Beach, Florida, were obtained from the Miami Beach Police Department, which supplied documents and police photographs from Case No. 99-24196.

Sources for the Jason Richardson domestic-violence case are police records from the Saginaw Township Police Department (Michigan), Incident No. 718-0002366-03; records from the Saginaw County Prosecuting Attorney's Office, Case No. 2366-03; and court records for *Michigan vs. Richardson,* Case No. 061297-00, filed in the 70th District Court for the County of Saginaw.

Sources for the Anfernee Hardaway case were obtained from the Paradise Valley Police Department (Case No. 242615.A94) and records from *Arizona vs. Hardaway,* Case No. 22088-LFMC-2000, obtained from the Town Attorney's Office in Paradise Valley.

All information about Warren Moon's domestic-violence case comes from Benedict and Yaeger, *Pros and Cons: The Criminals Who Play in the NFL,* Warner Books, 1998.

PAGE

175 *I'll be out there* "Complaint," *French vs. Robinson,* Case No. 2003-L-007427.

176 *now, don't you* "Offense Report," Chicago Heights Department of Police, Event No.01-02-025973.

176 *what the f——I say,* "Complaint.".

176 *ready to die* "Offense Report.".

176 *we are going* "Complaint.".

177 *away my baby* Ibid.

177 *rounds of ammunition* "Offense Report," Chicago Heights Police Department.

178 *displayed a gun* "Affidavit of Probable Cause," Commonwealth of Pennsylvania, Case No. 02-18-44613.

178 *fourteen-count indictment* Jasner, "Sixers Proceeding," July 12, 2002.

179 *judge dismissed twelve* Associated Press, "Judge Drops Felony Charges," July 31, 2002.

179 *this kind of case* San Diego Union-Tribune, "No Charges for Iverson," September 13, 2002.

180 *superstar Warren Moon,* See Benedict and Yaeger, *Pros and Cons.*

182 *You stupid bitch* "Incident Report," Saginaw Township Police Department, Incident No. 718-0002366-03, April 29, 2003.

183 *head on the wall* Ibid.

183 *Thomas offered Richardson* Interview with prosecutor Michael Thomas.

184 *never provided it* Ibid.

184 *he admitted grabbing* Tucker, "'He Pushed me,'" *Saginaw News,* August 28, 2003.

184 *judge sentenced him* "Sentencing Agreement," *Michigan vs. Richardson,* October 22, 2003.

185 *the Chicago Tribune* Hirsley, "Athletes and Guns," February 9, 2003.

185 *the New York Times* Freeman, "More N.F.L. Player Turn to Guns," December 26, 2003.

185 *Warriors' Byron Houston* Shirk, "Warriors Didn't Know Houston," May 20, 1993.

186 *to protect yourself* Hirsley, "Athletes and Guns.".

187 *out of the truck* "Continuation Report," Paradise Valley Police Department, Report No. 242615.A94, November 20, 2000.

187 *I'm sick of you* Ibid.

187 *Prosecutors offered him* Interview with prosecutor Andrew Miller.

187 *have been misrepresented* Gomez, "Hardaway Ruling Won't Resolve Case," Arizona Republic, January 13, 2001.

188 *prepared to go to trial* Interview with Miller.

188 *I ain't talking to you* "Complaint/Arrest Affidavit," Miami Beach Police Department, Case No. 99-24196, June 28, 1999.

188 *I don't have shit to say* Ibid.

189 *for disorderly conduct* *Tampa Tribune,* "Robinson cited," December 4, 1997.

189 *Indiana, police investigated* Associated Press, "Sports News," September 21, 1995.

189 *Connors was surprised* Interview with prosecutor Tammy Connors.

189 *Connors reminded jurors* Ibid.

191 *miss three games for it* Associated Press, "Glenn Robinson hopes to make an impact," July 25, 2003.

CHAPTER TWELVE: POUND OF FLESH

The scene descriptions and dialogue pertaining to the Paul Pierce stabbing incident come from over 2,000 pages of documents from the Boston Police Department, Boston Police Homicide Unit, crime-scene photographs, Suffolk County grand jury transcripts, grand jury photographs, transcripts of tape-recorded interviews with police, and Suffolk County court records. Due to the unusually high number of police and court documents needed to piece together the scenes detailed in the chapter, I've only listed those sources that do not come from the police and court documents.

PAGE

194 *Man enough to pull*   Zicarelli, "The Answer Is," *Toronto Sun,* November 22, 2002.

194 *ain't real to me*   Olson, "Keeping it Real," *Daily News,* July 17, 2002.

194 *an edgy street reputation*   Nichols, "Toil and Trouble," *Washington Post,* October 29, 2002.

194 *Get Rich or Die Tryin'*   Press Release, "Reebok and 50 Cent Announce the Successful Launch of New 'G-Unit Collection by RBK,' Reebok, November 25, 2003.

195 *bad boy out there*   Wilstein, "Iverson Shows His Arrogance," Associated Press, July 15, 2002.

195 *Governor Douglas Wilder*   Bailey, "Sports News," Associated Press, June 6, 1994.

195 *marijuana in the car*   Asher, "Iverson Trial Date Set," *Washington Post,* August 14, 1997.

196 *possession of cocaine*   Buffalo News, "Iverson's Car Impounded," July 14, 1998. Also see *Washington Post,* "Two Men in Iverson's Car Are Arrested," July 14, 1998.

196 *What is your emergency?*   Transcript of 911 call, September 25, 2000.

199 *Ragland shot and killed*   Latour and Kurkjian, "Two Suspects Held," *Boston Globe,* September 28, 2000.

204 *Battie pleaded no contest*   Associated Press, "Battie Enters Plea," August 4, 1999.

205 *be careful*   Boston Herald, "Coach Pitino to Players," September 28, 2000.

207 *unfortunate incident for all*   Gelzinis, "Despite Little Call," *Boston Herald,* October 8, 2002.

CHAPTER THIRTEEN: SEE NO EVIL

The primary sources for the incident at Walt Disney World Institute involving the Indiana Pacers are documents from Case No. 97-409829 at the Orange County Sheriff's Office in Orlando, photographs of the victim and her injuries that were taken at the hospital and obtained by the author from the forensics lab at the Orange County Sheriff's Office, as well as interviews.

PAGE

209 *crying and bleeding badly* "Incident Report," Orange County Sheriff's Office, Case No. 97-409829, October 8, 1997.

210 *small piece of bone* Police photographs, obtained from Forensics Lab, Orange County Sheriff's Office.

210 *wired in place* "Investigative Report," Orange County Sheriff's Office.

211 *Bird produced Smits* Ibid.

212 *he didn't care* Associated Press, "Pacers say Davis not Involved," October 10, 1997.

212 *in the incident* Ibid.

213 *couldn't have missed this* Interview with Orange County Sheriff's official.

215 *unbalanced journalism* Interview with Don Cronson.

215 *a loaded firearm* New York City Police Department, Queens Precinct, Arrest No. Q89023081.

215 *He pled guilty* Queens County Superior Court, Case No. 03224-89.

215 *a Manhattan restaurant* Associated Press, "Hornets' Mason Arrested for Fight," February 26, 2000.

215 *provoked by the police* Associated Press, Maull, "Former Knicks Forward Anthony Mason Pleads Guilty," November 5, 1996.

217 *being taken advantage of* Interview with Jeremy Randolph.

218 *rate below 50 percent* Fatsis, "URI Gets an Incomplete," *Wall Street Journal*, March 16, 2004.

219 *Strategies of Basketball* *USA Today*, "Harrick Jr.'s Test at Georgia a Slam Dunk," March 4, 2004.

BIBLIOGRAPHY

BOOKS

Benedict, Jeff. *Athletes and Acquaintance Rape*, Thousand Oaks, CA: Sage Publications, 1998.

Benedict, Jeff, *Public Heroes, Private Felons: Athletes and Crimes Against Women*, Boston, MA: Northeastern University Press, 1997.

Benedict, Jeff, and Don Yaeger. *Pros and Cons: The Criminals Who Play in the NFL*, New York, NY: Warner Books, 1998.

Carter, Craig, and Rob Reheuser. *Official NBA Guide: 2002–03 Edition*, St. Louis, MO: Sporting News, 2002.

Garrison, G., and R. Roberts. *Heavy Justice: The State of Indiana vs. Michael G. Tyson*, Reading, MA: Addison-Wesley, 1994.

Walton, David, and John Gardella. *Official NBA Register: 2002–03, Edition*, St. Louis, MO: Sporting News 2002.

ARTICLES

Ames Daily Tribune (Iowa). "Let Mack Now Rebuild his Life," Editorial, July 21, 1989.

Allen, Percy. "Forte Settles Assault Case," *Seattle Times*, August 19, 2003.

Asher, Mark. "Iverson Trial Date Set," *Washington Post*, August 14, 1997.

Associated Press. "Barkley Fined, Writes Letter of Apology to Settle Charges," June 26, 1998.

——. "Battie Enters Plea," August 4, 1999.

——. "Ex-Bearcat to Accept Attempted Rape Charge," May 8, 2001.

——. "Ex-Celtics Settle Lawsuit with Woman," January 12, 2000.

——. "Florida Files Charges Against Armstrong," August 20, 2003.

——. "Former NBA Player Says He's Innocent of Drug Charges," August 2, 2000.

——. "Former Pro Player Dontonio Wingfield Gets Year in Prison," September 10, 1999.

——. "Glenn Robinson Hopes to Make an Impact on Iverson's Team," July 25, 2003.

——. "Gold Club Stripper Admits Prostitution, Agrees to Testify in Racketeering Case," August 22, 2000.

——. "Griffin Indicted, TV Report Says," February 13, 2004.

——. "Hornets' Mason Arrested for Fight," February 26, 2000.

——. "Judge Drops Felony Charges vs. Iverson," July 31, 2002.

——. "Judge Sets Date for Armstrong Trial," September 3, 2003.

——. "Lowry Impeachment Proposed," March 30, 1995.

——. "Hornets' Mason Arrested for Fight," February 26, 2000.

——. "Nets Forward Griffin Stays Behind Bars," February 3, 2004.

——. "No Charges Filed Against LA Center," December 14, 2001.

——. "Pacers Say Davis Not Involved in Assault in His Townhouse," October 10, 1997.

——. "Prosecutors Decline to Bring Criminal Charges Against Mason," April 13, 1999.

——. "Rockets' Griffin Arrested on Drug Charges," April 8, 2003.

——. "Sonics Guard Forte Arrested on Drug, Gun Charges," April 26, 2003.

——. "Sports News," March 13, 1990.

——. "Sports News," September 21, 1995.

——. "Stoudamire Reinstated with Team, Fine Cleared," October 1, 2003.

——. "Trouble Continues for Former Cincinnati Star," June 12, 1997.

——. "Woman Claims Elden Campbell Assaulted Her in Lawsuit," August 30, 1997.

Bailey, Kate. "Sports News," Associated Press, June 6, 1994.

Banks, Lacy. "Laying Down the Law," *Chicago Sun-Times,* November 21, 2003.

Barnes, Sarah. "Mack Testifies White Forced Him to Rob Ames Restaurant," July 18, 1989.

——. "Prosecutor: Mack Sought Cash to Buy, Resell Cocaine," *Des Moines Register,* July 13, 1989.

Barr, Josh. "Forte Is Wanted for Questioning," *Washington Post,* May 3, 2003.

Beck, Howard. "Kobe, Shaq Let Their Feud out in Public," *Los Angeles Daily News,* January 11, 2001.

Blauvelt, Harry. "Shooting for a Better Life," *USA Today,* November 30, 1994.

Bondy, Filip. "Ex-Champ Dokes Beat Fiancée: Cops," *New York Daily News,* September 1, 1998.

Boston Globe. "Nets' Griffin Will Enter Rehab," February 1, 2004.

Brachowski, Matt. "Charge vs. Peeler Dropped," *The Missourian* (Columbia, Missouri), June 24, 1992.

Brown, Tim. "Bryant Is Talking It Up," *Los Angeles Times,* October 28, 2003.

———. "Fined Bryant Sits It Out," *Los Angeles Times,* October 29, 2003.

———. "It's the Return of the Star Wars," *Los Angeles Times,* October 27, 2003.

Buffalo News. "Iverson's Car Impounded, Two Face Drug Charges," July 14, 1998.

Burgess, Mike. "County Attorney Declines to Charge Mack," *State Press* (Arizona State University's Morning Daily), November. 21, 1989.

———. "Mack Suspended over Assault Probe," *State Press,* November 9, 1989.

Burkhead, Jeff. "Jury Explains Mack Verdict," *Ames Daily Tribune* (Iowa), July 21, 1989.

———. "White Refuses to Testify About Ames Robbery," *Ames Daily Tribune* (Iowa), July 13, 1989.

Chicago Sun-Times. "Heat's Hardaway in Trouble with Law," June 24, 1997.

Clarkson, Michael. "Trent Brings Plenty of Baggage to Town," *Toronto Star,* February. 14, 1998.

CNN.com. "NBA's Davis Sues over Gold Club Claims," June 14, 2001.

———. "Sex, Sports and the Mob: The Gold Club Trial," June 15, 2001.

———. "Strip Club Boss Cops Plea in Rackets Trial," August 3, 2001.

Cour, Jim. "Art Long Works to Overcome Famous Temper as a Sonic," February 2, 2002.

Couture, Pete. "Seahawks' Gilbert Found Innocent of Rape Charges," *St. Petersburg Times,* June 2, 1988.

D'Angelo, Tom. "Hardaway 'Hostile' During Traffic Stop for Going 110," *Palm Beach Post,* June 24, 1997.

Demasio, Nunyo. "Patterson Plea May Also Bring Sonics Penalty," *Seattle Times,* May 9, 2001.

Eggers, Kerry. "Spit Didn't Exactly Polish Bonzi's Image," *Portland Tribune,* November 22, 2002.

Farmer, Tom and Jose Martinez. "Suspects in Pierce Stabbing Surrender," *Boston Herald,* September 28, 2000.

Fatsis, Stefan. "URI Gets an Incomplete," *Wall Street Journal,* March 16, 2004.

Forbes. "The 400 Richest People in America" (Special Edition), 2003 Edition.

Fowler, Veronica, and Tom Witosky. "ISU's White Arrested for Robbery in 1987," *Des Moines Register,* April 4, 1989.

Freeman, Mike. "More N.F.L. Players Turn to Guns," *New York Times,* March 26, 2003.

Fryer, Jenna. "Hornets' Mason Sorry About Arrest," Associated Press, July 7, 2000.

Gatlin, Greg. "No Flinch, Yet, over Iverson," *Boston Herald,* July 11, 2002.

Gelzinis, Peter. "Despite Little Call," *Boston Herald,* October 8, 2002.

Gomez, Pedro. "Hardaway Ruling Won't Resolve Case," *Arizona Republic,* January 13, 2001.

Grant, Peter. "Big Matri-Money Could Be at Stake," *Daily News* (New York), February 13, 1998.

Greensboro News & Record. "Forte Set to Receive Warrant for Assault," May 14, 2003.

Gregorian, Vahe. "Kansas City Woman Talks of Plans," *St. Louis Post-Dispatch,* June 25, 1992.

———. "KC Prosecutor Drops Charge Facing Peeler," *St. Louis Post-Dispatch,* June 24, 1992.

———. "Mizzou's Peeler Is Named League's Top Male Athlete," *St. Louis Post-Dispatch,* June 18, 1992.

———. "Peller Arrested Again," *St. Louis Post-Dispatch,* June 23, 1992.

Hall, Landon. "Blazers Sign Ex-Sonics Patterson," Associated Press, August 2, 2001.

Hefley, Diana. "Sonics' Patterson Charged in Rape Try," *East Side Journal,* May 9, 2001.

Hemphill, Jim. "White Enters Guilty Plea," *The Daily Tribune* (Iowa), April 29, 1989.

Henderson, Diedtra. "Warrior Star Mullin Questioned by Police: Woman Accuses Player of Assault," *Seattle Times,* April 4, 1994.

Hinkelman, Andrew. "Stoudamire, Prosecutors Agree to Settle Citation," March 20, 2003.

Hirsley, Michael. "Athletes and Guns," *Chicago Tribune,* February 9, 2003.

Houston Chronicle. "Mack Fights Demons from the Past," February 12, 1992.

———. "NBA Notes," February 2, 1993.

——. "Shaq Takes Shot at Law Enforcement," July 13, 2002.

Isola, Frank. "Lakers Think Sixers on Brink L.A.," *Daily News* (New York), June 15, 2001.

Ith, Ian, and Nunyo Demasio. "Sonics' Patterson Faces Rape Charge," May 8, 2001.

Jasner, Phil. "Sixers Proceeding as If Iverson Is Still a Sixer," *Philadelphia Daily News*, July 12, 2002.

Jenkins, Lee. "Griffin Released from Jail," *New York Times*, February 14, 2004.

Kelley, Steve. "Gale Gilbert Resurrects Life, Career," *Seattle Times*, January 23, 1991.

Kerr, Greg. "Six More Area Players Picked in Baseball Draft," *St. Petersburg Times*, June 4, 1988.

Ko, Michael. "Sonics' Patterson Sentenced to 15 Days in Jail," *Seattle Times*, May 15, 2001.

Latour, Francie, and Stephen Kurkjian. "Two Suspects Held in Pierce Assault: Third Man Sought," *Boston Globe*, September 28, 2000.

Lindy's "Complete Guide to the NBA," 2003–2004, D.M.D. Publications, Inc.

Los Angeles Times. "Charge Added Against Payton," July 20, 2003.

Maull, Samuel. "Former Knicks Forward Anthony Mason Pleads Guilty to Disorderly Conduct," November 5, 1996.

McCallum, Jack. "The Dark Side of a Star," *Sports Illustrated*, July 28, 2003.

McCallum, Jack, and Don Yaeger. "'I Know He's Gone Off Before,'" *Sports Illustrated*, April 21, 1996.

Murphy, Shelley. "Celtic Walker Settles with Accuser," *Boston Globe*, March 7, 2000.

Nack, William, and Lester Munson. "Sports' Dirty Secret," *Sports Illustrated*, July 31, 1995.

NBA.com. "Bonzi on the Move," December 3, 2003.

New York Times. "Guilty Plea for Blazer," May 30, 1990.

——. "Mason Is Guilty of 2 Misdemeanors," June 26, 1998.

Nichols, Rachel. "Toil and Trouble," *Washington Post*, October 29, 2002.

Nish, Caitlin. "Webber Avoids Jail, Pleading Guilty on a Contempt Charge," *New York Times*, July 15, 2003.

Olson, Lisa. "Keeping It Unreal," *Daily News* (New York), July 17, 2002.

Paulson, Michael, and Kathy George. "Harassment Claim Cost Lowry $97,500," *Seattle Post Intelligence*, July 15, 1995.

Peterson, Kristine. "Former M.U. Basketball Player," *The Missourian* (Columbia, Missouri), January 6, 1992.

Rankin, Bill, and Steve Visser. "Braves' A. Jones Implicated in Gold Club Sex Case," *Atlanta Journal-Constitution,* June 4, 2001.

Robbins, Liz. "Bucks Had Court Woes Extending Beyond Nets," *New York Times,* April 21, 2003.

Runk, David. "Chris Webber's Guilty Plea Ends Michigan Booster Probe," Associated Press, July 15, 2003.

Rush, George, and Joanna Molloy. "Divorce Fight? Ewing Seen Nothing Yet," *Daily News* (New York), May 8, 1998.

San Antonio Express-News. "NBA Notes: Probe Continues of Clippers Center," December 4, 2001.

San Diego Union-Tribune. "No Charges for Iverson," September 13, 2002.

Sandoval, Greg. "Ex-DeMatha Star Forte Arrested by Md. Police," *Washington Post,* April 26, 2003.

——. "Wizards' White Won't Face Charges," *Washington Post,* May 28, 2003.

Schmaltz, Brad. "Trent Steered Clear of Trouble," *Columbus Dispatch* (Ohio), March 9, 1993.

Seattle Times. "Still No Answers About Iverson," July 11, 2002.

Shelman, Jeffrey, and Bob Queenan. "Patterson Suspension: 14 Games," *Cincinnati Post,* December 3, 1997.

Shirk, George. "Warriors Didn't Know Houston, Gatling Had Brushes with Law," *San Francisco Chronicle,* May 20, 1993.

Simon, Jim, and David Postman. "Settlement Carries a Price: Threat of Suit in Harassment Case Forced Lowry to Act," *Seattle Times,* July 15, 1995.

Singleton, Don. "Unlike Knicks, Ewing's Wife Does Fine Without Him," *Daily News* (New York), February 14, 1998.

Smith, Ben. "Wells' Focus Self-image, Not NBA's," *Journal Gazette* (Fort Wayne, Indiana), July 31, 2003.

Somers, Kent. "Mack Linked to Sexual Assault, Suspended from ASU Basketball," The *Arizona Republic,* November 9, 1989.

Sports Illustrated. "They Said It," Scorecard, November 17, 2003.

Sullivan, Tim. "Are We Being Told Crime Pays?" *Cincinnati Enquirer,* November 8, 1997.

——. "Patterson Aggravates Image," *Cincinnati Enquirer,* December 7, 1996.

——. "Too Harsh a Penalty? Hardly." *Cincinnati Enquirer,* December 3, 1997.

Sutton, Larry, and K. C. Baker. "Hoop Skirts: Mrs. Ewing Tells All," *Daily News* (New York), September 4, 1998.

St. Petersburg Times. "Around the NBA," December 6, 2001.

Tampa Tribune (Florida). "Robinson cited," December 4, 1997.

The Columbian (Vancouver, Washington). "Settlement Casts Doubt on Lowry's Political Life," July 18, 1995.

Thomas, Karen. "Jackson Challenges $60 Million Lawsuit," *USA Today,* June 12, 1996.

Toronto Star. "Clipper's Not in the Clear Yet," December 6, 2001.

——. "Three Bucks Charged in Assault at Strip Club," April 20, 2003.

Tucker, Darryl. "'He Pushed Me,' Richardson's Ex-girlfriend Testified," *Saginaw News* (Michigan), August 28, 2003.

United Press International. "Felony Charges Dropped Against Mason," June 25, 1998.

——. "Houston's Eddie Griffin Accused of Assault," October 25, 2003.

USA Today. "Bryant: Shaq Would Be Major Reason If He Left," October 28, 2003.

——. "Harrick Jr.'s Test at Georgia a Slam Dunk," March 4, 2004.

——. "Trail Blazers Make Statement with Dumping of Wells," December 4, 2003.

——. "Trail Blazers Sit Wells, Strip Co-captain Title," November 19, 2003.

Vivanco, Liz. "Ex-NBA Star Mack Faces Drug Charges," *Chicago Sun-Times,* July 12, 2000.

Voisin, Ailene. "Pro Basketball: NBA Western Conference," *Atlanta Journal and Constitution,* March 30, 1997.

Washington Post. "NBA Notes: Signings," January 30, 1999.

——. "No Charges Against Coleman," July 27, 1994.

——. "Trail Blazers' Randolph Is Charged with DUI," December 3, 2003.

——. "Two Men in Iverson's Car Are Arrested," July 14, 1998.

Weber, David. "Woman Claims She Was Assaulted at Celt's Home," *Boston Herald,* December 4, 1997.

Wells, Mike. "Cassell Enjoying All-Star Season," *Saint Paul Pioneer Press,* February 3, 2004.

Wilstein, Steve. "Iverson Shows His Arrogance," Associated Press, July 15, 2002.

Wise, Mike. "In Lakers' Dysfunctional Family," *New York Times,* October 28, 2003.

——. "Lakers' Star Bryant Is Charged with Sex Assault at Colorado Spa," *New York Times,* July 19, 2003.

——. "O'Neal-Bryant Feud Haunts Lakers' Title Drive," *New York Times,* January 14, 2004.

Wolff, Alexander. "Breaking Through," *Sports Illustrated,* December 2, 1996.

Wyche, Steve. "Wizards' Brown Arrested for DUI," *Washington Post,* August 20, 2003.

Youngmisuk, Ohm. "Griffin Guilty in Pot Case," *Daily News* (New York), January 21, 2004.

Zicarelli, Frank. "The Answer Is Badass or Victim of Bad Press," *Toronto Sun,* November 22, 2002.